EXPLORE

MAUI

An Independent Traveler's Guide

Blair Pruitt

Mutual Publishing

*For her assistance, proofreading and most of all, her support, this book is dedicated to **Amanda Jones**, Ph.D.*

Copyright © 2001
by Mutual Publishing

Library of Congress Catalog Card
Number: 2001088534

First Printing August 2001
1 2 3 4 5 6 7 8 9

Design by Mardee Domingo and Julie Matsuo
Cover Design by Jane Hopkins

Except where otherwise credited, all
photographs in this book are by Blair Pruitt

ISBN 1-56647-343-8 softcover

Mutual Publishing
1215 Center Street, Suite 210
Honolulu, Hawai'i 96816
Ph: (808) 732-1709
Fax: (808) 734-4094
e-mail: mutual@lava.net
www.mutualpublishing.com

Printed in Korea

FOREWORD

Visitors to Maui find that their time on this marvelous island is always too short. With its many attractions, activities and natural beauty, Maui offers more adventures than most people can experience in one stay. This book is written as a guide that will enrich the readers' Hawaiian experience and aid them in making the most of their precious time here.

The concise text serves up vivid descriptions, accurate directions and insights for the curious and adventurous traveler. Hikers can use their GPS receivers by inputting the coordinates of latitude and longitude provided for many destinations and waypoints. Clear, large maps make it easy for drivers and hikers to find their way by omitting extraneous detail. Highway mile markers are shown on the maps as well as important landmarks.

The Hawaiian language is covered early in the book with the hope that a basic background in Hawaiian pronunciation and meanings will lend further understanding when reading the following chapters. I have given history particular importance because an understanding of how things were and came to be leads to an appreciation of the culture and sights the traveler samples. Recounts of history begin with the birth of the Hawaiian Island chain 70 million years ago. Maui's history is given prominence as it intertwines with the history of the rest of the Hawaiian Islands.

This book is for travelers who want to know more about the land and sea they are visiting, the people who live here and how events shaped the island into what it is today. It is meant to be your guide while you explore Maui, and later, a reminder of your visit that will bring back treasured memories until you can return to the Magic Isle.

"No alien land in all the world has any deep strong charm for me but that one, no other land could so longingly and so beseechingly haunt me, sleeping and waking, through half a lifetime, as that one has done. Other things leave me, but it abides; other things change, but it remains the same. For me its balmy airs are always blowing, its summer seas flashing in the sun; the pulsing of its surfbeat is in my ear; I can see its garlanded crags, its leaping cascades, its plumy palms drowsing by the shore, its remote summits floating like islands above the cloud rack; I can feel the spirit of its woodland solitudes, I can hear the splash of its brooks; in my nostrils still lives the breath of flowers that perished twenty years ago."

—Mark Twain

TABLE OF CONTENTS

INTRODUCTION

Maui's oft-quoted motto is "Maui no ka oi"—"Maui is the best." Endorsing this boast, the readers of *Condé Nast Traveler* magazine voted Maui the "Best Island in the World" six times. For two years running they also named Maui the world's "Top Travel Destination." Each of the Hawaiian isles is unique and has something exceptional to offer. Maui just seems to have it all.

Golden-sand beaches scallop its coasts, luring the weary traveler to relax. Those who don't need to relax can swim, sail, windsurf, paddle a kayak or SCUBA dive to coral reefs inhabited by fish painted in colors more vivid than a Hawaiian rainbow. Ten thousand feet above the sea rests a caldera whose eerie landscape resembles the moon's surface. Burnt cinder cones rise hundreds of feet above the crater floor and rivers of frozen lava bear witness to the island's birth by fire in the not-so-distant past. Between the sea's waves and the volcano's crown live plants and animals found nowhere else on earth. Tens of thousands of acres on Maui and vast areas of its coastal waters have been proclaimed protected areas. Sugarcane carpets Maui's Central Valley green, and pineapple, the enduring symbol of Hawai'i, thrives in the hills above. Higher still,

M.V.B. / Ron Dahlquist

horticulturists nurture the otherworldly protea, and cattle and horses graze in pastures that roll across Haleakalā's slopes amid cactuses and purple-blossomed jacaranda trees. Haleakalā's south flank, where lava last flowed on the island, has a beauty that is stark and rugged. To the north, rainforests cloak the steep, eroded valleys with plants still to be discovered.

Maui is an adventurer's paradise waiting to be explored. This book is a guide for the traveler who wants to see and experience the best that Maui has to offer. Its detailed descriptions and accurate directions are written to help readers make their own discoveries.

TURTLE
XING

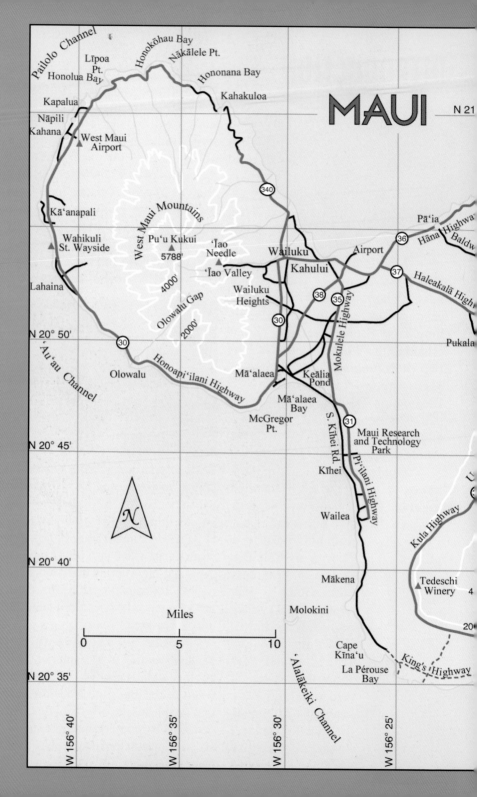

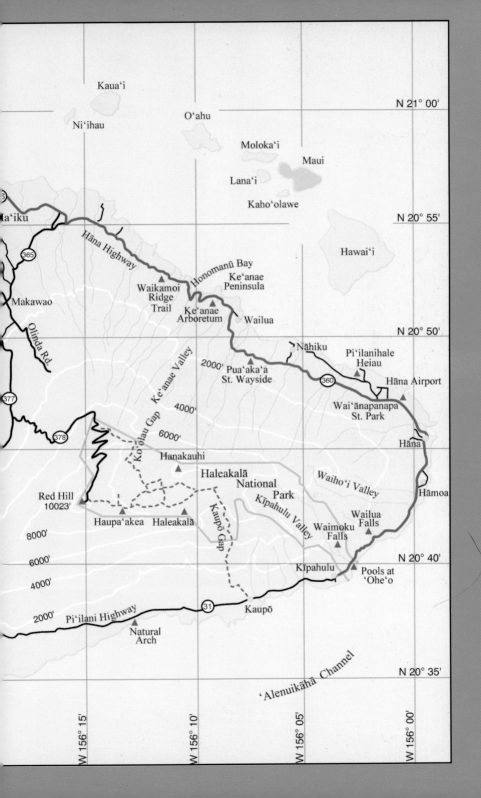

Kaua'i

Ni'ihau

O'ahu

Moloka'i

Maui

Lana'i

Kaho'olawe

Hawai'i

N 21° 00'

N 20° 55'

N 20° 50'

N 20° 40'

N 20° 35'

a'iku

Hāna Highway

365

Makawao

Olinda Rd.

377

378

Red Hill
10023'

8000'

6000'

4000'

2000'

Pi'ilani Highway

Natural
Arch

Waikamoi
Ridge
Trail

Ke'anae
Arboretum

Honomanū Bay

Ke'anae
Peninsula

Wailua

Ke'anae Valley

Ko'olau Gap

2000'

Pua'aka'a
St. Wayside

4000'

6000'

Hanakauhi

Haleakalā
National
Park

Kaupō Gap

Haupa'akea

Haleakalā

Kīpahulu Valley

Nāhiku

Pi'ilanihale
Heiau

360

Hāna Airport

Wai'ānapanapa
St. Park

Hāna

Waiho'i Valley

Hāmoa

Wailua
Falls

Waimoku
Falls

Kīpahulu

Pools at
'Ohe'o

31

Kaupō

'Alenuikāhā Channel

W 156° 15'

W 156° 10'

W 156° 05'

W 156° 00'

IMPORTANT THINGS FOR TRAVELERS TO KNOW

North American Airlines Serving Maui

All the scheduled airlines that connect Hawai'i to the U.S. mainland have flights to Honolulu, while some have direct flights to Kahului, Maui. Kahului's airport runway is not as long as Honolulu's—ruling out nonstop flights to Asia or the Midwest United States. Plans to lengthen the runway from 7,000 to 9,600 feet have met with opposition from some Maui residents who fear it may cause environmental damage and increased visitor traffic, which would negatively impact island life.

Aloha Airlines and Hawaiian Airlines operate short-hop flights between the Hawaiian Islands. They have aircraft taking off and landing on Maui every few minutes. Passengers can check schedules and book their flights directly on the airlines' websites. Maui's main airport is at Kahului, airport code OGG, with smaller airports at Kapalua, code JHM, and at Hāna, code HNM. The airport code for Honolulu International Airport is HNL.

With airlines recently operating at more than 96 percent capacity on flights from the mainland to Hawai'i, it is prudent to book your flight a few months in advance if possible. During the Christmas season, spring break, Thanksgiving and the summer months it might be necessary to book several months in advance.

Internet travel services can search for the best flight for you at no charge. They are connected to the airlines' schedules and fares much as a travel agency is. Four of them are: Microsoft's Expedia at <www.expedia.com>, Sabre's Travelocity at <www.travelocity.com>, TheTrip at <www.thetrip.com>, and <www.Previewtravel.com>.

Air Canada
(888) 247-2262
Website: www.aircanada.ca
Air Canada offers direct flights to Maui from Vancouver.

Aloha Airlines
(800) 367-5250, (808) 877-2737
Website: www.alohaair.com
Aloha Airlines controls about 60 percent of Hawai'i's interisland market, flying a fleet of eighteen 737s between Hawai'i's main islands. They have just expanded their service to the Bay Area with daily roundtrip flights between Maui and Oakland on Boeing 737–700s.

Aloha Island Air
(800) 323-3345
Aloha Island Air is owned and operated by Aloha Airlines and flies to many of Hawai'i's smaller airports. They have connections to Lāna'i, Moloka'i and Hāna from Kahului and

connect West Maui's Kapalua airport with Honolulu and Kona on the Big Island. Their full schedule is included in Aloha Airlines' website.

American Airlines
(800) 223-5436
Website: www.americanair.com

Canada 3000
(888) 226-3000
(416) 259-1118
Website: www.canada3000.com
Offers direct flights to Maui from Vancouver and Edmonton.

Canadian Airlines International
(800) 665-1177
Website: www.cdnair.ca

Continental Airlines
(800) 525-0280
Website: www.flycontinental.com

Delta Air Lines
(800) 221-1212
Website: www.delta-air.com

Hawaiian Airlines
(800) 367-5320
Website: www.hawaiianair.com
Hawaiian Airlines flies their DC-9s between the main Hawaiian islands and DC-10s to the mainland. Direct flights to Maui are available from several western U.S. airports.

Northwest Airlines
(800) 225-2525
Website: www.nwa.com

Pacific Wings
(808) 873-0877
Website: www.pacificwings.com

Flies eight-passenger Cessna 402C aircraft on scheduled interisland flights and a four-passenger Cessna 172 on charter flights. Scheduled flights from Kahului to Moloka'i, Honolulu and Kamuela on the Big Island are available. A flight from Kahului to Hāna can be chartered for $129.

Trans World Airlines
(800) 221-2000
Website: www.twa.com

United Airlines
(800) 241-6522
Website: www.ual.com

Car Rentals

Maui has no public-transportation system so the only way to get out and about without tour companies is to rent a car. All the major rental companies have outlets in Maui. Car-rental agencies based at Kahului Airport have shuttle buses to take customers to their car lots. Look for their signs on the road outside the baggage claim area. Be ready for a shock when you buy gasoline. Prices are about 40 percent higher than on the mainland.

If you don't have a favorite car-rental company and aren't sure which one has the best deal, there are free travel planning services on the Internet that can help. After inputting the dates of your stay and the type of car you want you just wait while they search all the rental-company records, then list the rates of available cars by company. Try <www.expedia.com>,

<www.travelocity.com>, or <www.thetrip.com>. Car-rental companies, like airlines, like to change their rates depending upon demand and availability. Often the first rate quoted is not their best rate for that car. Be armed with quotes from other companies and ask if they have any specials for that time period.

Alamo Rent a Car
Kahului (808) 877-3466
Kā'anapali (808) 661-7181
Website: www.goalamo.com
The Kahului Airport location is open 5:00 a.m.–11:00 p.m. Kā'anapali's location is open 7:00 a.m.–5:30 p.m.

Avis Rent a Car
(800) 831-8000
Website: www.avis.com
Avis has rental locations at Kahului Airport, Kā'anapali, Kapalua, Kīhei and Wailea. Hand-controlled vehicles are available at all locations with 48 hours notice.

Budget Rent a Car
(800) 572-0700
Website: www.drivebudget.com
Hand controls for most vehicles are available at no extra cost with reservations made 72 hours in advance.

Dollar Rent a Car
Reservations (800) 800-4000
Kahului (808) 877-6526
Kā'anapali (808) 667-2651
Hāna (808) 248-8237
Website: www.dollar.com

Hertz Rent a Car
Reservations (800) 654-3131
Kahului (808) 877-5167

Website: www.hertz.com
Hand controls are available with advance notice. Open 5:30 a.m.–10:00 p.m.

National Rent a Car
Reservations:
U.S. (800) 227-7368
Canada (800) 387-4747
Website: www.nationalcar.com

Thrifty Car Rental
Reservations:
(800) 367-2277
Kahului (808) 877-2333
Website: www.thrifty.com

Word of Mouth Rent a Car
150 Hāna Highway
(800) 533-5929, (808) 877-2436
You can look more like a local driving one of Word of Mouth's used cars and save money too. They offer airport pickup.

Motorcycle Rentals

Specialty Rentals Island Riders
126 Hinau Street, Lahaina
(808) 661-9966;
1975 South Kīhei Road, Kīhei
(808) 874-0311
Website: www.islandriders.com
Charge up your vacation with a rental of a Harley-Davidson. Reservations a week in advance are recommended and a valid motorcycle license is required. Hawai'i does not have mandatory helmet laws. Harley-Davidson Sportster 1/2 day $75, 24 hours $109; Big Twins 1/2 day $99, 24 hours $149. You're on vacation, so why not tour the island in an exotic car? Airport or hotel pickup is available.

Viper 5 hours $250, 24 hours $400; Hummer 5 hours $250, 24 hours $350; Prowler 5 hours $275, 24 hours $425; BMW Z-3 Roadster 24 hours $225.

Wheels U.S.A.
741 Waine'e Street, Lahaina (808) 667-7751; 75 Ka'ahumanu Avenue, Kahului (808) 871-6858 Wheels U.S.A. rents adventure vehicles like dune buggies, dirt bikes and mountain bikes. A dune buggy or Jeep Wrangler rents for $50/day. A 250 Enduro is $60 and a 750 Yamaha Virago is $90/day. Mopeds and mountain bikes can be rented from 8:30 a.m.–4:30 p.m. for $26 and $9 respectively.

Shuttles

TransHawaiian Airporter Shuttle
(800) 231-6984, (808) 877-7308 Their buses leave Kahului Airport, on the hour, 9:00 a.m.–3:00 p.m., in front of Baggage Claim 3, bound for Lahaina and Kā'anapali. Departure trips from West Maui to the Kahului Airport run from 10:00 a.m.–4:00 p.m. Reservations, which are required for the departure trips, should be made 24 hours in advance by calling their toll-free number. Office hours are 8:00 a.m.–5:00 p.m. They recommend that departure time be reserved for three and one half hours before your flight. One-way fare from the airport is $13, one-way to the airport is $7 and a return fare is $19. Add an extra dollar for golf bags.

SpeediShuttle
(808) 875-8070 Their vans provide door-to-door service to and from the Kahului Airport and most Maui resort locations. They claim that 80 percent of their transfers are exclusive with a maximum of three stops. For pickup at the airport use the courtesy phone at the baggage-claim area and dial 65. The rate for two people to Kā'anapali is $32, to Kapalua $44, to Kīhei $18 and to Wailea $22.

West Maui Shopping Express
877-7308 A colorful, trolley-like shuttle picks up passengers from every major resort north of Kā'anapali starting at the Ritz Carlton in Kapalua and brings them to waiting shops at Whalers Village. Rides are one hour apart starting at 9:00 a.m. Another shuttle starts at the Royal Lahaina in Kā'anapali, stops at Whalers Village and continues on to Lahaina, stopping at Lahaina Cannery Mall, Hilo Hattie's and the Wharf Cinema Center. This shuttle also runs hourly starting at 9:45 a.m. Fare is $1 each way.

Maui Ocean Center Trolley
270-7000 This shuttle makes several stops in Wailea and Kīhei before finishing at the Maui Ocean Center in Mā'alaea. It then heads to Whalers Village in Kā'anapali to shuttle West Maui visitors to the Ocean Center. The runs from the south begin at the Maui Prince Hotel at 8:30 a.m., 11:45 a.m. and 3:00 p.m., reaching the Maui Ocean Center in one hour. Shuttles leave Whalers Village at 10:15 a.m., 1:30 p.m. and 4:45 p.m. reaching the Ocean Center in half an half hour. It then continues back to South Maui. A round-trip fare is $7.00.

Taxis

Maui has several taxi companies but they are an expensive way to get around the island. Approximate fare from Kahului Airport to Kā'anapali is $49, to Kīhei $24 and to Wailea $32. To use a taxi for a shorter ride it's best to contact a company based in that area.

A B Taxi
Lahaina, 667-7575

Ali'i Cab
Lahaina, 661-3688

Ali'i Cab, Kīhei
874-4895

Central Maui Taxi
Wailuku, 244-7278

Excellent Taxi Services
Kula, 878-3407

Grand Central Taxi
Kahului, 877-7758

Jake's Taxi
Kahului, 877-6139

Kā'anapali Taxi
661-5285

Kapalua Executive Transportation Services
Kapalua, 667-7770

Mākena-Kīhei Taxi Ltd.
Kīhei, 879-3000

Maui Airport Taxi
Kahului, 877-0907

The Best Limo Taxi
Kīhei, 871-5559

Yellow Cab
Kīhei, 877-7000

Medical Assistance

Doctors on Call
667-7676 (24 hours)
Same-day care, seven days a week for visitors and residents in West Maui. They have an in-house pharmacy, X-ray, laboratory and EKG. Locations in the Hyatt Regency, Westin Maui and the Ritz Carlton.

Maui Memorial Hospital
221 Mahalani, Wailuku, 244-9056
Maui's largest hospital, with 24-hour emergency service.

Hāna Medical Center
Hāna Highway, Hāna, 248-8294

Kīhei Clinic
2349 South Kīhei Road, Suite D
879-1440
Serves walk-in clients and is geared toward caring for visitors.

Kula Hospital
204 Kula Highway, Kula
878-1221

Poison Control Center
Honolulu, (800) 362-3585

West Maui Healthcare Center
Suite H-7, Whalers Village
Kā'anapali, 667-9721
Open daily from 8:00 a.m. to 10:00 p.m.

Telephone Calls

The area code for all of Hawai'i is 808. Calls made anywhere on the same island are toll-free. Calls made to another Hawaiian island are considered long distance and the area code must be used. The cost to use pay phones on Maui is 35 cents.

Weather Forecasts

For a recorded forecast of weather conditions for all parts of Maui, call the National Weather Service at 877-5111.

Crime

Maui is a reasonably safe place to visit. Compared to the rest of the nation, Maui has a low rate of violent crime. Recent statistics reported by the *Maui News* show that the number of incidents of violent crime such as murder, rape, robbery and serious assaults has dropped. Most of these cases relate to the trade of illegal drugs. Use of crystal methamphetamine and heroin has become a serious social problem for a few Maui residents.

Visitors to Maui are clearly marked as targets for property crimes. Each week, the police report in the *Maui News* lists the incidents of thefts against visitors. The cases often involve unlocked rooms being entered or watchful culprits lifting unattended purses in public places. Awareness and common sense by potential victims can reduce opportunities for these criminals considerably. A chronic crime problem is theft from visitors' rental cars. The shiny new cars are easily

identified, and usually so are the visitors driving them. Don't leave valuables unattended in your car. Trouble areas are beaches, where the car is left unwatched for hours. Placing items in the trunk doesn't help at all. In ten seconds, a thief can break the passenger-door window, reach in and pull the trunk release, empty the trunk and take off. Some people suggest leaving items like cameras under the hood. That might help if you aren't being watched when you hide the items. Also, don't forget about your secret hiding place when you return and drive away.

Concerned citizens in conjunction with the Maui Police Department recently formed the Maui Citizen's Patrol to deter crimes against visitors and their property. The patrol, constituting volunteers dressed in blue shirts and armed with cellular telephones that give them a direct line to police, cruise the coastlines of Maui reporting any suspicious activity they observe. Patrol members receive training through the department's auxiliary policing program. They undergo background checks and are given a four-hour training course and on-the-job instruction by other volunteers before becoming full-fledged members. Their job is not to confront criminals, but rather to serve as eyes and ears of officers who can't be everywhere at once. With uniforms and marked vehicles, their overt presence acts as a deterrent. They are also there to help anyone in need of assistance, from visitors who have locked their keys in their cars to people needing medical attention.

Radio Stations

KAOI, 95.1, 96.7 FM
Rock and contemporary music.
KONI, 104.7 FM
Contemporary hits.
KPOA, 93.5, 107.3 FM
Hawaiian and contemporary Hawaiian music.
KLHI, 101.1 FM
"The Point" Alternative rock.
KKUA, 90.7 FM
Hawai'i public radio.
KDLX, 94.3, 95.9 FM
Country music.
KMVI, 98.3 FM
Rock music.
KNUI, 99.9 FM
Light rock and Hawaiian music.
KMVI, 550 AM
Island music.
KNUI, 900 AM
Oldies.
KAOI, 1110 AM
Contemporary Music.

Pets

It's not feasible to bring pets along with you for a Hawaiian vacation. Dogs and cats must undergo a 30-day quarantine when entering Hawai'i, even if they are fully vaccinated.

Agricultural Inspection

Before you can leave Hawai'i for the mainland all your bags are subject to an agricultural inspection at the airport. You will be asked if you have any agricultural products to declare and your luggage will be examined with low-level X ray. Failing to declare an item results in confiscation of it and possibly a fine of up to $250. Items that are allowed include: coconuts, unless they are going to Florida; roasted coffee; fresh flowers, excepting mauna loas, gardenias, jade vines or roses; dried or preserved insects; meats; nuts; papayas, but only if they have been officially certified; and sugar but not sugarcane. One ounce of beach sand can be taken for decorative purposes but not soil or potted plants.

Hawai'i at a Glance

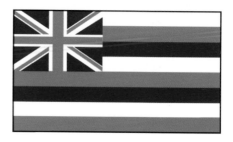

Nickname:
The Aloha State

Capital: Honolulu

Size: 6,425 sq. miles

Entered Union: August 21, 1959 as 50th State

State Bird: Nēnē

State Tree: Kukui (candlenut)

The Hibiscus, Hawai'i's State Flower

State Flower:
Ma'o hau hele
(yellow flower hibiscus)

State Fish:
Humuhumunukunukuāpua'a

State Mammal:
Humpback Whale

State Anthem: Hawai'i Pono'ī

State Gem: Black Coral

State Motto: Ua mau ke ea o ka 'āina i ka pono (The life of the land is perpetuated in righteousness)

State Flag: Designed prior to 1816 for King Kamehameha I, the flag has served the Kingdom,

Republic and State of Hawai'i. The Union Jack in the corner honors Hawai'i's early ties with Britain; the eight horizontal stripes represent Hawai'i's eight main islands.

Population: 1,211,537

Five Largest Cities:
Honolulu, O'ahu 377,060
'Ewa, O'ahu 230,190
Hilo, Hawai'i 46,180
Kailua, O'ahu 36,800
Kane'ohe, O'ahu 35,450

Most Remote Point from Coast:
28.5 miles—Hawai'i

Highest Peak:
Mauna Kea, Hawai'i— 13,796 feet

Lowest Temperature:
9°F, Mauna Kea, Hawai'i

Highest Temperature:
100°F, Pahala, Hawai'i

Wettest Place:
460", Mt. Wai'ale'ale, Kaua'i

Driest Place:
14", Mahukona, Hawai'i

Average Daily Visitor Census:
158,850

Governor:
Ben Cayetano (D)

Lt. Governor:
Mazie Hirono (D)

U.S. Senators:
Daniel Inouye (D)
Daniel Akaka (D)

State Taxes: Excise Tax, 4.167%, added to purchases; Transient Accommodations Tax (T.A.T.), 7.25%, added to hotel and condo rates in addition to the excise tax.

Maui at a Glance

Nickname:
The Valley Isle (now marketed as The Magic Isle)

Size: 728.8 sq. miles

County Seat: Wailuku

Flower: Lokelani

Population: 91,361

Five Largest Cities:
Kahului 16,889
Kīhei 11,107
Wailuku 10,688
Lahaina 9,073
Pukalani 5,879

Miles of Shoreline: 120

No. of Beaches: 81

Major Industries: Tourism, Sugar, Pineapple, Cattle, Diversified Agriculture

No. of Hotel Rooms: 10,660

No. of Vacation Condominium Units: 7,340

Highest Peak: Haleakalā Volcano— 10,023 feet

Most Remote Point from Coast: 10.6 miles

Average Daily Visitor Census: 42,640

Lowest Temperature:
9°F, Haleakalā

Highest Temperature:
98°F, Kīhei

Geographic Opposite:
Kalahari Desert, Botswana, Africa

Maui County Mayor:
James "Kimo" Apana (D)

U.S. Representative:
Patsy Mink (D)

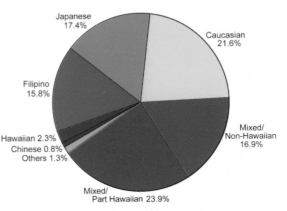

Ethnic Origin of
Maui County Residents

Japanese 17.4%
Caucasian 21.6%
Filipino 15.8%
Mixed/ Non-Hawaiian 16.9%
Hawaiian 2.3%
Chinese 0.8%
Others 1.3%
Mixed/ Part Hawaiian 23.9%

THE MYTH OF MĀUI

THE ISLAND OF Maui is named after Māui the demigod, a prominent figure in Polynesian folklore born of the goddess Hina. Māui was characterized as being a trickster who used his imagination to invent novel methods of making life easier and his superhuman strength to make them happen. One story carried down through generations in Hawaiian chants tells of Māui's greatest trick. Māui's brothers often went fishing but never took him because of his tricks. When his brothers came back one night without catching any fish, they agreed that Māui could go with them the next day and use the new fishhook he had carved. When the brothers were again unsuccessful catching fish, Māui told them to paddle home and not to look back. The brothers could not help looking back as they paddled and saw Māui give a mighty pull on his fishhook.

Out of the sea, attached to the hook, emerged a large piece of land. But when the brothers looked back the land mass fell, shattering the magic and the land with it into several pieces. Today you can see those pieces in the sea as the Hawaiian islands. Māui's great fishhook shines in the sky as the constellation Scorpius.

GEOGRAPHY

The Tropic of Cancer bisects the 132 protuberances of lava and coral that make up the Hawaiian archipelago. At the northwest end, at 28.15° N latitude and rising only 20 feet above the sea, is Kure Atoll. Anchoring the chain at the southeast end is the largest island, Hawai'i, which soars to 13,796 feet. With the exception of the five Midway Islands (administered by the U.S. Navy), this chain of shoals, reefs, islets and islands is the State of Hawai'i. Maui is the second island from the southeast end and follows the island of Hawai'i in size, height and newness. A semi-tropical island, most of Maui lies between 20.5° N and 21° N latitude. Hong Kong, Mecca and Calcutta share the same latitudes.

More than 99 percent of the state's land area of 6,425 square miles is contained in the eight main islands clustered at the southeast end. In order of size they are: Hawai'i, Maui, O'ahu, Kaua'i, Moloka'i, Lāna'i, Ni'ihau and Kaho'olawe. Ni'ihau is privately owned and off limits to the public. Uninhabited Kaho'olawe was,

until recently, used as a practice target by the U.S. Navy.

Sitting alone in the North Pacific, the Hawaiian Islands are the most isolated land masses on Earth. Maui lies 2,300 miles from both California and Alaska and 3,850 miles from Tokyo, Japan. Tahiti is 2,500 miles away and Sydney, Australia, 5,070.

It is two hours earlier in Maui than in North America's Pacific Time Zone, three hours earlier than Mountain Time, four hours before Central Time and five hours earlier than the Eastern Time Zone. Since Hawai'i does not observe daylight-saving time, the differences with North America become one hour greater from April to October. In the other direction, Sydney, Australia, is four hours earlier than Maui, and Tokyo, Japan, is five hours earlier.

The landscape of Maui is dominated by the two volcanoes that formed the island with their overlapping lava flows. At 5,788 feet, Pu'ukukui is the highest point of the older West Maui Mountains. To the southeast, the younger and less eroded Haleakalā volcano rises above the clouds to 10,023 feet. Between lies the fertile plain of the Central Valley, planted in sugarcane and pineapple. Sloping up Haleakalā is Upcountry Maui, which hosts cattle ranches, vegetable farms, exotic flower farms, horses, artists and homes with grand views. The prevailing trade winds from the northeast bring the moisture that feeds the rain forests and waterfalls of the windward side of

Maui. Arid weather and sunshine on the leeward side favor development of resorts and golf courses. Maui has numerous streams, but no lakes.

At its extremes, Maui measures 26 miles by 48 miles. The mean elevation is 2,390 feet with 75 percent of the land above 500 feet and 41 percent above 2,000 feet. Three quarters of the land is within five miles of the coast and 36 percent of the land has a slope greater than 20 percent.

There are no large cities in Maui. Together, the contiguous towns of Kahului and Wailuku form the largest metropolitan area. Situated on the north coast of the Central Valley, Wailuku is the administrative seat of Maui County and Kahului has Maui's busiest harbor and airport. Other important towns are Lahaina, the historic town in West Maui, Kīhei, a popular visitor destination, Pukalani and Makawao in Upcountry and Hāna on the eastern point of the island.

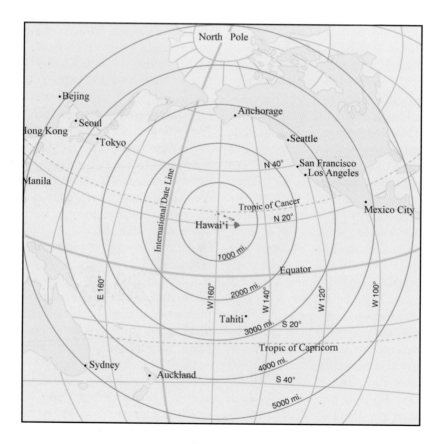

CLIMATE

It's hard to imagine a climate more agreeable than Maui's. Daytime high temperatures consistently reach the 80s, cooling to the high 60s at night. Sunshine is plentiful and the humidity is moderate. In fact, the climate is a principal reason Maui attracts more than two million visitors a year.

Maui experiences only two seasons, summer and winter. The warmest months are August and September and the coolest months are January and February, but the average maximum temperature between the warmest and coolest months ranges only seven degrees. The least precipitation falls from June to September and the rainiest months are December to February. These are averages and trends however; hot, dry days and cool, wet days will occur in every month. Maui's equable climate is credited to a number of factors. Its location is semitropical, mostly

south of 21° N. The Hawaiian Islands are surrounded by the vast waters of the Pacific Ocean, which acts as a climatic thermostat, warming cool air masses and cooling warm air currents. Ocean temperatures around Maui range from 77–80°F. The trade winds, which regularly blow at 10–20 mph, provide a moderating effect on the temperature and humidity.

Despite a lack of strong seasonal variation, Maui is host to an extraordinary diversity of microclimates, from desert to rain forest. Temperature drops three degrees for every 1,000 feet of altitude, an important factor to remember when traveling to the summit of Haleakalā, where at 10,023 feet, snow can fall in the winter months. Rainfall varies more with location than with season. The northeast shores are the windward side of the island when the trade winds are blowing. When the winds, laden with moisture, blow over the island they are forced up by the land. As the temperature of the air drops with altitude so does its ability to hold

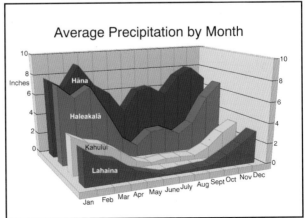

Average Precipitation by Month

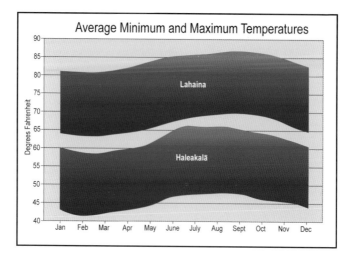

Average Minimum and Maximum Temperatures

moisture. The moisture in the cooler air condenses into rain, mainly in the higher altitudes of the windward side. The air, depleted of much of its moisture, is pushed over the mountains, warming as it descends to the island's leeward side. The resorts of Lahaina and Kā'anapali are in the lee of the West Maui Mountains and Kīhei and Wailea are in the lee of Haleakalā. Hāna, on the windward side, receives five times as much rain as Lahaina. Sometimes the trade winds are replaced by kona winds that can carry rain and humid, uncomfortable weather from the southwest.

It rains every day somewhere on Maui. Most rain showers are isolated and of short duration. Nasty storms can occur, particularly in the winter. If you plan on hiking in the backcountry pay heed to flash-flood warnings given in local weather forecasts. The West Maui Mountains and Haleakalā create a funneling effect, increasing the velocity of the trade winds as they blow through the Central Valley. Gusty afternoons are common at Mā'alaea and north Kīhei.

Winter storms in the north Pacific create swells and large surf on Maui's north shores. Twenty-foot waves are possible. They are extremely dangerous, but from a safe distance they provide spectacular ocean-watching. Hurricanes and tsunamis are possible but are very rare. Weather forecasts can warn of approaching hurricanes several days in advance. Tsunami warning sirens are positioned throughout the island. They are sounded as a test at 11:45 a.m. on the first government work day of each month.

Good weather is far more likely to embrace you than bad weather. You can appreciate the weather even more during your visit as you scan the newspaper for temperatures back home.

THE HAWAIIAN LANGUAGE

The prevailing language of Hawai'i today is English, liberally peppered with Hawaiian words and phrases. All of a visitor's requests for services can be understood as well as answered in English. An elementary understanding of the Hawaiian language, however, is the foundation of appreciating all of Hawaiian culture and your attempts to correctly pronounce words will show respect to the people who are your hosts. Hawaiian place names are commonly used, so familiarity will breed less contempt when traveling. Some words such as *aloha, lū'au* and *lei* you already knew before you became a *malihini* (newcomer); other words such as *mahalo* (thank you) you will probably add to your vocabulary of the *'ōlelo Hawai'i* (Hawaiian language) on the first day of your visit.

Hawaiian belongs to the Polynesian family of languages, related closely to Tahitian, Marquesan and Māori, and more distantly to Fijian, Malagasy and Malay. The first European to listen to the Hawaiians speak, Captain James Cook, found he was able to communicate with them thanks to his rudimentary grasp of Tahitian. The Hawaiian that Cook heard evolved from the language of the Tahitian voyagers who populated the Hawaiian Islands centuries earlier.

The Hawaiians were rich in unwritten literature that included poems, songs, genealogies and mythologies. Hawaiian existed only in its oral form until the early 19th century. Christian missionaries, anxious to have Hawaiians read their teachings, took up the daunting task of creating a written language. The Hawaiian language, in both oral and written forms, continued as the language of general use for the government, business and social circles for several decades. As their monarchy died, so did usage of the Hawaiians' language. Hawaiian is no longer spoken as the mother tongue except on the privately owned island of Ni'ihau and in the homes of a few old Hawaiians. Some local churches hold services in Hawaiian.

Recently, Hawaiian began receiving renewed attention by the state government and the school system. In 1978 Hawaiian was again made an official language by the State of Hawai'i, the only state to officially use a native language. The government reestablished schools in 1987 that teach in Hawaiian, and the University of Hawai'i offers degree programs in Hawaiian language studies.

Listeners to Hawaiian delight in painting it with such flattering but vague adjectives as melodious, soft, fluid, gentle and mellifluous. Gushing metaphorically, Hawaiian sways like a palm tree in a gentle wind and slips off the tongue like a love song. There are two unvarnished reasons for Hawaiian sounding this way. First, unlike English, Hawaiian has no consonant clusters, and every syllable ends with a vowel, resulting in a high vowel-to-consonant ratio. Second, Hawaiian has no sibilants (s-like sounds), an attribute endearing to singers.

The missionaries assigned only twelve letters to the alphabet when they phonetically rendered the Hawaiian language. The consonants are: h, k, l, m, n, p and w. Five vowels are used: a, e, i, o and u. The consonants are pronounced the same as in English, except for the *w*, which is often pronounced as a *v* when it appears in the middle of a word and follows an *e* or an *i*. When *w* follows an *a* it can be pronounced as either *w* or *v*, thus you will hear either Hawai'i or Havai'i. Hawaiian vowels come in both short and long forms. Long-duration vowels are stressed with a bar above the letter called the *kahakō* in Hawaiian and macron in English. The vowels are pronounced: *a* as in "father" when stressed and as in "above" when not stressed; *e* as in "they" when stressed and as in "let" when not stressed; *i* as in "marine"; *o* as in "boat"; and *u* as in "true." In addition to the *kahakō*s, Hawaiian uses the diacritical mark called an *'okina* and is represented with ' which looks like a backwards apostrophe. The *'okina* indicates a glottal stop and is used as an additional consonant. In English it would approximate the sound between the vowels in the expression "oh-oh." Use of the *kahakō* and the *'okina* are crucial to correct pronunciation of the words in which they appear. Their usage has become more prevalent in recent years; in older guide books and maps they were sometimes omitted.

There's just one more rule you need to learn. Consonants aren't, but vowels can be, clustered into diphthongs. A diphthong is created when two vowels join to form a single sound. The vowels glide together with stress being placed on the first vowel. In English, examples are t<u>oi</u>l and <u>eu</u>phoria. Examples in Hawaiian are *lei* (lay) and *heiau* (hay-ee-ow). The eight vowel pairs that make up Hawaiian diphthongs are: ae, ai, ao, au, ei, eu, oi, ou.

Some words are doubled to emphasize their meaning. *Wiki* means quick, *wikiwiki* means very quick. Hawaiian appears formidable when you are attempting to pronounce many long and similar-looking words. The long words are usually combinations of shorter words and if you divide the long words into their shorter components, pronunciation becomes more easily achievable. Several words begin with *ka,* meaning "the," which is attached to the word itself. Therefore Kā'anapali, which means "the rolling precipices," should be broken down to Ka-a-na-pa-li. The name for Hawai'i's state fish is so long it will barely fit on a T-shirt, but when you break down *humuhumu nukunukuāpua'a* into humu-humu-nuku-nuku-apu-a-a, it <u>is</u> easy!

Glossary of Hawaiian Words

ʻaʻā: rough clinker lava, accepted as the correct geological term

ʻāina: land

aliʻi: chief, royalty

aloha: love, affection, hello, to greet, goodbye

ānuenue: rainbow

ʻapōpō: tomorrow

aʻu: swordfish

hale: house

Hana-: bay

haole: Caucasian, recently come to mean any foreigner.

hapa haole: half Caucasian

hau: hibiscus tiliaceus

hauʻoli: happy

heiau: ancient terrace or platform for worship

he mea iki: you are welcome

hoaloha: friend

Hono-: bay

honu: sea turtle

hukilau: pull-net fishing

hula: Hawaiian dance with chants where a story is told with the hands

ʻiʻiwi: scarlet honeycreeper

imu: underground earthen oven used in cooking at a lūʻau

ka: the

kā: belonging to, of

kahiko: ancient, old

kahuna: priest, expert

kai: sea water, seaward

kālua: to bake in an underground oven; kālua pig is the featured entrée at a lūʻau

kamaʻāina: native, literally "child of the land"

kanaka: human being, man, person

kānaka: human beings, men, persons

kāne: male, man, husband; used to indicate a public men's restroom

kapu: taboo, forbidden, sacred; keep out, if it appears on a sign

keiki: child, children

koa: a type of hardwood

kōkua: to help, assist

Kona: leeward or a leeward wind

kukui: candlenut tree

kula: plain, upland

kuʻu ipo: my sweetheart

lae: point (geographic feature)

lānai: porch, terrace, balcony

lani: heavenly

lei: garland of flowers

lilikoʻi: passion fruit

limu: seaweed

lomilomi: salt salmon minced with onion and tomato

lūʻau: traditional feast

mahalo: thanks, to thank, admiration

makai: toward the sea (used when giving directions)

mahimahi: dolphin fish (not a dolphin!)

maiʻa: banana

maikaʻi: good, fine, beautiful

makaʻāinana: public, common people, citizen

malihini: newcomer, visitor, tourist

mana: supernatural power

manō: shark

Maui nō ka ʻoi: Maui is the best!

mauka: inland (used when giving directions)

mauna: mountain

mele: song

Mele Kalikimaka: Merry Christmas

moana: open sea, ocean

moku: island

muʻumuʻu: long loose-fitting dress introduced by the missionaries

nā: the (plural), by, for

nani: pretty

nēnē: Hawaiian goose

niu: coconut

nui: big, large, important, many, much

'ohana: family, including extended family

'ono: delicious

pāhoehoe: smooth and ropey lava, accepted as the correct geological term

pakalōlō: marijuana, literally "crazy smoke"

pali: cliff, precipice

paniolo: cowboy

pau: finished, completed

poi: starchy paste made from taroroots

poke: cubed, marinated and spiced raw fish

pono: righteous, honest, moral

pua: flower

pua'a: pig

puna: spring, creek

pūpū: hors d'oeuvre

pu'u: hill

'ukulele: small stringed instrument

wa'a: canoe

wahine: woman, wife, female, Mrs.; used to indicate a public women's restroom

wāhine: women

wai: fresh water

wailele: waterfall

wikiwiki: very quick, in a hurry

Meanings of Maui Place Names

Ha'ikū: broken apart

Haleakalā: house of the sun

Hāmoa: Perhaps an old name for Samoa.

Hāna: Poetic for "rainy land, low-lying cloud"

Honokōhau: bay drawing dew

Honokōwai: bay drawing water

'Īao: cloud supreme

Kā'anapali: "Kā'ana cliff;" Kā'ana meaning "division"

Kahana: cutting

Kahului: Probally "the winning"

Kalama: the torch

Kama'ole: childless

Kapalua: two borders

Kaupō: night landing

Ke'anae: the mullet

Keawakapu: the sacred harbor

Kepaniwai: the water dam

Kīhei: shoulder cape

Kula: "plain"

Lahaina: cruel sun

Lahainaluna: upper Lahaina

Mākena: abundance

Maui: name of a demigod

Molokini: many ties

Nāpili: the pili grass

Olowalu: many hills

Pā'ia: noisy

Pukalani: sky opening

Pu'unēnē: goose hill

Pu'uōla'i: earthquake hill

Wai'ānapanapa: glistening water

Waikapū: water of the conch

Wailea: water of Lea, goddess of canoe makers

Wailua: two waters

Wailuku: water of slaughter

Pidgin

Pidgin is the spicy Creole tongue that borrows from other languages. Hawaiian pidgin has roots in the plantation days of the 19th century when European and American owners had to communicate with recently arrived Chinese, Japanese and Portuguese laborers. It was designed as a simple language, born of necessity and stripped of dispensable words.

Modern pidgin is a vernacular of mainly Hawaiian and English words with a unique syntax and a rising inflection that can change the meaning of what is being said. It is a colorful, ever-changing dialect as regionally distinct as the speech of Louisiana Cajuns. No longer plantation talk, pidgin is learned at school and on the streets.

Hip young locals are the main pidgin speakers. They choose to speak pidgin as a private "in" language and are perfectly capable of speaking English. Whole conversations can take place in pidgin or one or two words can be dropped into conventional English. You might not be able to understand what the locals are saying in pidgin (that's the idea), but you should get a sense of what is meant. Pidgin is the mark of the local; newcomers shouldn't attempt to speak it. You won't sound cool—just stupid.

A Sampling of Hawaiian Pidgin

an den?: and then?

any kine: anything, any kind

ass right: that's right, you're correct

beef: fight

brah/bruddah: friend, brother

broke da mout: delicious tasting

buggah: guy or thing that is a pest

bumbye: later on, after a while

chicken skin: bumps on your skin when you get the chills, goose bumps

cockaroach: steal, rip off

da kine: used as filler when the speaker can't think of the right word to use

garans: guaranteed

geevum: go for it, try hard

grind: to eat

grinds: food

Hawaiian time: to be late

howzit?: how is it going? how are you?

lolo: dumb, crazy

Maui wowie: particular type of marijuana

mo bettah: good stuff, great idea

moke: big, tough local guy

pau hana: finish work, quitting time

poi dog: a mutt, a person of mixed ethnic background

stink eye: a dirty look

tita: a tough girl

talk story: a conversation

shahkbait: pale, white-skinned person

yeah yeah yeah yeah: yes I know already so shut up

GEOLOGY

The Hawaiian chain of volcanic peaks—consisting of 132 islands, islets, reefs and shoals—stretches 1,523 miles northwest to southeast across the center of the Pacific Ocean. There is more to the Hawaiian Islands than the land you see. If the ocean were drained of its water, this chain would appear as a lofty mountain range. Maui, second in size, lies second from the southeastern end.

Each volcanic cone is built of dark, iron-rich rock that poured out of vents as highly fluid lava in countless eruptions spanning millions of years. The result is the tallest mountains in the world, which break the surface of the ocean at about 18,000 feet. Haleakalā cone measures five miles from sea floor to summit.

Like most of the world's volcanoes, the Hawaiian cones spawned from a zone of weakness. Weaknesses occur where giant, slow-moving tectonic plates—segments of the Earth's crust—rub and collide as they drift like icebergs atop the mantle. A hot spot is a place where an extraordinary amount of molten rock is generated. Its source is a huge upwelling column of mantle rock. The plume of mantle rock ascends because it is hotter than the surrounding rock, chemically different, or both. When the temperature is high enough, or its pressure has been reduced enough, the rising rock partially melts and pushes through the earth's crust.

The stationary hot spot in the earth's mantle that caused Maui's birth now remains beneath the island of Hawai'i. For 70 million years, a plate of the earth's crust has been moving over that hot spot. Again and again, molten rock has risen from the hot spot to build volcanic islands, and in the seemingly endless procession of geologic time they have drifted away, riding aboard the plate. The oldest volcanoes created by this event are the submerged Emperor Seamounts, which now lie north of the island of Midway. The youngest volcano is a burgeoning seamount named Lō'ihi, 20 miles southeast of the island of Hawai'i. This embryonic island must grow another 3,180 feet before it emerges from the ocean—60,000 years from now.

Sometimes, separate cones were close enough to each other for their lava flows to merge and form a single island. Maui is such an island. Sea levels have been restless, see-sawing with the thaws and freezes of ice-age glaciers and continental ice sheets. In the last million years, four great ice sheets moved out from polar regions, then retreated, causing sea level to fluctuate. The islands of Maui, Lāna'i, Moloka'i and Kaho'olawe form the Maui group, which stands as a pedestal on the Hawaiian ridge. During the cold periods, the sea level dropped enough to expose the "saddles" between the islands of the Maui group. This single, large island, Maui Nui, was about half the size of the present island of Hawaiʻi.

Maui is a high island. One quarter of its surface lies above the 2,900-foot contour and three quarters of it lies above the 500-foot contour. Maui's coastline is 140 miles long with 29 miles of that being sea cliffs higher than 100 feet. The most remote point from the sea is 10.6 miles.

The two volcanoes that form Maui are sisters, not twins. The West Maui Mountains resulted from the older cone and are heavily dissected. Rising twice as high above sea level, the more recent cone formed Haleakalā, which has a relatively smooth surface. The West Maui Mountains, covered in vegetation, rest upon an extinct cone. Haleakalā, bare rock at high altitude, last erupted a few centuries ago.

Maui takes the shape of an asymmetric figure eight with two large bays at its waist. Lava flowing down Haleakalā pooled against the pre-existing West Maui volcano. Streams coursing their way out of West Maui canyons covered those flows hundreds of feet deep with sediment called alluvium. The isthmus that resulted lies between Kahului Bay at the north and Māʻalaea Bay at the south. This area is often referred to as the Central Valley.

The volcanoes of the Hawaiian chain are rounded, dome-shaped masses, broad for their height. In profile, they resemble the shields of medieval warriors, and are known as shield volcanoes. These emerge from vents that effuse highly mobile lava that runs swiftly and spreads widely, accreting a cone of gentle slope.

Around the rim of the Pacific Ocean more viscous lava flows have produced the classic upswept form of a composite volcano. The lava does not flow far before it solidifies, building higher and higher around its vent. Famous composite volcanoes are Fuji in Japan and Rainier, Hood, Shasta and St. Helens in the United States.

Hawaiian volcanoes generally erupt along cracks in the cone's flanks. Movement within the earth's crust tears open a series of fissures, forming a rift zone. Pressing through the cracks, magma fountains onto the land as lava. When an eruption is over, the lava remaining in the fissure hardens into a wall-like mass called a dike. These half-yard wide formations surface prominently in Ukumehame Canyon on West Maui and in the summit depression of Haleakalā.

Volcanic activity built the shield of West Maui; running water shaped it. The peak, Puʻukukui, receives about 390 inches of rain a year, ranking it among the wettest places on Earth. Waiheʻe, Waiehu, ʻĪao and Waikapū streams have cut deeply into the West Maui volcano, transporting its core material and depositing it in fan-shaped banks, called alluvial fans, at the mouths of canyons. The fans have joined to form an alluvial plain, which is now partly planted in sugarcane.

At a height of 10,023 feet above sea level, Haleakalā still only exposes seven percent of its mass. Fifteen times more than what we see lies beneath the waves. Haleakalā is shaped like a triangle with its apex eroded away. The ridges sloping downward mark its three major rifts—north, east and southwest. The summit is an oval-shaped depression seven miles long and 2.5 miles wide.

Haleakalā is not capped with a volcanic crater, although the term crater is often used. A volcanic crater forms either as material is blown out of the top of a cone, or as a vent region sinks to become a caldera. Haleakalā is the result of neither explosive activity nor of sinking. Once, its peak was 3,000 feet higher than it is now. A long period of erosion occurred as streams worked headward, toward their source, enlarging and deepening the valleys.

The heads of Ke'anae and Kaupō Valleys came nearly to the point of joining. When lava flooded the region between the heads of the greatly eroded valleys it created the summit depression atop Haleakalā.

Maui, which appeared late in geological history, is doomed to extinction, but on a time-scale of a magnitude that defies comprehension. It will be eroded to a shoal as the plate that carried it past the hot spot of its birth inches inexorably toward the edges of the Pacific. Like a conveyor belt, the plate trundles to the Aleutian Trench, where the sea floor bends into the earth's interior. Maui's cycle will be complete as its remnants are reincorporated into the crust of the earth.

HISTORY

People Come to Maui

People did not rush to settle in the world's most remote place. Humans have inhabited other parts of the earth 60 times longer than they have lived in Hawai'i. The first migrations to Maui and the other Hawaiian islands likely came from the 11 islands that make up the Marquesas, 2,000 miles to the southeast. The Marquesans were masters at building great double-hulled canoes. The two hulls were fastened together to form a catamaran with a cabin built in the center. At 60-80 feet long, these voyaging canoes could carry an extended family of 30 people as well as all the staples they would need in a new land.

As new evidence comes to light, anthropologists have pushed the date of the first journey to Hawai'i back to about 400 A.D. The Polynesians sailors had neither charts nor navigational instruments, but relied on an internal navigational system programmed by intuition, knowledge and experience.

The first settlers came prepared. With them they brought useful plants such as taro, ti, sugarcane, ginger, yams, bamboo and the breadfruit tree. They also brought the small pigs of Polynesia, dogs, fowl and stowaway rats. Native lowland forests were cleared with slash-and-burn techniques to plant crops. The new Hawaiians started to irreversibly and profoundly alter their environment. Habitat loss, competition for food, and predation by the introduced animals wrought havoc upon the native animals. Many species of birds had already become extinct before the arrival of Europeans.

Likely the southernmost island of Hawai'i was the first to be settled. To the northwest, Maui could be easily accessed by crossing the narrow channel and the migration would have continued across the Hawaiian chain.

For seven centuries the Marquesans continued their voyages to Hawai'i. They lived peacefully on the new land and the tribes coexisted

Man of the Sandwich Islands *by John Webber*

Hawai'i State Archives

Hawaiian war canoe with masked paddlers *by John Webber*

Hawaiʻi State Archives

in relative harmony since there was no competition for land.

In about the 12th century, an exodus of aggressive Tahitians arrived and subjugated the settled Hawaiians. On the southern shore of Maui there are ancient ruins called Kahiki-nui, the Hawaiian word for Tahiti (or horizon). The Tahitian priest Paʻao introduced the warlike god Ku and replaced basic animistic beliefs with the rigid *kapu* (forbidden) system. Deciding that the Hawaiian blueblood was too diluted, Paʻao summoned Pili, a Tahitian chief, to establish a new royal lineage. With Pili as ruler and Paʻao as high priest, a new dynasty was formed. It was to last seven centuries.

The Tahitian migration lasted for about a century. Their intricate system of beliefs and practices was transformed into a stratified and rigid Hawaiian culture. This caste system placed the *aliʻi* or noble class at the top. Slightly below in prestige were the *kāhuna*, which included priests, healers and astrologers. Lower down were the *kanakawale*, the craftsmen and artisans who made the canoes, calabashes and lei. Next were the *makaʻāinana* or common people who worked the land, and at the bottom were the *kauwā* or untouchables. The noble class had lower chiefs within it who provided the higher chief with taxes and commoners to serve as soldiers. Land was divided among the chiefs into wedge-shaped plots, called *ahupuaʻa*, which extended from the ocean inland to the mountain peaks. The tightly circumscribed bloodlines could not be crossed. Most people were at death what they had been at birth. Life centered on the *kapu*, a complete set of rules that dictated what was sacred or forbidden. A *kapu* forbade women to eat pork, bananas and shark meat; nor could they eat in the company of men. According to the 19th century Hawaiian scholar, David Malo, a person could not allow his shadow to fall upon the house of a chief, or pass through that chief's stockade or doorway.

Kapu-breakers were believed to be violating the will of the gods and could be executed. While many *kapu* may seem strange, some were founded as conservation measures, such as seasons being established for the gathering or catching of scarce food. The word *kapu* is believed to be the Hawaiian version of the Tahitian *tapu*, from which the word taboo is also derived.

Hawaiians generally worshiped privately at small shrines or in their homes. The focal points of most major religious observances were large open-air temples known as *heiau*. Ruins of these *heiau* can still be found throughout Hawai'i. Today what remains are usually simple platforms, terraces and walls made of lava stones.

Because ancient Hawaiians did not have a written language, their past was kept alive with by the voices of *kahuna* who chanted the sacred *mele*. The most important *mele* was called the Kumulipo and it retold the genealogies of the *ali'i*. It was by their direct lineage to the progenitor gods, Wakea and Papa that the *ali'i* claimed divine right to rule. They believed the union of these gods gave birth to the islands of Maui, Kaho'olawe, Hawai'i, Kaua'i and Ni'ihau, and the rest of the Hawaiian Islands were created when these gods took other mates.

The Kumulipo tells that 20 generations before the great Maui chief, Pi'ilani, ruled in the 16th century, the prince Maui-Loa held reign as the first independent sovereign of Maui. He was born in Kaupō and waged battles with many of the district chieftains; establishing his authority at a young age. In return for the help of his uncle, Prince Haho, the king of Hawai'i, Maui-Loa ceded the district of Hāna to Hawai'i. This cession was the root cause of many fierce battles between Hawai'i and Maui for generations to come.

The ten kings of Maui who succeeded Maui-Loa consolidated their strength, built up their armies and created an island-nation that at times threatened even the might of the powerful kings of Hawai'i. It was said that the prince Kamalu-Ohua took more pleasure from the company of women than from the responsibilities of government. He was lulled into a false sense of security—unconcerned with the ambition of his cousin in Hawai'i. Across the 'Alenuihāhā Channel, Prince Kalunui-Ohua set his covetous eyes towards the other islands of the archipelago. Kalunui-Ohua gathered provisions, assembled a fleet of war canoes and moved against the island of Maui. The powerful army from the island of Hawai'i conquered Maui and then quickly took Moloka'i and O'ahu. Next in line was Kaua'i, but the invading army was soundly defeated by forces lead by Prince Kukona.

Following his defeat on Kaua'i, Kalunui-Ohua returned to Hawai'i to rule and Kamalu-Ohua again ruled Maui. The Hawaiian monarchs of this era carried the epithetic title of "Ohua," which means manservant. It was a description borne proudly by the descendants of the sacred Prince Kanipahu, King of Hawai'i. Kanipahu was overthrown from power by his half-brother and was forced to labor as a servant. The title "Ohua" memorializes this period of humiliation and servitude and bestows royal sanctification upon menial labor.

Prior to the 16th century, the domains of Maui rulers shifted periodically, sometimes reaching beyond Maui's shores. West Maui chief Kaka'alaneo, along with his brother, Kaka'e, ruled over Lāna'i as well from a court in Lahaina. Kaka'alaneo, known for his thrift and energy, had a reign free of strife and want.

In the 1500s, Pi'ilani, a great-grandson of Kaka'e, pushed Maui to the fore politically. He is the most revered of the Maui monarchs and is credited with being the 130th-generation descendant of Wakea, the god of light. Pi'ilani's power extended from Hāna to West Maui and included the neighboring islands of Lāna'i, Moloka'i, and Kaho'olawe, and his reign inaugurated a long period of peace, stability and prosperity. He constructed the only ancient road to encircle a Hawaiian island. Known as the King's Highway, this rock-paved passageway was four to six feet wide and 138 miles long. It facilitated travel

and communication throughout the realm. Sections of the King's Highway still exist and can be traveled on foot as they were four centuries ago.

A long-standing alliance with the island of Hawai'i dissolved during the reign of a chief named Kekaulike, but he was able to repel the invaders and maintain power. His son lost Hāna to the armies from Hawai'i, but his brother and successor, Kahekili, returned the east Maui region to the fold.

In the late 18th century, Kahekili, Maui's ruthless and fierce chief, held court in Wailuku. He appeared likely to be the first chief powerful enough to conquer the entire island group. Kahekili appropriated the island of O'ahu from his own adopted son, killed him in the process, and placed his brother on Kaua'i as ruling chief. His most formidable opponent was Kamehameha from the island of Hawai'i—rumored to be his son. Before they could battle, at dawn on January 18, 1778, sailors from an unimagined land sailed into Hawaiian waters. Two ships under the command of Captain James Cook appeared on the horizon. An event marking the onset of the modern age of Hawaiian history had occurred.

Strangers From a Strange Land

Captain Cook departed Plymouth, England in 1776. His mission was to find the long-sought Northwest Passage. For more than two centuries, European

Captain James Cook

The first Hawaiian island that Cook sighted was Oʻahu. Calm winds held his ships offshore during the night while he drifted west until he was in view of Kauaʻi. As the ships worked their way closer to Kauaʻi's shore, natives paddled canoes out to meet them. The intrepid Englishmen were given a friendly although timid reception. Cook found a suitable place to drop anchor at Waimea Bay.

Cook went ashore with a guard of armed marines. He was surprised that his presence caused the natives to fall face down to the ground, rising only with his encouragement. Captain Cook didn't understand that the islanders prostrating themselves in his presence and his reverential treatment resulted from the propitious timing of his arrival. Every year during the winter months a festival called *makahiki* was held throughout the Islands. It was a period of rejoicing and festivity dedicated to honoring Lono, the fertility god of the earth. The islanders celebrated by feasting, dancing, playing games and freely exchanging sex partners. According to legend, Lono was to someday arrive on moving islands. Cook's appearance, commanding ships larger, and like no other the natives had seen, was interpreted as the coming of a god.

explorers had tried unsuccessfully to map a link between the Atlantic and Pacific Oceans via a route atop the North American continent. Cook had been instructed to find the theorized passage from a western approach by The Earl of Sandwich, First Lord of the British Admiralty. The sea passage was officially to be the sole object of his search, but it was Captain James Cook's destiny to turn prosaic instructions into accounts of history.

Cook commanded the 100-foot flagship, HMS *Resolution*, and her companion, the 90-foot HMS *Discovery*. Among Cook's crew were midshipman George Vancouver and William Bligh, who was sailing master on the *Resolution*. Vancouver would go on to captain his own voyages in the Pacific and along the west coast of North America. Ten years later, Bligh became the infamous commander of the HMS *Bounty*.

The *kāhuna* wanted to test the force of this apparition. A real god, they believed, had no want of women; men did. With the approval of the Hawaiian men, throngs of women swarmed the ships to offer their bodies to please Lono and his attendants; whereby the sailors quickly failed their test of divinity. Cook gave strict orders prohibiting sexual relations with the Hawaiians. Of the 112 members of Cook's expedition, 66 showed symptoms of venereal disease. The infected crewmembers were not allowed ashore. The attempt to keep the native population free of this disease, to which they had never been exposed, proved futile. Despite the exhibition of ungodlike behavior from his crew, Cook did not associate with any of the women. Whether this interloper was a deity was something the Hawaiians could ponder in his absence.

The stores of the *Resolution* and the *Discovery* were replenished and on January 23, 1778, five days after first sighting a Hawaiian island, they sailed north—the Northwest Passage once again the object of their quest. In honor of his patron in the British Admiralty, Cook christened the islands he came upon by chance the Sandwich Islands.

The next leg of Cook's journey took him through the Bering Strait into the Arctic Ocean. In the middle of summer, at a latitude of N 70° 44', an impenetrable wall of pack ice halted Cook's progress. Disappointed, he decided to return to the warmth of the Sandwich Islands.

On the return trip, winds carried Cook to the east of Kaua'i. At daybreak on November 26, 1778, Cook sighted the island of Maui. In his logbook, Cook described what he saw:

> We were now satisfied, that the group of the Sandwich Islands had been only imperfectly discovered; as those of them which we had visited in our progress Northward, all lie to the leeward of our present station.
>
> In the country was an elevated saddle hill, whose summit appeared above the clouds. From this hill, the land fell in a gentle slope, and terminated in a steep rocky coast, against which the sea

An offering before Captain Cook *by John Webber*

broke in a dreadful surf. Finding that we could not weather the island, I bore up, and ranged along the coast to the Westward. It was not long before we saw people on several parts of the shore, and some houses and plantations. The country seemed to be both well wooded and watered; and running streams were seen falling into the sea in various places.

The natives on Maui spotted the ships and paddled their canoes out to greet him. Maui's principal chief, Kahekili, paid a visit to Charles Clerke, who captained the *Discovery*, and brought a red feather cloak as a gift. The island of Hawai'i's king, Kanaliopu'u, who was battling in the Hāna district of Maui, brought some of his people to stay overnight on the *Resolution*. Some of those who stayed aboard had venereal sores and were given medicine. In less than a year, the infection brought by the English sailors had spread throughout the islands.

The rocky and exposed north coast of Maui offered no safe anchorage. The English continued sailing to the last and largest island of the chain. For a month Cook sailed along the northern and eastern shores of the island the natives called Hawai'i. He was frustrated in his search for a safe anchorage until he rounded South Point and sailed into the shelter of Kealakekua Bay on January 17, 1779. The two ships anchored in the bay and were received by 10,000 Hawaiians who lined the shore and filled a flotilla of 3,000 canoes.

By an even greater coincidence, Cook's second visit to the Hawaiian Islands was again during *makahiki* and he chose Kealakekua Bay. According to Hawaiian legend, Kealakekua Bay was considered Lono's private, sacred harbor. Natives from around the island came to pay homage to what they were sure was a returning god.

Congenial relations prevailed for the next two weeks. But the English overstayed their welcome when restocking supplies for another voyage north nearly exhausted the resources of the islanders. On the morning of February 4, the English set sail along the coast to the north followed by a canoe entourage. After the ships cleared the north point of the island, a violent winter storm broke the foremast of the *Resolution*. Cook's flagship limped back to Kealakekua Bay so that the carpenters could make repairs.

Cook found that the time of the *makahiki* had expired when he returned. The Hawaiians began to share their doubts that a true god would return after the *makahiki*. While repairs to the mast were being made, some natives stole a cutter from the *Discovery*. An infuriated Cook went ashore with Lt. James King and nine marines with the intent of taking Kalaniopu'u hostage in exchange for return of the boat. As Cook and his party searched for the chief, a large crowd of natives gathered around them. When Cook decided to leave, a skirmish erupted at the water's edge. A native menaced Cook with a stone and a long iron spike. Cook fired at the native, but the shot could not penetrate the heavy straw mat that he wore as armor. The native turned triumphantly to the crowd to show them he was unharmed. Emboldened, the crowd of Hawaiians threw stones at the marines who were lined up against the water. When the crowd

winds moved the ships off the dry and uninviting shore of Kaho'olawe. Later they were able to tack along the shore near Lahaina, where they spent time trading with natives who paddled out in canoes. Captain Clerke sailed to the north shore of O'ahu before he made another futile attempt at finding the

Death of Captain Cook *by John Webber*

Hawai'i State Archives

surged forward, Cook turned toward his boat and was stabbed in the neck by a native with a dagger. He fell face down in the shallow water, where several natives stabbed and clubbed him to death. Four marines were killed as they struggled back to their boat. As the six survivors rowed to safety, they saw their captain's bludgeoned body being dragged away by the Hawaiians.

Charles Clerke succeeded to command the expedition. He intended to explore Maui further but adverse

Northwest Passage, dying of tuberculosis before he reached home.

The return of the *Resolution* and the *Discovery* to England caused little fanfare in a nation whose attention had been focused on the war with the American colonies. Maps and accounts of their voyages did spawn European and American expeditions of discovery and trade. Although he sighted Maui, Cook never set foot on its soil. The distinction of being the first European to land on Maui's shores went, seven years later, to the seasoned French explorer, Admiral Jean-Francois de Galaup, Comte de La Pérouse.

Commanding the frigates *Astrolabe* and *Boussole*, La Pérouse sighted the island of Maui on May 28, 1786. The next morning, rough seas prevented a landing along the Hāna coastline. La Pérouse continued south, deciding on Keoneʻōʻio as a site to land and trade with the natives. Within a few hours, 300 squealing pigs were loading onto the decks of the French ships. La Pérouse and an armed party reconnoitered four small villages. Security precautions proved unneeded. On his encounter with Hawaiians, La Pérouse wrote:

> …the women showed by the most expressive gestures that there was no mark of kindness they were not disposed to confer upon us, and the men in the most respectful attitude endeavored to discover the motive of our visit in order to anticipate our desires…I had no idea of a people so mild and attentive.

Bolstered by provisions and frustrated by the lack of a safe harbor, La Pérouse set sail, never to return to Maui. The fleeting, three hour tour by Maui's first visitor was commemorated by renaming Keoneʻōʻio as La Pérouse Bay.

By the end of the 18th century, ship captains from all over the world were dropping anchor in Hawaiʻi to replenish supplies and repair their vessels. In January 1790, the American merchant ship *Eleanora*, commanded by Capt. Simon Metcalfe, sailed into the waters of Honuaʻula, Maui. One night, natives stole a boat that was tied to the *Eleanora*, killing the sailor on watch in the process. Upon discovering the theft the next day, an angry Metcalfe bombarded the village of Honuaʻula with grapeshot and sent his men ashore to set fire to the huts and heiaus. The *Eleanora* moved down the coast to Olowalu, a beach five miles east of Lahaina, and Metcalfe planned a more terrible revenge to vent his malevolence. Under the ruse of wanting to trade peacefully, Metcalfe enticed 200 canoe loads of natives out to the ship. When they were in range, the captain ordered point-blank cannon fire on the innocent natives. Metcalfe supervised the carnage from his post on deck as 100 Hawaiians were slain and another 150 were seriously wounded. Simon Metcalfe then sailed away to the island of Hawaiʻi, unrepentant of what has been termed the Olowalu Massacre.

From Force and Might Come Unity

Captain Cook met his end trying to capture chief Kalaniopuʻu. Injured by gunfire in the skirmish was Kamehameha, nephew of the Hawaiian chief. Towering above others at six feet, six inches, Kamehameha was soon to become Hawaiʻi's greatest warrior-chief.

Hawaiʻi became a port of call for the newly opened fur trade between North America and China. In exchange for provisions, the Hawaiians were demanding guns in trade.

Hawai'i State Archives

A man of the Sandwich Islands in a mask *by John Webber*

Kamehameha did well in the Hawaiian arms race. Looting an American ship for its cannons and firearms and kidnapping two skilled seamen to advise him were what he needed to tip the balance of power with competing chiefs in his favor.

After the death of his uncle, Kalaniopu'u, from whom he received his early military training, Kamehameha formed a shaky truce with his cousins. This gave the ambitious Kamehameha time to aim his aggression at Maui. His forces' canoes heavy with firearms, Kamehameha confronted the warriors of Maui. Kalanikupule, the son of Kahekili, who was on O'ahu, led the defenders. Kamehameha landed first on the shores of Ko'olau district at Hanawana. Successful in this battle, Kamehameha sailed his forces to Kahului to engage in another battle. Kalanikupule's army was forced to retreat to the deathtrap that was steep-sided 'Īao Valley. Kamehameha's firepower overwhelmed the doomed warriors of Maui. So many men were slaughtered that their bodies dammed the bloodied waters of 'Īao Stream. A plaque erected in the valley commemorates this battle called *ka pani wai*, meaning "the damming of the waters."

Kamehameha could savor his victory for only a short time. His domain on the island of Hawai'i was under siege from his enemies, necessitating his return. In Kamehameha's absence, Kahekili returned from O'ahu to regain control of Maui. Not satisfied, Kahekili loaded his canoes with newly acquired guns and backed by a fearsome-looking battalion with eyelids turned inside out, attacked Kamehameha in the waters surrounding the Big Island. The two great warriors fought Hawai'i's first armed sea battle to an indecisive conclusion.

In the midst of the strife between the kings of Maui and Hawai'i the English explorer, George Vancouver, returned to Hawai'i and Maui in 1793. Vancouver, promoted from his duties as James Cook's midshipman, now led his own expedition for the British and commanded his own flagship—also named the *Discovery*. After visiting Kamehameha, with whom he formed a friendship, Vancouver sailed to Maui, following the path taken by La Pérouse seven years earlier. Sailing past La Pérouse Bay, Vancouver met with a

Hawai'i State Archives

Kamehameha I at spear practice

chief who came out to the ship in a canoe. Vancouver used the chief as a messenger to send a gift and message of friendship to Maui's King Kahekili. Setting anchor at Lahaina, Vancouver observed the western shores of Maui to be in a state of devastation from the depredations of years of warfare waged between Kamehameha and Kahekili. The few Hawaiians who did come out to trade did so in worn or inferior canoes and had little livestock or produce with which to barter. Vancouver presented repeated arguments to the Maui chiefs to reach a peaceful settlement with Kamehameha. The Maui chiefs held Vancouver in high regard but would not trust Kamehameha. Vancouver sailed on, refusing requests to take sides in the dispute or to sell firearms.

Kahekili returned to O'ahu and died peacefully in 1794 at the age of 81. His half-brother, Ka'eokūlani, assumed the rule of Maui but was subsequently killed in a battle on O'ahu. Kamehameha, now with complete control over the island of Hawai'i and fortified once again by Western expertise and firearms,

invaded and easily conquered Maui and then Moloka'i. When a small civil war broke out on O'ahu, Kamehameha took advantage of the disorder. Landing at Waikīkī in 1795, Kamehameha's warriors steadily drove the defenders, led by Kalanikupule, who had escaped from the slaughter at 'Īao Valley, back into the surrounding mountains. The beleaguered army from O'ahu made its last stand at Nu'uanu Pali, a great precipice in the mountains behind present-day Honolulu. Kamehameha's army claimed final victory by literally pushing the retreating warriors over the top. The king of Kaua'i, Kaumuali'i, accepting the inevitable, recognized Kamehameha as supreme ruler and thereby spared his people the ravages of a needless war. By 1810, Kamehameha undisputedly ruled all the islands—a first in Hawaiian history.

United under Kamehameha's rule, the islanders enjoyed a time of peace unlike what they had ever experienced. The king moved his royal court to Lahaina, where in 1803 he built the "Brick Palace," the first permanent building in Hawai'i. Although Kamehameha retained the *kapu* system and readily applied its punishments, he also learned the ways of the foreigners whose ships he supplied with provisions. These foreigners were expressing great interest in Hawai'i's sandalwood forests.

The lucrative market for the beautiful and fragrant wood was in China. To reap the greatest gain from trading the wood, the king made the business a government monopoly, requiring all trade to go through him. Realizing that the forests would soon be depleted, he put *kapus* on young trees to protect them. Even so, the depletion that would eventually decimate the sandalwood forests had begun.

During his life, Kamehameha had 21 wives. In 1795, he married highborn Keōpūolani, with whom he fathered 11 children. Two of those sons survived to maturity and eventually succeeded him as Hawaiian monarchs. Even though she bore his heirs, Keōpūolani was not the king's favorite wife. That honor belonged to Ka'ahumanu, the only daughter of Maui High Chiefs Ke'eaumoku and Namahana.

Ka'ahumanu was born in a small cave near Hāna, Maui in about 1773. At six feet tall and 200 pounds, the king thought her to be a beautiful and desirable woman. On May 8, 1819, when Kamehameha the Great died, Ka'ahumanu was at his bedside. She charged that with his last breath, he had named her *kuhina nui*, the person who would run his kingdom and take care of his heir, 20-year-old Liholiho.

Queen Ka'ahumanu

Hawai'i State Archives

Seven days after the bones of Kamehameha had been laid away, the chiefs of the kingdom gathered in a great half circle at the seashore, clothed in feather cloaks and helmets. Ka'ahumanu addressed the assemblage. She proclaimed Liholiho as the "Divine One" and said the will of Kamehameha was that she and Liholiho would jointly rule the kingdom. Liholiho became Kamehameha II and Ka'ahumanu was the powerful Queen Regent.

Immediately, Ka'ahumanu made an incredible demand on the new, young king. She petitioned him to lead the way to the abandonment of the foundation of Hawaiian society's beliefs and conduct—the *kapu* system. It was *kapu* for women of any rank to enter the *luakini heiau*s, where political as well as religious decisions were made. Thus, while her relationship to the Kamehamehas, father and son, gave her a position of power, her gender kept her from wielding her power fully. Liholiho hesitated at first, but after two days of drinking rum he gave way to her sizeable will. He attended a feast arranged by Ka'ahumanu and, by eating with women, he broke the onerous *kapu* forbidding men and women to eat together. When the king ordered that *heiau*s and religious images throughout the kingdom be destroyed, his subjects knew he was serious. The Hawaiians, whose belief system had been seriously eroded, were a people adrift in a spiritual vacuum.

Two weeks before Liholiho had abolished the *kapu* system, a ship carrying Protestant missionaries left Boston bound for Hawai'i. They were in search of souls to save.

All God's Children Must Go to Heaven

The attention of the American Board of Commissioners for Foreign Missions was drawn to Hawai'i by a young Hawaiian visitor they called Henry Obookiah. The young Christian convert expressed anguish for his unredeemed countrymen before he died of typhus. This inspired the American Board to organize a missionary company to go to Hawai'i. Six months and 18,000 miles later, the missionaries landed on the island of Hawai'i and presented themselves to Liholiho. In 1823, they established a mission on Maui.

Queen Regent Ka'ahumanu treated the missionaries with regal haughtiness before she fell gravely ill. Hiram Bingham's wife, Sybil, nursed her back to health, and Ka'ahumanu emerged the unfailing friend of the missionaries, much more receptive to Christian teachings. In April 1824, she publicly announced her conversion to Christianity. Soon many prominent chiefs converted and thousands of commoners listened to the missionaries' preachings.

Wanting the Hawaiians to read the gospel for themselves, the missionaries decided they must reduce the Hawaiian language to written form. Again, they focused on the leaders by first teaching the chiefs to read and write. The mass of Hawaiians eagerly followed. In 1831 a high school was founded in the hills overlooking Lahaina on Maui. The school was called Lahainaluna, and its purpose was to train young men to become assistant ministers and teachers. Lahainaluna High School stands today at the same location.

The Rev. William Richards and Rev. Charles Stewart led the crusade against the debauchery that whalers were perpetrating upon Lahaina. After a 15-year career at the Lahaina mission, Richards could lay claim to having translated a third of the Bible into Hawaiian. Richards left the mission to become the king's teacher and translator, focusing on the teaching of politics and government to the chiefs and native scholars. As a result, Richards' students composed a declaration of rights in 1839, followed in 1840 by Hawai'i's first constitution. In 1842, representing the king, he met with world leaders and secured American, French and British recognition of Hawaiian independence.

In the 19th century, the American Board of Commissioners for Foreign Missions dispatched 37 missionaries to Maui, not counting the wives who labored beside their husbands. Not all missionaries were ordained ministers, nor were they all white men. Betsey Stockton, a former slave, taught at Lahaina. Maria Ogden spent almost 30 years instructing children at Lahaina and Wailuku. Lydia Brown came independently as a

missionary and spent five years teaching native girls how to spin and weave Maui-grown cotton and wool. The board sent the multi-talented Edward Bailey as a teacher, but he also served as an agriculturist, physician, architect, engineer, businessman, botanist, surveyor, poet, musician, and artist during his years at Wailuku. His house still stands, now a museum dedicated to his work and talents.

To the missionaries' dismay, the Roman Catholic Church broke the monopoly on Hawaiian souls. Called the "Apostle of Maui," Hawaiian layperson Helio Koaeloa introduced Catholicism in the late 1830s. The first official Catholic mission on Maui was formed in 1846 and in 1858 they constructed Lahaina's landmark Maria

Hawai'i State Archives

An officer of the king *by Jacques Arago,*

Lanakila Church. Following just a few paces behind were the Mormons. In 1851, in the village of Kealahou, Elder George Q. Cannon founded the first Hawaiian branch of the Church of Jesus Christ of Latter Day Saints. By 1853, almost every Hawaiian was a member of some church. Before the century ended, Mormons and Catholics combined outnumbered Protestant church members six to one.

The Whalers' Tale

When Maui's sandalwood forests were spent, whaling took over as the important economic activity. In 1820, Captain Joseph Allen of Nantucket commanded the first whaling vessel to put into Honolulu Harbor. The only two ports in Hawai'i that were suitable anchorages for the whaling ships were Honolulu and Lahaina. In 1846, 429 whaling ships visited Lahaina, bettering Honolulu's 167. In one record-breaking season, more than 100 vessels crammed the shallow waters off Lahaina at one time.

The entire island of Maui benefited from the economic impact of whaling. Rural Hawaiians supplied produce, meat and firewood to replenish the ship's stores. The American whalers' appetites for potatoes lead to its extensive cultivation in Kula.

Crews on whaling ships lived wretched lives. The officers were often brutal men who enjoyed the iron hold they had on men at sea. After a four-year voyage, a seaman might walk away from his ship with as little as $100 for his labors. To make a voyage more profitable, a ruthless captain might persecute a crewmember to the point where he would jump ship at the next port and his pay would revert to the ship. One young whaler who came ashore at Lahaina on May 2, 1843, never returned to his ship, the *Charles and Henry*. At the age of 24, he had his fill of life aboard a whaling ship. After a brief period of employment in Honolulu, Herman Melville returned to the United States and wrote *Moby Dick*.

Most whale men that came ashore did not behave as sober, law-abiding citizens. They had endured months of bullying and hardships at sea and were inclined to celebrate to excess. The whalers' ports of call were rife with drunkenness and prostitution. The Rev. Lorrin Andrews wrote to a fellow clergyman about the situation: "the Devil is busily engaged in Lahaina." Conditions degraded to a point where Maui Governor Hoapili, a Christian convert, forbade prostitution and drinking alcohol in 1826. Ship arrivals decreased for the 12 years this prohibition was in effect, but with Hoapili's death, Lahaina again bloomed as a center of vice and debauchery.

Whaling's decline began in the 1850s, owing to the scarcity of whales. The death knell of the industry rang when the first commercially successful oil well was drilled in Pennsylvania in 1859. Petroleum and its derivative, kerosene, proved to be a better and more cheaply produced fuel than whale oil.

Add Sugar to the Mix

The Polynesians who settled Maui brought with them cuttings of sugarcane. Soon, the cane was growing wild on the island. Early Chinese residents brought knowledge of sugar production with them and in 1828, two merchants established the Hungtai sugar works at Wailuku.

As whaling declined in Maui, business interests turned to sugarcane. Whereas whaling had been a boon to merchants, sugarcane would sprout wealth for the land barons. Included in those who were snapping up Maui land were missionaries and their offspring. The plantation system, with its concept of growing crops for profit rather than subsistence, celebrated capitalism and marked the introduction of wage labor to Maui.

Sugar plantations are labor intensive and the native population of Maui was in decline, due largely to imported diseases. The pragmatic islanders that were left saw little value in the backbreaking, low-paying work of harvesting sugarcane, especially when the land and the sea offered them plenty of food staples. Plantation owners recruited workers accustomed to working long days in hot weather from overseas. In 1852, the first group of indentured workers came from China. In the decades to follow, immigrants from Japan, Portugal, the Philippines and Korea came to toil in the cane fields and to add to the ethnic mix of the Islands.

In 1854, a sea captain brought a better variety of cane from Tahiti, which became known as Lahaina cane. By 1861 the number of sugar plantations on Maui had risen to twenty-two. A boom in demand resulted when the supply from Louisiana was cut off during the American Civil War. The Wailuku Sugar Company was organized in 1862 by a syndicate lead by the C. Brewer Company. Hired as manager of the company was Edward Bailey, who had arrived on Maui as a missionary 25 years earlier.

A millionaire sugar baron from California named Claus Spreckels set sail for Hawai'i aboard the steamer *City of San Francisco* in 1876. The ship also carried the first news of the passage by Congress of the Reciprocity Treaty. Spreckels speculated that the treaty, which allowed importation of Hawai'i sugar without tariff, would drive up prices. Ever the opportunist, he proceeded to buy over half of the sugar crop of 1877 before the price rise had time to take effect. Using his profits, Spreckels bought a part interest in the Waihe'e Plantation on Maui in 1878. He then secured the rights to purchase and lease 40,000 acres of Maui land. More importantly, he needed the water rights for the northern slope of Haleakalā and the right to build a ditch to conduct the water to his plantation in the central valley. Spreckels petitioned the cabinet for the water rights but they wanted time to study the matter. Luckily for Spreckels, a crony of his was none other than King David Kalākaua. After a night of sharing a few bottles of champagne with the Spreckelses, Kalākaua awakened the cabinet in order to accept their resignations. For his favors, Spreckels gave the king a gift of $10,000 plus a loan of $40,000. But the manipulative sugar magnate wasn't done yet. He bought the purported claim to one half of the crown lands of Hawai'i held by Princess Ruth Ke'elikolani for $10,000. The princess' claim was tenuous but Spreckels was able to use it a bargaining tool. In trade for relinquishing his claim, Spreckels obtained outright title to the 24,000 acres of land he leased in Maui. He then built a mill at Pu'unēnē and organized under the name of the Hawaiian Commercial and Sugar Company.

Pineapple emerged as Hawai'i's second major cash crop in the early 1900s. James Dole, a cousin of Sanford, purchased the island of Lāna'i and developed it into the world's largest pineapple plantation. Maui pineapple pioneer Dwight David Baldwin first shipped the fruit fresh to the mainland in 1900 and four years later, with his brother Henry, built Maui's first cannery.

Maui and the Military

When Japan attacked Pearl Harbor on December 7, 1941, Hawai'i was immediately placed under martial law and remained so until 1944. In Maui, invoking of martial law resulted in the establishment of the Maui Military District, headquartered in Wailuku School. The Army usurped civilian authority by instituting curfews and placing controls on driving, consumer prices and the local media. A military court presided over offenses ranging from traffic violations to serious crime.

Maui took a direct hit, if not off-target, from the Japanese aggression. On December 15, 1941, a Japanese submarine skulking about Kahului Bay launched five shells. Two shells landed in the harbor and three grazed the Maui Pineapple Company cannery. Again on December 31, a Japanese submarine wasted its ammunition, first by undershooting into the harbor and then overshooting Kahului and landing its unexploded shells near Pu'unēnē. Property damage from both of these attacks was slight and the death toll amounted to one chicken.

Maui's varied terrain, from coastal to mountainous, provided excellent training grounds for the fighting men headed for the South Pacific. Men in uniform outnumbered Maui civilians four to one during the war years. As many as 200,000 soldiers, sailors and marines inundated the island for training, as well as rest between missions.

Welcome Visitors

In 1959, the same year as statehood, Qantas inaugurated

commercial jet service between Hawai'i and San Francisco, cutting travel time to five hours. A few months later, Pan Am connected Honolulu with Tokyo. Jets conveyed increasing numbers of visitors, spurring resort development. Waikīkī hotels pushed skyward and agricultural land in Maui shifted to use for visitor accommodations. Sugarcane workers were fashioned into hotel staff.

When the Royal Lahaina Beach Hotel opened in 1962, in the Kā'anapali area of Maui, it spearheaded the development of Hawai'i's destination resorts in the 1960s. Providing a combination of hotel, restaurants, shopping center and golf course, the visitor was attracted to the resort as much as to the location. Further development built Kīhei and Wailea into key visitor destinations.

Tourism entered a period of unparalleled expansion with the influx of Asian capital. In the early 1980s, tourism overtook the government, the military and agriculture as the state's largest industry.

U.S. sailors land during the revolution of 1893

Hawai'i State Archives

MAUI TIMELINE

2 million years ago: West Maui emerges from the sea.

900,000 years ago: Haleakalā rises above the ocean waves. Eventually, lava flowing from the east meets with West Maui and one island is formed.

400-500 A.D.: The first Polynesians arrive, likely from the Marquesan Islands.

1100: A second wave of settlers arrives from Tahiti.

1500: Chief Pi'ilani comes to power and starts construction of the King's Highway.

1773: Queen Ka'ahumanu is born in Hāna.

1778: Captain James Cook spots Maui on his return voyage to the Hawaiian Islands.

1786: The first non-Hawaiian sets foot on Maui when French explorer Admiral La Pérouse lands at the bay later named for him.

1790: American captain Simon Metcalfe commits the Olowalu Massacre, killing 100 Hawaiians. Forces of Kamehameha I from the Big Island defeat the army of Maui's Kahekili in a bloody battle in 'Īao Valley.

1803: Kamehameha I moves his royal court to Lahaina and builds the Brick Palace.

1819: The first whaling ship stops at Lahaina.

1823: Christian missionaries build the first mission of the Congregational Church at Lahaina.

1832: The oldest school west of the Rockies, Lahainaluna Seminary, is formed.

1834: The Baldwin House is built in Lahaina and remains as Lahaina's oldest standing building.

1840: Kamehameha III officially decrees Hawai'i's first constitution from Lahaina.

1846: Maui's first Catholic mission is formed.

1851: George Wilfong starts Maui's first sugarcane plantation at Hāna.

1862: Pioneer sugar mill is built at Lahaina.

1873: Lahaina's famous banyan tree is planted.

1876: Samuel Alexander and Henry Baldwin begin construction on the Hāmākua Ditch to bring irrigation water to their sugarcane fields.

1901: The Pioneer Inn opens in Lahaina and remains West Maui's major hotel for more than 50 years.

1927: The road to Hāna is built.

1929: Inter-Island Airways, later to become Hawaiian Airlines, lands its first aircraft on Maui.

1946: San Francisco industrialist Paul Fagan develops the Hāna Ranch and builds the Hotel Hāna Maui.

1959: Development of Kāʻanapali as Hawaiʻi's first planned resort begins.

1961: A National Park is designated for Haleakalā.

1962: Lahaina is designated a National Historic Landmark.

1969: Kīpahulu Valley is added to Haleakalā National Park.

1974: Famed aviator Charles Lindbergh dies at his home in Hāna.

President Sanford Dole and U.S. Minister Sewall at annexation ceremony, August 12, 1898

A SUCCESSION OF MONARCHS

Hawai'i State Archives

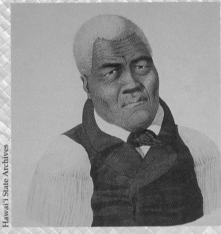

Kamehameha I

Kamehameha I, 1795–1819

Towering above others at six feet, six inches, Kamehameha was to become Hawai'i's greatest warrior-chief. He was royal born in the Kohala district of the island of Hawai'i. Perhaps Halley's comet, which in 1758 marked the year of his birth, foreshadowed his destiny as an unusual and auspicious man. In 1791, Kamehameha became the sole chief of the island of Hawai'i. After conquering Maui and Moloka'i, he invaded O'ahu in 1795 and established his reign there as well. Stormy seas and an outbreak of disease turned his troops back on two attempts to invade Kaua'i. Accepting the inevitable and wanting to avoid bloodshed, the king of Kaua'i yielded to Kamehameha's rule in 1810. With his grand design of unification completed, he had earned the title Kamehameha the Great. The first Hawaiian to rule all the Islands died in 1819. His bones were buried at a secret location on the island of Hawai'i.

Kamehameha II, 1819–1824

Liholiho bestowed upon himself the title of Kamehameha II, but he did not mirror his father's image of a strong and autocratic ruler. With the overbearing influence of Ka'ahumanu, his father's favorite wife, he disassembled the kapu system.

During his reign, foreign trade decimated the sandalwood forests and whalers and missionaries strengthened

Hawai'i State Archives

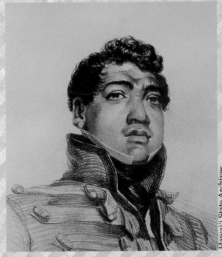

Kamehameha II, 1824

their holds on his kingdom. Seeking the advice of King George IV, Liholiho set sail for England, accompanied by Queen Kamamalu. Before the couple could enjoy an audience with the British monarch, Liholiho and his wife contracted measles and died.

Kamehameha III and Kalama, 1846

Kamehameha III, 1825–1854

At 30 years, Kauikeaouli was Hawai'i's longest-reigning monarch. Ka'ahumanu continued as Queen Regent when the nine-year-old brother of Liholiho became king. The child received a Christian education from Rev. Hiram Bingham, who attempted to instill in him a love for Western values. Kamehameha III grew up, however, to be steadfastly pro-Hawaiian in culture and beliefs. His most significant act was an edict issued in 1848 which became known as the Great Mahele. The act divided Hawai'i's land ownership among the monarchy, the government and the common people.

Hawaiians, who were not used to the concept of land ownership, allowed foreigners to buy two thirds of all land sold by 1886.

Dr. Gerrit Judd, Prince Alexander Liholiho (Kamehameha IV), Prince Lot (Kamehameha V), 1849

Kamehameha IV, 1854–1863

Before his death, Kamehameha III named his nephew and grandson of Kamehameha the Great, Alexander Liholiho, to succeed him. While a prince, Alexander traveled in Europe and America. His experiences in Europe were pleasant and enriching, but he was insulted and humiliated by being ordered off a train in New York City because of his race. During his short reign he tended to shift Hawai'i closer to the British Empire in both spirit and policy. After his son, Prince Albert, died at four years, the 29-year-old king, run down by grief, guilt and alcohol, died during an asthmatic attack.

Kamehameha V, 1863–1872

Lot Kamehameha was the older brother of Alexander Liholiho and the last Hawaiian monarch to carry the lineage of Kamehameha the Great. He baptized his strong, autocratic style of leadership by refusing to take an oath to uphold the constitution of 1852, believing it weakened the powers of the monarchy. In its place he offered a new constitution that established a one-chamber legislature for nobles and elected representatives, and required that persons pass literacy tests and own property before being allowed to vote. His determination to strengthen the monarchy sparked resentment among non-royalists, fueling the forces that would later bring down the monarchy. The "bachelor king" died without leaving a successor. Future kings would be elected.

Lunalilo, 1873–1874

"Whiskey Bill" Lunalilo was a favorite of the Hawaiian commoners and the fact that he was a drunkard did little to diminish his charm. Three of his four cabinet ministers were Americans and were instrumental in paving the way for a treaty of reciprocity whereby the Hawaiian government would lease Pearl Harbor to the United States in return for duty-free access to the American sugar market. Lunalilo died after just 13 months as monarch.

William Lunalilo, 1873

David Kalākaua, 1874–1891

After defeating Queen Emma, the widow of Kamehameha IV, in a colorful campaign, David Kalākaua put high priority to reviving Hawaiian heritage. He resuscitated the hula, which had been banned for many years by the missionaries—even contributing his own new dances. He ushered in a renewed appreciation for Hawaiian music and composed "Hawai'i Pono'i," Hawai'i's state song. Because of his jovial style and his love for the performing arts, the haoles dubbed him "The Merrie Monarch." Kalākaua elevated his critics' rancor by incurring huge debts to build the opulent 'Iolani Palace and treating himself to a lavish coronation ceremony nine years after becoming king. An armed insurrection in 1887 forced Kalākaua to accept a "Bayonet Constitution" that stripped the Chinese of the vote and limited Hawaiian political power while shifting more power to the land-owning American and British residents. Kalākaua died in San Francisco, leaving his sister to become queen of what was essentially an American-controlled nation.

Lydia Lili'uokalani, 1891-1893

Like her brother, Lydia Lili'uokalani had a talent for music and wrote some of the most beautiful and delicate songs in the Hawaiian language, including "Aloha Oe." Lili'uokalani charged that the constitution of 1887 was illegally forced upon King Kalākaua. She penned a new constitution that promised only true Hawaiians could vote and they would not have to be rich men to cast a ballot or run for office. The Queen, however, could not effect her new constitution. Anti-royalist forces made Lili'uokalani the last Hawaiian monarch and the first to take leave before death.

Queen Lili'uokalani

Hawai'i State Archives

David Kalākaua

Hawai'i State Archives

ECONOMY & GOVERNMENT

The most important segment of Maui's economy is tourism, as it is to the rest of the state of Hawai'i. Maui is the second most popular Hawaiian destination after O'ahu. Following behind tourism in importance and losing ground are agriculture and government expenditures.

Yearly visitor arrivals to Maui number 2.3 million, 80 percent of them westbound. The westbound visitors stay an average of 7.4 days and the eastbound visitors' stay averages 3.6 days. The eastbound visitors from Japan spend $287 for every day they visit Maui, while visitors from the mainland U.S.A. contribute $137 to Maui's economy each day. On a typical day there are 42,000 visitors in Maui, 43 percent of whom are making their first visit. For the repeat visitors the average number of trips to Maui is 3.8. Hotel rooms enjoy 72-percent occupancy with an average rate of $156.

A recent survey conducted by the Maui Visitors Bureau confirmed that Maui's scenery and environment are highly rated attractions to visitors. Following closely with high approval are the island's quality of service and aloha spirit. Maui's beaches, activities, local culture and quality of accommodations and restaurants earned impressive ratings as well.

Sugar continues to be important to Maui's economy, but struggles as a viable cash crop. Maui and Kaua'i are the only Hawaiian islands that still grow sugarcane. Other significant agricultural products are pineapple, livestock, vegetables and nursery-grown flowers.

Ranking high in cash revenues is the illicit production of pakalōlō, or marijuana. In its heyday, marijuana was likely Maui's largest cash crop. Two decades of aggressive eradication programs such as "Green Harvest" and "Operation Wipe-Out" have made the homegrown "Maui Wowie" scarce and expensive.

Maui is making a serious stab at diversifying its economy with high-tech ventures. The Maui Research and Technology Park is a 330-acre Kīhei facility credited with generating $30 million in new business revenues and creating 400 new jobs. Its flagship tenant is the Maui High Performance Computing Center, which boasts one of the 30 most powerful computers in the world.

Nation of Residence of Visitors to Maui

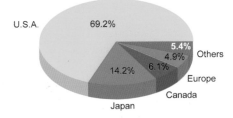

U.S.A. 69.2%
5.4% Others
4.9%
14.2% 6.1%
Europe
Canada
Japan

The computing center is a government-funded operation, managed by the University of New Mexico under a cooperative agreement with the Air Force Research Laboratory. The Air Force uses the supercomputer for advanced imaging for its Maui space surveillance work from the top of Haleakalā. It is also used for weather modeling research by the University of Hawai'i and the Scripps Institution of Oceanography, for Marine Corps battle simulations and for a variety of private-business applications.

Government

Hawai'i has three levels of government: federal, state and county. Hawaiians are represented in Washington D.C. by two senators and two representatives. The seat of state government is in Honolulu. The state's executive power is vested in a popularly elected governor who serves a four-year term as do the lieutenant governor, state legislators and county mayors. The state legislature is comprised of a 25-member Senate and a House of Representatives with 51 members. Maui County is represented by three state senators and six state representatives. For the past several decades the dominant political party at all levels has been the Democratic Party.

Hawai'i is divided into four county governments, but unlike mainland states, it has no municipal government. Maui County consists of the islands of Maui, Moloka'i, Lāna'i and Kaho'olawe. The county is governed by a mayor and county council and provides services such as police and fire protection that are usually assigned to cities.

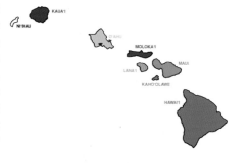

FACTS ABOUT SUGARCANE

- Polynesian settlers brought sugarcane to Hawai'i more than 1,000 years ago.
- Sugarcane is a giant grass that can produce stalks that range from 8 to 30 feet tall.
- Hawaiians chewed on the stalks for the sweet juice but did not make sugar.
- Fields of sugarcane start off as 12-inch slips cut from a stalk of cane.
- Machines cut furrows into the ground, drop in the seed cane, insert drip tubing and cover the furrows in one operation.
- Young plants are constantly watered with drip-irrigation pipes. This more efficient irrigation system has reduced the water needed to produce a ton of sugarcane to one ton.
- In some fields, stands remaining after harvest are used to grow a new crop. This is called ratooning.
- A&B's East Maui Irrigation Company brings water from rainy east Maui to dry central Maui through a system of ditches 74 miles long.
- It takes 24 months for the young plants to grow to harvest height.
- An acre of land yields 90 tons of cane or 12.5 tons of raw sugar.
- Cane fields are set afire to clear excess leaves from the cane before harvesting.
- Cane burning is scheduled to take advantage of favorable winds and weather conditions.
- Do not stop your car near a cane burn.

WEST MAUI SIGHTS

When you see the whale's tale, it is about to dive.

West Maui is home to tony resorts, condominiums, golf courses, the historic town of Lahaina, rugged coastlines, sandy beaches and sugarcane and pineapple fields all linked by the Honoapi'ilani Highway (Highway 30). Inland from the highway, slopes rise to the deeply eroded West Maui Mountains. The coastline edging the northern part of West Maui is indented with six bays noted for once belonging to Chief Pi'ilani. His rule of the bays and the neighboring islands of Moloka'i, Lāna'i, and Kaho'olawe is recognized in the name of the road circling West Maui—Honoapi'ilani, "the bays acquired by Chief Pi'ilani." Starting

The 'Au'au Channel separates Lahaina from the island of Lāna'i

from the south the bays are: Honokōwai, Honokeana, Honokahua, Honolua, Honokōhau and Hononana.

On the southern tip of West Maui the lower slopes of desert brown give way to the greens of rain forest at higher elevations. The Honoapi'ilani Highway skirts several lava flows here, the first occurring seven-tenths of a mile past Mile Marker 7 at **McGregor Point**. A trail leads down to the lighthouse and the remains of what used to be **McGregor's Landing**.

One mile farther along the highway is the turnoff to the viewpoint of **Papawai Point**. Visible from this lookout are the islands of Lāna'i and Kaho'olawe and the South Maui coastline with Haleakalā looming above. This is an excellent spot for watching for the humpback whales that winter in Hawaiian waters from December to May. During whale season **Pacific Whale Foundation** research naturalists are on hand from 8:30 a.m. to 4:30 p.m. to assist in locating whales and to answer

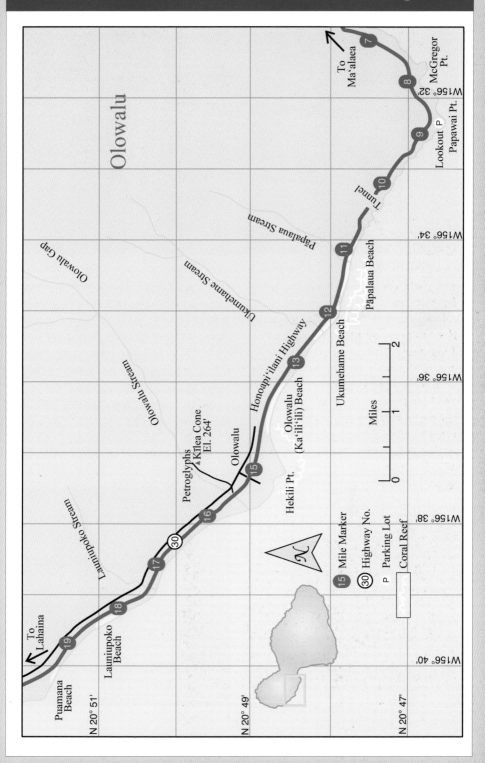

Olowalu

Olowalu Gap

To Ma'alaea

McGregor Pt.

W156° 32'

Lookout P
Papawai Pt.

Tunnel

Papalaua Stream

W156° 34'

Papalaua Beach

Ukumehame Stream

Honoapi'ilani Highway

Ukumehame Beach

Olowalu Stream

Petroglyphs
Kīlea Cone
El. 264'

Olowalu

Olowalu
(Ka'ili'ili) Beach

W156° 36'

Hekili Pt.

Miles

2

1

0

Launiupoko Stream

30

W156° 38'

15 Mile Marker

30 Highway No.

P Parking Lot

Coral Reef

15

30

P

Launiupoko Beach

To
Lahaina

N

Puamana
Beach

N 20° 51'

N 20° 49'

N 20° 47'

W156° 40'

Petroglyphs at Kīlea Cone

questions. When the parking lot at Papawai Point is full, other vantage points for whale watching are available between Mile Markers 9 and 10. The two dirt pullouts are never busy but can only be entered safely from the west with a right-hand turn.

The highway follows the outlines of 100-foot-high sea cliffs, passing through the only tunnel on Maui before opening up at the foot of **Ukumehame Gulch**. Starting with Mile Marker 11, the highway closely follows the coastline at sea level, offering opportunities to stop at Pāpalaua, Ukumehame and Olowalu Beaches.

In the vicinity of Mile Marker 15 the West Maui Mountain's **Olowalu Gap** can be sighted. Below the gap, planted in sugarcane, is a prominent alluvial fan created by eroding material carried out of the mountains. Irrigation ditches arc across the arid fan. Rectangular piles of boulders dotting the cane fields look like heiau platforms but were actually deposited by plantation workers clearing the fields.

At Mile Marker 15 are the **Olowalu General Store**, **Chez Paul Restaurant** and pay phones. Behind the building and to the left, next to a water tank, is a dirt road leading six-tenths of a mile to the **Kīlea cinder cone**. Ancient Hawaiians carved petroglyphs on a smooth, flat slab of the cinder cone. The carvings of animals, boats and people were chiseled in the rock two or three centuries ago.

The Waiheʻe River continues to erode the West Maui Mountains

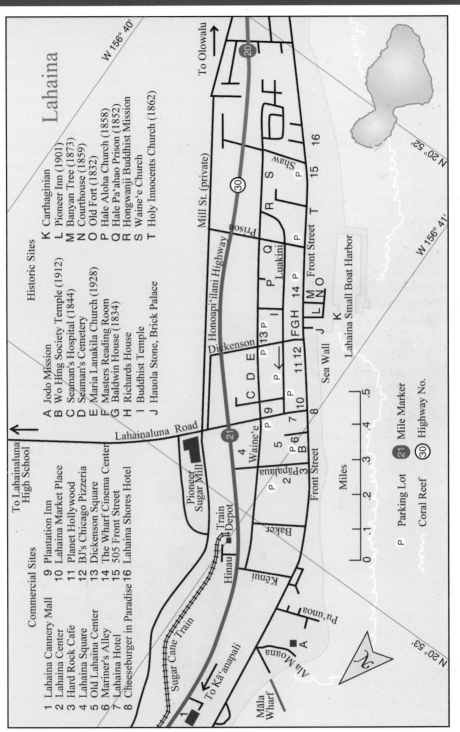

Lahaina

Commercial Sites

1 Lahaina Cannery Mall
2 Lahaina Center
3 Hard Rock Cafe
4 Lahaina Square
5 Old Lahaina Center
6 Mariner's Alley
7 Lahaina Hotel
8 Cheeseburger in Paradise
9 Plantation Inn
10 Lahaina Market Place
11 Planet Hollywood
12 BJ's Chicago Pizzeria
13 Dickenson Square
14 The Wharf Cinema Center
15 505 Front Street
16 Lahaina Shores Hotel

Historic Sites

A Jodo Mission
B Wo Hing Society Temple (1912)
C Seaman's Hospital (1844)
D Seaman's Cemetery
E Maria Lanakila Church (1928)
F Masters Reading Room
G Baldwin House (1834)
H Richards House
I Buddhist Temple
J Hauola Stone, Brick Palace
K Carthaginian
L Pioneer Inn (1901)
M Banyan Tree (1873)
N Courthouse (1859)
O Old Fort (1832)
P Hale Aloha Church (1858)
Q Hale Pa'ahao Prison (1852)
R Hongwanji Buddhist Mission
S Waine'e Church
T Holy Innocents Church (1862)

To Lahainaluna
High School

Lahainaluna Road

Pioneer Sugar Mill

Train Depot

Sugar Cane Train

To Kā'anapali

Māla Wharf

Ala Moana

Pu'unoa

Hinau

Kēnui

Baker

Papalaua

Waine'e

Front Street

Dickenson

Luakini

Shaw

Front Street

Sea Wall

Lahaina Small Boat Harbor

Honoapi'ilani Highway

Mill St. (private)

Prison

To Olowalu

W 156° 40'

N 20° 52'

W 156° 41'

N 20° 53'

Miles

P   Parking Lot
21 Mile Marker
30 Highway No.
    Coral Reef

Lahaina

Lahaina has preserved the nautical flavor of a mid-nineteenth-century Hawaiian seaport so well that the town was declared a National Historic Landmark. The lively town and bustling seaport retain much of their lusty whaling past. Along **Front Street**, the main artery skirting the harbor, old two-story wooden buildings that once housed grog shops now sell T-shirts, souvenir gifts, art of every form depicting breaching whales, and more T-shirts. Lahaina may be a low-rise town but no one would accuse it of being low-key. Yet somehow, its old charm remains intact.

Lahaina was formerly known as Lele. Hawaiian lore says that a chief looking for a shady area cursed the heat with: "He keu ho'i ke'ia o ka lahaina," which means, "What an unmerciful sun." With the retelling of the story, the place became known as Lahaina.

Coconut grove, Lahaina, 1912

Hawai'i State Archives

Before the whalers arrived, Lahaina gained historical importance when Kamehameha I established his headquarters here in 1802 and resided in the **Brick Palace**, the first Western-style building in Hawai'i. American missionaries established **Lahainaluna Seminary** in 1831, making it America's oldest school west of the Rockies. Lahaina became the capital of Hawai'i in 1820, and remained the seat of government until it was moved to Honolulu in 1854. Under Kamehameha III, Hawai'i's first constitution was promulgated from Lahaina in 1840. This constitution, which provided for representational government, was drafted by a group of progressive Maui Hawaiians, including **David Malo**, one of the first students at Lahainaluna Seminary and often referred to as the first modern native Hawaiian scholar.

The whalers and the missionaries both came to Lahaina in the 1820s. Lahaina with its grog shops and uninhibited women must have seemed like heaven on earth to sailors after years at sea. To the stiff-collared missionaries it was an abominable pool of degradation. The cultures of the zealous missionaries, hellbent on salvation, and the profligate whalers, hellbent on a good time, clashed in the streets of Lahaina. The confrontations climaxed when whalers aboard the ship *John Palmer* tried to send Rev. Richards, who was responsible for a ban on naked Hawaiian women swimming out to greet the ships, to his eternal reward by firing cannonballs at his residence.

With whaling's decline in the 1860s, the economic void was filled with the emergence of the sugar industry. In 1862, what was to become the **Pioneer Mill Company** was founded. Lahaina evolved into a sleepy plantation town and remained quiet until Amfac Inc. developed the tourism industry on the nearby beaches of Kā'anapali in the 1960s. Again, Lahaina is Maui's most energetic town.

The best way to enjoy the sights of Lahaina is on foot. Most attractions are downtown, on or close to Front Street (where pedestrians generally can move quicker than cars). Traffic is congested and parking can be a problem. A free parking lot is situated a couple of blocks south of downtown at the corner of Front and Shaw streets. A block north, at Front and Prison streets, is a free parking lot with a three-hour time limit. The **Old Lahaina Shopping Center**, to the north of downtown, has a pay lot. Merchants at the shopping center will validate parking if you make a purchase. Other pay lots are available and a limited amount of street parking is available. Pay heed to the parking restriction signs as the parking police are especially efficient at issuing tickets and towing.

A good place to start a tour of Lahaina is at Front and Canal under the largest banyan tree in the state. Shading more than two-thirds of an acre and reaching upward to 60 feet, the **Banyan Tree** has been a Lahaina landmark for nearly 13 decades. The tree has spread over the area via aerial roots which, when they reach the ground, grow into thick trunks. The banyan tree, which came from India when it was only eight feet tall, was planted in 1873 to commemorate the founding of Lahaina's first Protestant Christian Mission fifty years earlier. Many years of caring by members of the community have helped the tree create its symmetrical shape. Japanese gardeners would hang large pickle jars full of water under the aerial roots that they wanted to grow as trunks. As the roots grew down, the ropes around the jars were lengthened. Other aerial roots would be trimmed off, thus controlling the shape and symmetry of the tree. Every day its shade offers respite to Lahaina visitors and residents and in the evenings it becomes the roosting place for most of the local mynah bird population. At sundown the tree comes alive with the raucous tunes of these birds.

Almost in the shade of the banyan tree is the **Old Courthouse**.

Lahaina Courthouse and Post Office, 1935

Hawai'i State Archives

Hawai'i State Archives

Lahainaluna Missionary Seminary *by Hiram Bingham, 1847*

Built in 1859 from coral blocks recycled from King Kamehameha III's unfinished palace, it is currently under restoration.

The stone ruins next to the courthouse are the remains of the **Old Fort**, built from 1831 to 1832 to guard against cannonballs and other aggressions directed at the town from angry whalers. Constructed of coral blocks hacked and sawed from the reef beyond the beach, it covered one acre and was enclosed by 20-foot-high walls. Cannons salvaged from a warship stood on guard outside the fort.

North of the courthouse and right on the waterfront is the **Pioneer Inn** (661-3636, 800-457-5457). It was built in 1901 by George Freeland, a dedicated member of the Royal Canadian Mounted Police, who tracked a criminal to Lahaina. So enamored was he with Lahaina that he stayed for the rest of his life. For many years it was the only hotel in Lahaina and it still functions as one today. The bar and dining rooms feature an impressive collection of whaling artifacts and other salty memorabilia.

Berthed in front of the Pioneer Inn is the *Carthaginian*, a replica of a 19th-century brig, typical of the small, fast freighters that brought commerce to these islands. The silhouette of this majestic ship against the sky is a sentimental reminder of Lahaina's heritage. It serves now as a floating museum containing exhibits on whales and whaling, audiovisual displays and an original whale boat. Open daily, 10:00 a.m. - 4:00 p.m., admission $3.00 adults, $2.00 seniors and $5.00 families.

Lahaina's Pioneer Inn and the Carthaginian

A small fishing boat moored off Lahaina

Next door to the Baldwin home is the **Master's Reading Room**, which is home to the Lahaina Restoration Foundation and is not open to the public. During the whaling years the building provided a home to officers wishing to stay ashore where they could view ships at anchor, passing boats and village activity.

Built in 1834, the **Baldwin Home**, at Front and Dickenson, is the oldest standing building in Lahaina. It was built with thick walls of coral, stone and hand-hewn timbers. A second story was added in 1849 to accommodate the Baldwin's six children. The missionary and Harvard-trained physician, Rev. Dwight Baldwin, and his bride of a few weeks sailed from New England to Hawai'i in 1830. He was assigned as pastor of Lahaina's old Waine'e Church. The Baldwin home served as a medical office and center of missionary activity. Restored to exacting detail by the Lahaina Restoration Foundation, the house contains period pieces and family heirlooms, including some of the doctor's fiendish-looking medical implements. Impressive furnishings include the Baldwin's Steinway piano, four-poster bed fashioned out of native koa wood and china that survived the voyage around Cape Horn. Admission is $3.00 adults, $2.00 seniors.

Two blocks up Front Street is the restored **Wo Hing Temple**. In 1912 a Chinese fraternal society built the hall, which became the social center for hundreds of Chinese men who were imported to work in the sugarcane fields. In 1983 the Lahaina Restoration Foundation restored the

Top: Wo Hing Temple decked out for Chinese New Year

Bottom: Statue of Buddha sits serenely in front of West Maui Mountains

Sugar Cane Train

building and installed a display of the history of the Chinese in Lahaina. The cookhouse was separate from the main building as a precaution against fire. In addition to displays, the Cookhouse Theater offers an unique visual history lesson, showing movies of Hawai'i taken by Thomas Edison in 1898 and 1903.

A change of pace from the frenetic downtown is a few blocks north at the Buddhist enclave of **Lahaina Jodo Mission Cultural Park**. Drive north on Front Street and turn left at Ala Moana. The largest statue of Buddha outside of Japan sits serenely among flowering oleander bushes, its back to the mountains, facing Japan. It was erected in 1968 to commemorate the centennial of Japanese immigration to Hawai'i. The compound includes the temple shrine, a pagoda and a large ceremonial bell. Inside the temple, five outstanding Buddhist paintings by noted Japanese artist, Haijin Iwasaki adorn the walls. A copper roof covers the 90-foot-high pagoda. Niches in the walls of the pagoda's first floor hold cremation urns. At 3,000 pounds, the bronze bell is the largest temple bell in the state of Hawai'i.

North of the mission is the **Māla Wharf**, built in 1922 to handle vessels that could not dock in the shallow waters off Lahaina. As soon as the wharf was completed, however, it was found to be unusable. Powerful currents made the landing too dangerous. The wharf is condemned and the sea is gradually claiming it.

A fun attraction is a ride aboard the **Lahaina-Kā'anapali & Pacific Railroad**, or **The Sugar Cane Train** (661-0089). Once the narrow gauge railway hauled sugarcane to the mill. Now the restored, oil-fired steam engines pull cars full of tourists to Pu'ukoli'i and back, guided by a singing conductor. The shaky, four-mile ride from Lahaina takes 30 minutes to reach the northern terminal at Pu'ukoli'i where it loops around for a stop at Kā'anapali to take on water before returning to Lahaina. The Lahaina depot is inland of the highway off of Hinau Street. Shuttle buses also pick up passengers at the Banyan Tree square and from Kā'anapali. The one-way fare for adults is $10.50 and for children, $6.00. Round trip tickets are $14.50 for adults and $8.00 for children.

DAVID MALO

HAWAIIAN SCHOLAR DAVID Malo is remembered as an energetic man with an inquiring mind. He was born in Keauhou on the Big Island in 1793. Malo moved to Lahaina in 1823, where he came to know people at the royal court and studied Hawaiian lore.

Under the influence of the Rev. William Richards, Malo converted to Christianity and learned to read English and to write in the Hawaiian language. In 1831, at the age of 38, he entered the newly opened Lahainaluna Seminary and graduated four years later.

Lahaina was the capital of Hawai'i in the 1830s when Malo provided guidance to Kamehameha III. He helped the king draft the declaration of rights of 1839 and the next year produced the first constitution for the kingdom.

Concerned about the wave of westernization, and seeing the passing of old Hawaiian ways, Malo felt it important to record his recollections of history, legends and traditions of the Hawaiian people. Around 1835, Malo and other students put to paper Hawaiian chants, genealogies and Hawaiian oral traditions in the book, *Mo'olelo Hawai'i*, now titled *Hawaiian Antiquities*.

Malo continued to pursue his varied interests in his later years. He tried to introduce cotton growing and cloth manufacturing in Hawai'i. He became a licensed preacher in 1852, spending the last year of his life ministering at Kalepolepo.

Each spring, David Malo Day celebrates the Maui scholar in an event renowned for its Hawaiian food, games and entertainment. Twice a year, the students of what is now Lahainaluna High School visit Malo's gravesite high above their school on the slopes of Pu'u Pa'upa'u, also known as Mount Ball. They refurbish the giant "L" that is visible for miles around Lahaina and remember him with leis and songs. Malo picked that elevated site because it was, as he penned, "beyond the rising tide of foreign invasion."

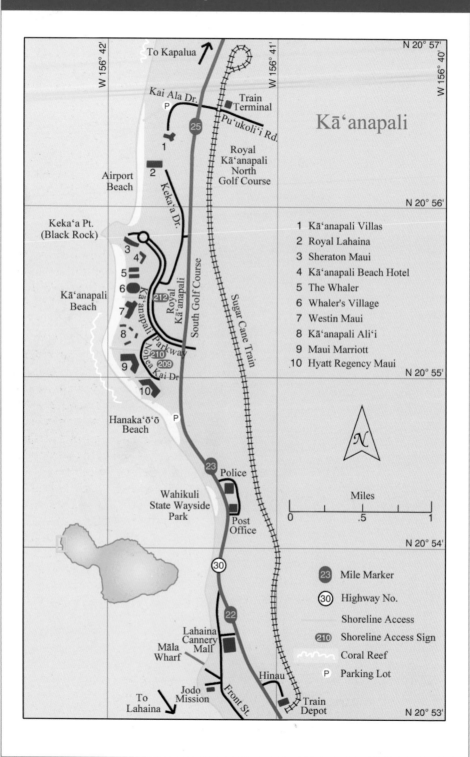

Kā'anapali

1 Kā'anapali Villas
2 Royal Lahaina
3 Sheraton Maui
4 Kā'anapali Beach Hotel
5 The Whaler
6 Whaler's Village
7 Westin Maui
8 Kā'anapali Ali'i
9 Maui Marriott
10 Hyatt Regency Maui

Miles

23 Mile Marker
30 Highway No.
     Shoreline Access
210 Shoreline Access Sign
     Coral Reef
P Parking Lot

Kāʻanapali

Three miles north of Lahaina is the famous resort area of Kāʻanapali, where high-rise, high-rate resorts separate golf courses from the beach. The long sandy beach of Kāʻanapali is bisected by **Kekaʻa Point** or **Black Rock**. Less than 125,000 years ago an eruption a short distance offshore sent cinder and spatter into the air to build the 90-foot-high cone. Kekaʻa was a sacred place for the Hawaiians, who constructed a heiau on it. They believed that the souls of the dead departed for ancestral spirit worlds from this point. The great Maui chief Kahekili was said to prove his bravery by leaping into the ocean from the cliff.

In 1963, the Sheraton Maui was built near Black Rock and resort development soon spread in both directions. Now Kāʻanapali Beach is lined with grand and expensive hotels. Other than the resorts and fabulous beach, the most compelling attraction to visit in Kāʻanapali is the **Whalers Village Museum**, located in the **Whalers Village Shopping Complex**, 2435 Kāʻanapali Parkway; 661-5992. Admission is free to this museum dedicated to what was once Maui's most important industry. Hundreds of artifacts, photo murals and interpretive graphics provide a self-guided tour of the business of whaling and the hardships endured by the men who lived "before the mast." While your sympathies may lie with the whales, it is easy to be engrossed in the world of 19th century whaling—the cramped quarters, the seasonal runs from Maui

Harpoons of every description displayed at Whalers Village Museum

to Arctic whaling grounds and back, and the industry's final decline as whale oil is supplanted by kerosene and the newly invented light bulb. The museum is open daily from 9:30 a.m. to 10:00 p.m.

The first of Piʻilani's bays, **Honokōwai**, "the bay drawing water," is found one mile north of Kāʻanapali. This bay is no more than a long, slight curve in the coastline. The edge of the land here is beach sandstone, hardened by the chemical cementing of its grains.

Five miles north of Kāʻanapali, condominiums line **Nāpili Bay**, "the joining or pili grass," and the next of Piʻilani's bays, **Honokeana**, which has the small, deep indentation of a cove rather than a bay. On the mountain side, the irrigated sugarcane fields give way to the lush, green fields of pineapple.

Kapalua

Kapalua is the northernmost resort area in West Maui and has established an enviable reputation as a visitor destination. The area encompasses two hotels, three golf courses, four beaches, seven residential complexes and 22 tennis courts. In the 1970s this 1,500-acre portion of pineapple plantation was developed by the Kapalua Land Company from the holdings of the Maui Land & Pineapple Company, which has roots tracing back to the missionary Baldwin family, and is still shepherded by descendants of that clan.

Kapalua was once part of the Honolua Ranch, complete with herds of Hereford cattle. An early manager of Honolua Ranch, D. T. Fleming, experimented with many different crops to see what best suited the land. He introduced pineapple to the ranch in 1912 and grew mango, avocado and aloe, which still can be seen lining some of the area's older roads. Fleming's house is now the Restaurant at Pineapple Hill and Fleming Beach and County Park is named for him.

Honokahua gives its name to both the next bay and the small plantation village across the highway from it. Above the village of cottages with rust-red roofs a double line of Norfolk Island pines, planted 25 feet apart, line the road to Nāpili.

The highway has a lookout point over the popular snorkeling beach of **Mokulē'ia Bay**. Dropping behind the bay at Mile Marker 33, the highway winds behind the next of Pi'ilani's bays, **Honolua**, "two harbors," which forms a twin with Mokulē'ia Bay. As the highway rises again, watch for two lookouts in three-tenths of a mile. Stop here for a view down into the water that is the **Marine Life Conservation District**, created to protect the reef and sea life of the twin bays. To the southeast are the series of beautiful bays separated by narrow fingers of lava that form the Kapalua coastline.

Moloka'i, nine miles across the Pailolo Channel

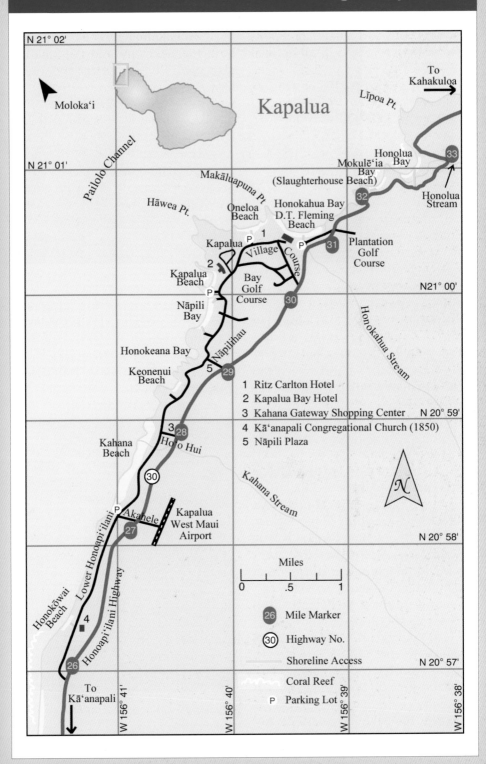

N 21° 02'

Moloka'i

Kapalua

To Kahakuloa

Līpoa Pt.

Paliolo Channel

N 21° 01'

Makāluapuna Pt.

Honolua Bay

Mokulē'ia Bay (Slaughterhouse Beach)

Honolua Stream

Hāwea Pt.

Oneloa Beach

Honokahua Bay D.T. Fleming Beach

Kapalua Village Course

Plantation Golf Course

N 21° 00'

Kapalua Beach

Bay Golf Course

Nāpili Bay

Honokeana Bay

Nāpilihau

Keonenui Beach

1 Ritz Carlton Hotel

2 Kapalua Bay Hotel

3 Kahana Gateway Shopping Center

4 Kā'anapali Congregational Church (1850)

5 Nāpili Plaza

Honokahua Stream

N 20° 59'

Kahana Beach

Hono Hui

N

Kahana Stream

N 20° 58'

Akahele

Kapalua West Maui Airport

Lower Honoapi'ilani

Honoapi'ilani Highway

Honokōwai Beach

Miles

0   .5   1

26 Mile Marker

30 Highway No.

Shoreline Access

N 20° 57'

Coral Reef

P Parking Lot

To Kā'anapali

W 156° 41'

W 156° 40'

W 156° 39'

W 156° 38'

Snorkelers float on Honolua Bay

As the highway heads east, **Līpoa Point**, which means "seaweeds," comes into view. The point, created from a broad, flat lava flow, is planted in pineapple. At the west end of the point is a red dirt entrance road where you can park and enjoy the view of cacti, surfers 120 feet below the basalt cliffs, and Moloka'i, nine miles across the Pailolo Channel.

One-half mile past Mile Marker 36, and still easily accessible, is the fifth of Pi'ilani's bays, **Honokōhau**, "the bay drawing dew." Emptying into the bay, **Honokōhau Stream** is West Maui's longest. The waterfall at the head of the nine-mile stream drops 1,600 feet, making it America's second highest waterfall after Yosemite in California.

Visible to the east of Honokōhau Bay is the 358-foot cinder cone, **Pu'u Ka'eo**. Erosion from the sea has exposed the brilliant red and lavender colors of its volcanic ash and pumice. From the east side of the bay,

look back into Honokōhau Bay and you will see a bright yellow layer of volcanic ash that runs a few feet above the water line.

Mile Marker 38 marks the parking area and trail to **Nākālele Point** light station. A row of stacked

Honokōhau Falls are the second highest in the United States

Cacti meet the ocean at Līpoa Point.

lava trails off into the ocean here at Maui's most northerly point. The wind, with nothing to stop it across thousands of miles of open ocean, blows so hard sometimes that you must lean into it to remain standing (nākālele means "leaning"). Vegetation struggles to take hold in the stark hills. To the right of Nākālele Point, the waves have carved a cave and a blowhole in the rocks. When air is trapped and compressed in the cave by advancing waves it is released from a hole in the chamber's roof with a whoosh and a white plume of water. You can see and hear the blowhole by hiking down the jeep trail to the light station and picking your way over the rocks to the cove on the right. The walk is about a third of a mile one way.

The last of Pi'ilani's bays, **Hononana**, appears below the highway at Mile Marker 41. The Honoapi'ilani Highway continues eastward as the Kahekili Highway (Highway 340), transforming itself into a rock-littered corniche susceptible to washouts after bad storms. The road passes through the small town of **Kahakuloa** and eventually connects with Wailuku in central Maui. If you dare take your eyes off the winding road that often narrows to one lane as it snakes around sharp corners, the drive will offer magnificent views of swells from the North Pacific eroding the red cliffs.

A mile before Kahakuloa, on the right side of the road, is a large boulder called **Pōhaku Kani**, "the bell stone," because when struck with a rock it gives forth a sonorous sound remotely resembling the ringing of a massive bell. The stone has shallow pits worn into it by the curious.

Appearing across Kahakuloa Bay are West Maui's most prominent seacoast features. The promontory, **Kahakuloa Head**, is a 630-foot volcanic dome butted up against the ocean like a fortress, and to its right is **Pu'u Kāhuli'anapa**, rising to 536 feet.

Windswept Kahakuloa Head and Pu'u Kāhuli'anapa

Kahakuloa

The tiny village of Kahakuloa is nestled in an overgrown valley beside a deep bay. Scattered about are a few wood-frame houses, a couple of churches, fruit vending stands, and 26 families of Hawaiian ancestry. In Maui's precontact days, Kahakuloa was one of the island's five most populous sites. The abundant flow of Kahakuloa Stream allowed Hawaiians to intensively cultivate taro, arrowroot, sweet potatoes, mulberry and olon, a plant used for fiber. Kahakuloa remains unique today as one of the state's few Hawaiian communities. Likely, the risks of driving the narrow road will deter heavy visitation and this valley will retain the qualities that lend it such charm.

The mile markers for Highway 340 count down as you drive east towards Wailuku. The road widens a mile east of Kahakuloa at Mile Marker 13 and just past that is the **Kaukini Gallery and Gift Shop**. This little shop does a good business selling nice samples of local arts and crafts, pottery and jewelry. They also sell "I Survived the Drive to Kahakuloa" T-shirts, a successful marketing idea borrowed from Hāna merchants.

For a few more miles the road continues to hug the precipices like windowsills on a skyscraper, but roadside pullouts are available for scenery viewing and photography opportunities. Modern houses start to appear above the road around Mile Marker 11 and the road returns to two lanes at Mile Marker 7 as you approach Waihe'e and 'Īao Valley.

Kahakuloa Congregational Church

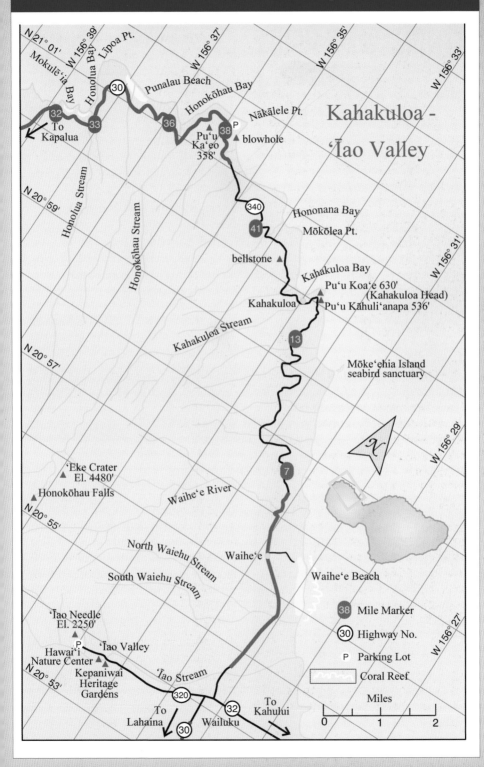

N 21° 01'
W 156° 39'
W 156° 37'
W 156° 35'
W 156° 33'

Honolua Lipoa Pt.

Mokulē'ia Bay

Honolua Bay

Punalau Beach

Honokōhau Bay

Nākālele Pt.

Kahakuloa -
'Īao Valley

To
Kapalua

30

32

33

36

38

P

Pu'u
Ka'eo
358'

blowhole

N 20° 59'

Honolua Stream

Honokōhau Stream

340

Hononana Bay

Mōkōlea Pt.

41

bellstone

Kahakuloa Bay

Pu'u Koa'e 630'
(Kahakuloa Head)
Pu'u Kāhuli'anapa 536'

Kahakuloa

W 156° 31'

N 20° 57'

Kahakuloa Stream

13

Mōke'ehia Island
seabird sanctuary

N

'Eke Crater
El. 4480'

Honokōhau Falls

7

Waihe'e River

N 20° 55'

W 156° 29'

North Waiehu Stream

Waihe'e

South Waiehu Stream

Waihe'e Beach

'Īao Needle
El. 2250'

P

'Īao Valley

Hawai'i
Nature Center

Kepaniwai
Heritage
Gardens

'Īao Stream

N 20° 53'

38 Mile Marker

30 Highway No.

P Parking Lot

Coral Reef

320

32

To Lahaina

Wailuku

To Kahului

30

W 156° 27'

Miles

0   1   2

CENTRAL MAUI SIGHTS

Bridging the two volcanoes that formed Maui is the isthmus created by their overlapping lava flows. Haleakalā gave Central Maui its underlying structure and the surface soils eroded from the West Maui Mountains. From a vantage point, Central Maui appears as a great curve sweeping down from Haleakalā and rising back to the mist-shrouded West Maui Mountains. Irrigated fields of sugarcane blanket the fertile plain and green pineapple crops cover the foothills. A web of highways destined for West Maui, Haleakalā, Hāna and South Maui crisscrosses the plain. Travelers quickly leave the area as soon as their flight lands but many attractions warrant a return visit.

Kahului

Anchoring Central Maui is the island's largest town and commercial center, Kahului. Maui's main airport is here along with a deepwater harbor bustling with cargo ships and occasionally a cruise ship. It also has the island's highest concentration of shopping centers.

J. Onishi Cash Store, Kahului, 1907

Hawai'i State Archives

In the 1790s Kahului was attacked by Kamehameha I when his warriors landed their war canoes here in preparation for battle at 'Īao Valley. The town was assaulted again in 1900, this time by a bubonic plague outbreak. In an attempt to wipe out the infestation of plague-carrying rats, the China Town district was purposely burned down and a corrugated steel fence erected around the town. After the second World War, the Kahului Development Company constructed a planned community where economical houses were built for sugarcane

Fields of sugar cane blanket the Central Valley

workers. Reflecting the enthusiasm of the workers who aspired to home ownership, the developers called the new district "Dream City." The popularity of Kahului's tract homes led to the closing of plantation camps and stores.

Lying in the heart of the town is the **Kanahā Pond Wildlife Sanctuary**. It is home to several species of birds, two of which are the Hawaiian stilt or ae'o and the Hawaiian coot or 'alae kea. The noisy ae'o wades upon long red legs and wears black and white plumage. White-beaked coots are close relatives of the "mudhens" from which Hawaiian legend says the demigod Maui stole the secret of fire. The pond is between the airport and downtown Kahului. Look for the entrance near the intersection of Highways 36 and 396. A trail from the parking lot leads 100 yards to an observation deck.

On the southern outskirts of Kahului at the intersection of Highway 35 and Hansen Road is the **Alexander & Baldwin Sugar Museum** (871-8058). This 2,000-square-foot museum, located in the plantation town of Pu'unēnē, occupies the former residence of the superintendent of Hawai'i's largest sugar factory. The still-active factory, built in 1900, is located across the road. Exhibits, which have won local awards, include coverage of Maui's geography and climate, water supplies, the history of sugar, industry entrepreneurs, immigration and the multiethnic labor force. Visitors can view artifacts dating back to 1878, photo murals, scale models and a video. Its hours are Monday–Saturday, 9:30–4:30; admission adults

$4.00, children $2.00; wheelchair accessible.

The local community is justifiably proud of the **Maui Arts and Cultural Center**. It is located in Maui Central Park off Kahului Beach Road. Completed in 1994, the $32-million complex features a 1,200-seat theater, an amphitheater with room for 4,000, an art gallery and a 200-seat studio theater. It has been the venue for performances of Hawaiian culture such as the hula and chanting. International artists, Tony Bennett, Bob Dylan, Carlos Santana and the Vienna Choir Boys have performed under the stars in the amphitheater. For information on what is playing, call (808) 242-SHOW or look for the "Showtime at The Center" ad in the Sunday or Thursday *Maui News*.

Wailuku

The main street in Kahului leads uphill to the older and more interesting town of Wailuku. Once centered around a now-defunct sugar mill, the town has managed to sustain itself without help from the tourist industry. The town is the seat of government for Maui County, which includes the islands of Maui, Lāna'i, Moloka'i and Kaho'olawe. There aren't any resorts here; the town forthrightly presents a local atmosphere. Outside of a few government buildings the streets are lined with a colorful mix of old shops, restaurants and small houses.

Tony Novak-Clifford

Ka'ahumanu Church in Wailuku

Long ago, the abundant flow of nearby streams nourished the densest area of taro cultivation in Hawai'i and sustained Maui's second-largest population. These agricultural and human resources were sources of wealth and power enjoyed by high-ranking chiefs. In 1781, covetous rivals such as Hawai'i chief Kalani'ōpu'u confronted the Maui chief Kahekili in Wailuku. The defenders persevered after a bloody two-day battle. Less than ten years later, Kamehameha the Great succeeded in conquering Maui in a battle in the nearby 'Īao Valley. He established Wailuku as Maui's second town after Lahaina.

Missionaries arrived in 1832 and founded a school for girls to complement the boys-only seminary at Lahainaluna. Immigrant sugar workers built churches and missions so they could worship as they did in their homelands.

The missionaries' pivotal convert was Queen Ka'ahumanu. The Queen attended services in 1832 at a Wailuku church, which was no more than a grass shack. She immodestly requested that the first permanent church at that site be named after her. An adobe church was built but rain eventually eroded it away. It was replaced by the island's first stone church in 1837. In 1876 the structure was reduced to about half its size and what remained was the **Ka'ahumanu Church** you see today on High Street. The white church with striking green trim and its lofty spire is a dramatic landmark in Wailuku's historic district. Visitors are welcome for Sunday services at 9:00 a.m., partially conducted in the Hawaiian language, but are not allowed inside during the rest of the week.

Along High Street, south of the church, is the **Civic Center Historic District,** which has four buildings that were added to the National Register in

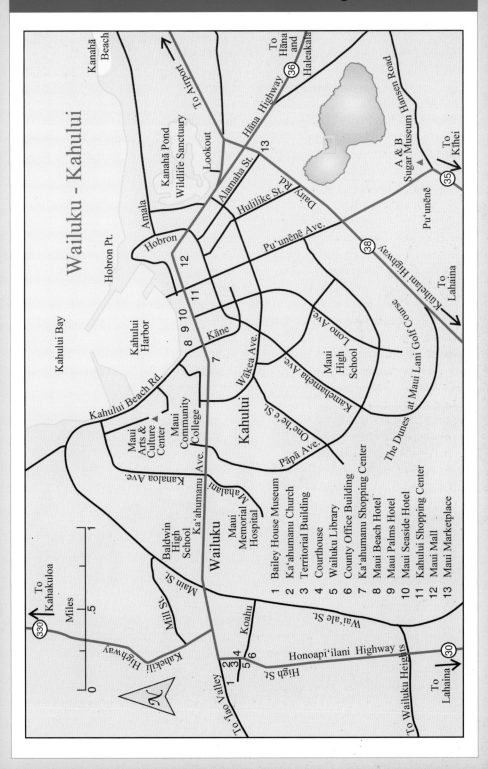

Wailuku - Kahului

Kanahā Beach

Kanahā Pond Wildlife Sanctuary

To Airport

To Hāna and Haleakala

Hāna Highway

36

13

A & B Sugar Museum

Sugar Museum Hansen Road

To Kīhei

35

Pu'unēnē

Lookout

Amala

Alamaha St.

Dairy Rd.

Hulilike St.

Pu'unēnē Ave.

38

Kīhelani Highway

To Lahaina

Hobron Pt.

Hobron

12

11

10 9 8

Kāne

7

Wakea Ave.

Lono Ave.

Kamehameha Ave.

Maui High School

The Dunes at Maui Lani Golf Course

Kahului Bay

Kahului Harbor

Kahului Beach Rd.

Maui Arts & Culture Center

Maui Community College

Kahului

One'he'e St.

Papa Ave.

Kanaloa Ave.

Ka'ahumanu Ave.

Mahalani

Maui Memorial Hospital

Wailuku

Baldwin High School

Main St.

Mill St.

Kahekili Highway

To Kahakuloa

330

Miles

.5

0

To Tao Valley

Koahu

Wai'ale St.

High St.

Honoapi'ilani Highway

30

To Lahaina

To Wailuku Heights

1   Bailey House Museum
2   Ka'ahumanu Church
3   Territorial Building
4   Courthouse
5   Wailuku Library
6   County Office Building
7   Ka'ahumanu Shopping Center
8   Maui Beach Hotel
9   Maui Palms Hotel
10 Maui Seaside Hotel
11 Kahului Shopping Center
12 Maui Mall
13 Maui Marketplace

1 2 3 4 5 6

N

1986. **The Wailuku Courthouse** is a Beaux Arts-inspired structure built in 1907, when Wailuku became the seat of county government. Down the street beside the banyan tree is the **County Office Building**. This Mediterranean-style building dates back to 1927 and currently houses the County Planning Department. Across the street, the **Wailuku Library** (1928) and the **Territorial Building** (1931) were designed by Maui-raised architect C. W. Dickey, who was known for developing a Hawaiian style of architecture characterized by a distinctive double-hipped roof.

A short distance from High Street, up Main Street, is the **Bailey House Museum**. It stands at the entrance to ʻĪao Valley on land given to the American Board of Commissioners for Foreign Missions by Governor Hoapili and King Kamehameha III in 1832. The rambling building, also called Halehōʻikeʻike (house of display), is the headquarters of the Maui Historical Society, which converted the former mission house into a museum. Rev. Jonathan Green began the mission station in 1833 and established the Wailuku Female Seminary and the Kaʻahumanu Church. Edward Bailey and his wife Caroline sailed from Boston in 1837 to teach at the female seminary. The house was built in 1841 and over the next 20 years was expanded, becoming known as the Bailey House. It was here that the couple lived for 45 years and raised their family of five sons. The 20-inch-thick walls of the house were built of

Former home of missionary Edward Bailey is now a museum

coral blocks covered with plaster. The binder used in the plaster was human hair donated by the young women who attended Rev. Bailey's seminary.

On the house's first floor is the Historical Society's collection of "precontact" Hawaiian artifacts such as stone and shell implements, tapa, cordage, woodwork and feather and bone articles. Another room is a gallery displaying Bailey's works. Edward Bailey was a missionary, teacher, builder, musician, writer, botanist and entrepreneur. It was as an accomplished artist that Bailey left a valuable record of nineteenth-century Maui through his oil paintings and engravings on copper.

Upstairs, a bedroom and a sitting room have been decorated with impressive Victorian furnishings. One room features a table inlaid with koa and other Hawaiian woods. It was made to be a gift to General U.S. Grant when he became President. Before it was finished Congress passed a law forbidding Presidents to accept gifts from foreign countries, i.e., Hawaiʻi. The table displays a large engraved silver bowl commemorating the Reciprocity Treaty of 1876, which made sugar Hawaiʻi's principal crop, tied Hawaiian economy to American markets and led to America's use of Pearl Harbor. The treaty provided for duty-free entry of Hawaiian sugar into the U.S. in return for Hawaiʻi's promise not to lease any port or harbor to another nation.

Outside, a lovely garden includes many rare plants, some of the original varieties of sugarcane brought to the Islands by the first Polynesians,

a hand-hewn koa outrigger canoe and a redwood surfboard used by the legendary Duke Kahanamoku. The museum hours are 10:00–4:30 daily; admission is $4.00 adults, $1.00 children 6–12.

Two miles south of Wailuku, on Highway 30, is the **Maui Tropical Plantation** (244-7643). It's an opportunity for an up-close look at a working plantation. A 35-minute narrated tram tour takes you through orchards of mango, coffee, macadamia, guava, banana and papaya trees. The tour strategically ends at the gift shop. It's very commercial and touristy. The tram tour costs $8.50 for adults and $3.50 for children and leaves every 45 minutes beginning at 10:00 a.m. until 4:00 p.m.

ʻĪao Valley

Don't miss taking the 3-mile drive into the beautiful and historically significant ʻĪao Valley. Follow the

Above: ʻĪao Needle

Opposite page: ʻĪao Valley

Kepaniwai Japanese Gardens

signs from Wailuku's Main Street, past the Bailey House Museum on Highway 320. The lush valley leads deep into the West Maui Mountains. In fact, ʻĪao Stream was the first, and so far the only stream, to reach to the old eruptive center of the West Maui volcano. Clouds pour over the summit, **Puʻu Kukui**, and spread a curtain out into the valley. ʻĪao means "cloud supreme." Puʻu Kukui is deluged with 400 inches of rain each year, making it the second wettest spot in the Hawaiian Island chain.

The valley widens at **Kepaniwai**, site of the 1790 battle between two powerful chiefs. Kahekili's ambition was to unite all of the Islands under his command. Kamehameha shared his ambition.

Kahekili was in Oʻahu and left his son Kalanikupule, in charge of Maui's defense. Kamehameha, who was rumored to be another son of Kahekili, led his forces from Hawaiʻi into the precipitous ʻĪao Valley. Bolstered with guns from other cultures, Kamehameha slaughtered his rival's followers. ʻĪao Stream was so choked with the bodies of the fallen that the area was called Kepaniwai, meaning "Damming of the Waters." Kalanikupule and a few of his chiefs escaped the carnage by fleeing over the ridge at the head of the valley and down the other side to Olowalu. Later, Kalanikupule engaged Kamehameha in Oʻahu and again suffered defeat.

Kepaniwai Heritage Gardens Park appears as a counterpoint to the ferocious battle that took place here two centuries earlier. This beautifully landscaped park in its magnificent setting is dedicated to the many ethnic groups that have populated and developed Maui. Tour the gardens on foot to see a Polynesian grass shack, a Filipino thatched house, a New England missionary home and a Portuguese garden. Best maintained are the Chinese and Japanese gardens. A bronze statue of two Japanese sugarcane workers commemorates the centennial of Japanese immigration to the Islands. Take time to read the poignant inscription on the plaque next to the statue. The park has picnic shelters with barbecues available. There is no admission charge.

Next door to the gardens is the **Hawai'i Nature Center**. The center features a brand-new interactive science arcade that will especially appeal to children. A favorite exhibit is a simulated "dragonfly ride" through the valley. Hours are 10:00–4:00 daily. Admission is $6.00 adults, $4.00 children. Proceeds go directly to support the center's environmental field education programs for elementary schoolchildren. Reservations for the daily guided nature walks can be made by phoning (808) 244-6500.

In a half mile, the road widens and a sign marks the **John F. Kennedy Profile** rock formation to the right. Erosion has coincidentally carved a reasonable likeness of the late president's profile into the hillside. Before America had presidents, the Hawaiians were told a different story by a kahuna named Kauaka'iwai, who

served the ali'i Kaka'e, ruler of Maui 500 years ago. This ali'i was of such high rank that persons would be put to death if they looked at him or if his shadow fell upon them. To protect his subjects, Kaka'e lived in a cave like a hermit, guarded by his likeness.

Less than half a mile farther up the road is the parking lot for **'Iao Valley State Park**. This is a well-visited destination and the lot is frequently full. Early mornings are less busy. The park is open daily from 7:00 a.m. to 7:00 p.m. The centerpiece of the park is the **'Iao Needle**, a moss-mantled pinnacle rising 1,200 feet above the valley floor and 2,250 feet above sea level. Tall, pointed and narrow, it appears to be an isolated spire, justifying its name. A hike up the valley or a flight above will reveal it to be the knob-like end of a sharp ridge. 'Iao Needle is an erosion-resistant chunk of West Maui's original caldera fill. The older volcanic material cracked as it was stressed from later geological events. Newer, fluid lava of a tougher mineral composition filled these cracks, forming dikes that strengthened the area. When streams flowing down the mountains scoured out the valley, 'Iao Needle and its supporting ridge withstood the water's cutting force.

Paths from the parking lot lead to short and easy hikes. Take the left fork just before the footbridge for the walk down to 'Iao Stream. Bordering the trail are guava and kukui trees, torch ginger, heliconia and numerous other tropical plants. At the bottom, you can look upstream to see several cascades. 'Iao

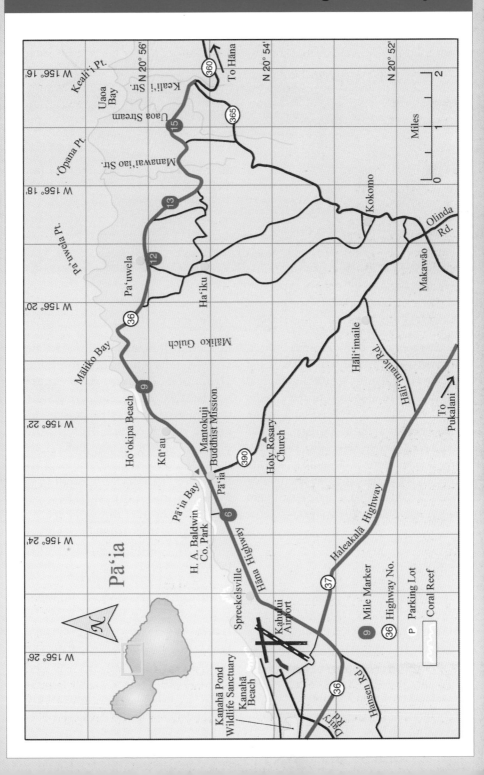

The Hāna Highway takes everyone through colorful Pā'ia

Needle appears even more ominous from this perspective. The trail loops at the bottom and returns to the footbridge. From here continue up to the Needle overlook. Stairs have been built as the trail steepens at the end where a shelter and benches have been built. Enjoy the magnificent views: a close-up look at the Needle, across the gap to the steep valley walls draped in foliage and downstream to the valley carved by water.

Pā'ia

Four miles east of the intersection of the Hāna and Haleakalā Highways is the funky town of Pā'ia. Its diverse population is only one quarter of what it was in its heyday as a sugar town. Many residents moved to Kahului when low-cost housing developments were built. Starting in the 1960s, Pā'ia has attracted denizens as diverse and colorful as its refurbished storefronts. Dropouts, hippies, new agers, windsurfers, artists and farmers mix with tourists making their first stop on the road to Hāna. This is a fun place to shop for vintage aloha shirts, unusual imported goods, or local arts and crafts. Pā'ia is the best place on Maui to shop for antiques and Hawaiian collectables. There are several good international restaurants and coffee shops to relax in while people-watching.

On the east side of town is the **Mantokuji Mission**, a Japanese Buddhist Temple built in 1921. It's fronted by a cemetery filled with more than 600 burial markers. The mission observes the Obon season each summer with services and dancers honoring their ancestors. Each sunrise and sunset is heralded with its huge gong sounding 18 times.

The Hāna Highway hugs the cliffs at Honomanū Bay

EAST MAUI SIGHTS

Road to Hāna

There are more than 50 miles, 50 bridges and 600 twists and turns awaiting those who drive the **Hāna Highway** (Highway 360) along East Maui's windward shore. Ranked as the most spectacular coastal drive in Hawai'i, the road winds deep into lush valleys and courses through vegetation so thick it seems to spill out from the mountainside. Ficus roots dangle overhead, waterfalls nearly splash onto the road and moss takes root on exposed rocks. Rain forests drip with ferns; philodendron and bamboo abound; and African tulip trees add a splash of color. Built in 1927, the paved and sometimes bumpy road hugs towering cliffs before dropping down to the rugged coastline and pounding surf.

The State Foundation on Culture and Arts declared the Hāna Highway as one of 50 Millennium Legacy Trails in the nation, the only route in Hawai'i selected for the honor.

Kahului to Hāna can be driven in three hours but you don't want to rush this experience. Take time to admire the views, take pictures or

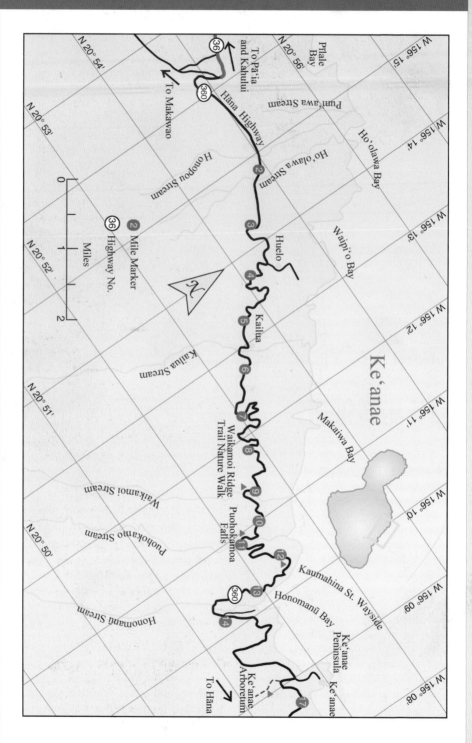

Patrick McFeeley

Windsurfer at Hoʻokipa

explore. Top up the gas tank before you leave as there are no gas stations between Pāʻia and Hāna. Bring food and plenty of drinking water as there are lovely spots to eat a picnic lunch en route and Hāna's dining choices are limited and expensive. Be prepared for it to rain at some point in the day and bring proper hiking footwear. Unless you are staying in Hāna or camping, allow a full day for the return trip.

The Hāna Highway begins in Central Maui as Highway 36, passing through the town of Pāʻia. Two miles east, at the nine-mile marker, is the entrance to **Hoʻokipa Beach Park**, one of the world's premier windsurfing spots. The overlook next to the parking lot is filled with spectators on windy afternoons (see Beaches).

One mile east of Hoʻokipa, the road runs along a 100-foot cliff then turns upstream to cross **Māliko Bay**. Above the bay, **Māliko Gulch** presented an almost impossible obstacle for the builders of Maui's first large irrigation system, the **Hāmākua Ditch**. In 1876, Samuel T. Alexander

and his partner, Henry P. Baldwin, began the construction of a series of irrigation ditches, siphons and tunnels that would divert the abundant flow from Haleakalā's watershed to the sugarcane fields of the Central Valley. Adding to their difficulty was the fact that they had a two-year deadline to meet or they would lose the rights to their rival, Claus Spreckels. When the construction workers reached Māliko Gulch they were to be lowered on ropes to prepare the channel and lay the pipes for the siphons. The walls of the gulch were so steep-sided that the workers refused to drop down the canyon. It was left to Baldwin himself to become the hero of the project. Not letting the loss of one arm in a sugar-mill accident hinder him, he grabbed the rope and lowered himself 300 feet to the floor of the canyon. Inspired by their leader's example, the workers followed Baldwin and continued working on the project. The Hāmākua Ditch was completed in the nick of time. The water was turned on and the

Waterfalls abound along the road to Hāna

Right:
View of the Hāna Highway from Waikamoi Ridge Trail

Opposite Page:
Painted bark eucalyptus trees at Keʻanae Arboretum

next day water was flowing into the Haʻikū Plantation—one day before the deadline.

From Māliko Gulch, Highway 36 winds gently through another six miles of pineapple fields and pastureland before intersecting with Highway 365. The road is relabeled Highway 360 and the mileage markers begin at zero.

Every shade of green is represented in the groves of mango, kukui, eucalyptus and bamboo that border both sides of the road. One-lane bridges are common—look upstream as you pass over them and you will likely be rewarded with views of waterfalls. One-half mile past Mile Marker 9 is a roadside turnout for the **Waikamoi Ridge Trail Nature Walk**. The trail, covered with exposed tree roots, leads to a lookout through a thick forest of paperbark trees and eucalyptus wreathed in philodendrons. Here you can turn back for a walk of three-tenths of a mile or you can continue up the ridge and through a

bamboo forest to a second lookout and picnic area. From there return via the Jeep road for a round trip of 1.2 miles and about half an hour.

At Mile Marker 11, park just before the bridge to take the short walk that leads to a pool and **Puohokamoa Falls**. Unless the stream is raging from a heavy rainfall, the pool is safe for swimming. As with all other streams in Maui, don't drink the water. Feral pigs living in the forests upstream make the presence of giardia a possibility.

A delightful spot to rest or have lunch is just past the 12-mile marker at the **Kaumahina State Wayside**. There are portable toilets here and picnic tables overlook a view of the ocean and Keʻanae Peninsula. Short trails from the rest area lead through hala trees perched upon aerial roots that look like stilts. Rainfall turns exposed roots and rocks on the trails slippery, making proper hiking footwear a good idea. This is about the halfway point to Hāna but the best scenery and the slowest part of the road are yet to come.

Bamboo shoots tower at Keʻanae Arboretum

Diver takes a plunge near Ke'anae

When you reach the 13-mile marker you are descending a 400-foot cliff into the rugged **Honomanū Valley**. The bay, exposed to the rough water of the North Pacific, indents the coastline by a third of a mile. Honomanū Stream carved walls 1,500 feet high where the canyon swells to an amphitheater two miles upstream. Much of the stream's flow is diverted from its outlet to irrigate sugarcane in the Central Valley. On the valley floor, a dirt entrance road at Mile Marker 14 leads to the boulder-covered beach (see Beaches).

The **Ke'anae Arboretum**, six-tenths of a mile before Mile Marker 17 (Mile Markers 15 and 16 are missing), covers six acres and displays native and introduced trees and ornamental and food plants along a nature trail. Stop in a small parking area shaded by monkeypod trees and follow the path for a round trip of three quarters of a mile. Photographers should bring fast film or a tripod because the path is shaded by a canopy of trees. At the entrance, note the unusual hau tree to the right. It has bright yellow blossoms and long, sinuous branches that interlock. Farther up the trail on the left, is a stand of towering bamboo. This is the arboretum's most photographed flora. Have someone stand in front to add perspective to the picture. Although the size of mature trees, bamboo is the tallest member of the grass family. African tulip trees can be identified by their bright red blossoms. Note the colors splashed on the trunks of the eucalyptus trees. These specimens are of a species native to the Philippines. The pathway culminates with a section of taro patches planted between lava-rock walls.

Mile Marker 17 and a tsunami siren locate a cliff-top pullout

Huge winter waves pound the Ke'anae Peninsla

A patchwork of taro fields cover the Ke'anae Peninsula

overlooking the beautiful **Ke'anae Peninsula**. The peninsula was built by a later flow of lava escaping Haleakalā Crater through the Ko'olau Gap and advancing down the valley. Below, sunlight glistens off the quilt work of rectangular taro patches fed by Ke'anae Stream. The community living there is mostly native Hawaiian who tend the taro fields and pound poi.

Just before the 19-mile marker, to the right, is the **Ke'anae Valley Lookout**. For a change, this lookout faces mauka (inland) up into the Ke'anae Valley. If the clouds aren't too low, you can see Ko'olau Gap, a break in the rim of Haleakalā Crater. This valley was once much deeper than what we see now. Repeated eruptions of Haleakalā in the past 10,000 years have sent many rivers of lava down this valley to the sea. Another lookout makai (to the sea) of the road stands over the settlements on the **Wailua Peninsula**.

The next section of road passes a succession of waterfalls. Whether they are trickles or torrents depends on the recent rainfall on the mountain.

Watch for **Waikani Falls** one-half mile past Mile Marker 19 and **Kōpili'ula Falls** just before Mile Marker 22.

If you need a rest, stop half a mile past Mile Marker 22, at the **Pua'aka'a State Wayside**. Restrooms, a pay phone, and drinking water are provided. Picnic shelters sit beside a waterfall and swimming ponds on two levels. Ferns, heliconias, guava and native trees backdrop this enchanting picnic ground.

If you have time, take a side trip to **Venus Pool**, a beautiful place that few people other than local residents know about. The return trip is five miles. At Mile Marker 31, turn left onto 'Ula'ino

Pua'aka'a State Wayside provides relaxation and swimming on the road to Hāna

A waterfall fills secluded Venus Pool

Road. After a mile and a half, you come upon the **Kahanu Gardens**, part of the National Tropical Botanical Garden. The Kahanu Gardens' focus is to collect and study plants at the Pacific and develop collections of rare and native plants, especially those endemic to Maui. Located on the garden grounds is **Pi'ilanihale**, the largest heiau on Maui. The heiau's stone platform is more than 100 yards long in each direction and 50 feet high. Small pebbles pave its surface and two sides are terraced. This was probably the royal home of the Pi'ilani family in the sixteenth century.

Tours of the garden and heiau are conducted at 11:00 a.m. and 1:00 p.m. each weekday. The price is $10 per person and reservations are required. Phone (808) 248-9812.

Continue on Ula'ino Road for another mile until it is crossed by a stream. If the water level is low, you can drive across, but if it has been raining hard you will have to ford the stream on foot or with four-wheel drive. The road ends in two-tenths of a mile at the mouth of **Helele'ike'ōhā Stream**. If large rocks are exposed in the streambed, it can be safely crossed; otherwise the water level is too high. Scramble along the boulder-covered beach on the other side of the stream for 200 yards to reach this lovely freshwater pool fed by a waterfall. It is nestled at the base of a fern-drenched lava wall with springs of weeping water.

Be sure to stop at **Wai'ānapanapa State Park**. The half-mile-long entrance road is at Mile Marker 32. Meaning "glistening water," Wai'ānapanapa is a 122-acre park with cabins, camping, restrooms, showers, and drinking water. Below the parking lot the water glistens over a stunning black sand beach (see Beaches). Signs at the parking lot point to a short trail to the **Wai'ānapanapa Caves**. The caves were formed when two lava tubes partially collapsed and filled with water. The water in the upper pool is usually stagnant, but the lower pool's water is great for a cold, refreshing swim. By swimming under the ledge at the back of the pool you can reach a hidden chamber. Sometimes the water in the pool is colored red from thousands of tiny shrimp called 'ōpae 'ula, which occasionally emerge from subterranean cracks in the lava.

Legend tells us Wai'ānapanapa Cave was the hiding place of a Hawaiian princess. Her jealous husband became angry when he thought she was consorting with another. The princess and her attendant entered the water-filled cave and swam under the rock ledge to the dry chamber to escape the husband's wrath. Searching for the princess, the husband entered the cave. Although they remained quiet, the image of the princess's kāhili, the bright royal emblem, reflected upon the surface of the pool, revealing their hiding place. The husband killed both women. Now the red water represents the blood of the victims.

Hāna

After parading past a plethora of road curves, bridges, waterfalls and rock walls, the highway unravels into the luxuriant district of Hāna. Nestled beneath the rainy slopes of Haleakalā, Hāna is surrounded by green pastures and a serrated black-lava coastline. Showered with 70 inches of rain a year, this Eden-like town is nicknamed "Heavenly Hāna."

Until the completion of the road from Kahului, Hāna, at the extreme east end of Maui, remained isolated from the rest of the island. Now, as the stream of rental cars flowing through town attests, Hāna is accessible, but it remains quiet and has changed little over the years. The pace of living is slow and relaxing. Hāna is about 90 miles and 90 years from the resorts of West Maui. Only 1,900 people call Hāna home, and of those more than half claim native Hawaiian descent.

Hāna's history is an illustrious and bloody one. Because of its strategic location, 35 miles across the 'Alenuihāhā Channel from the Big Island, Hāna has often been a battleground in the wars between the chiefs of Maui and the Big Island. King Kamehameha the Great was the last chief to utilize the strategic advantage of Hāna when in 1802 his fleet of double-hulled war canoes gathered in the bay to assault Maui. **Ka'uiki Head**, a 386-foot cinder cone, was the site of a fortress where battles were fought in

Grass houses and buildings are recreated at Hāna's Cultural Center and Museum

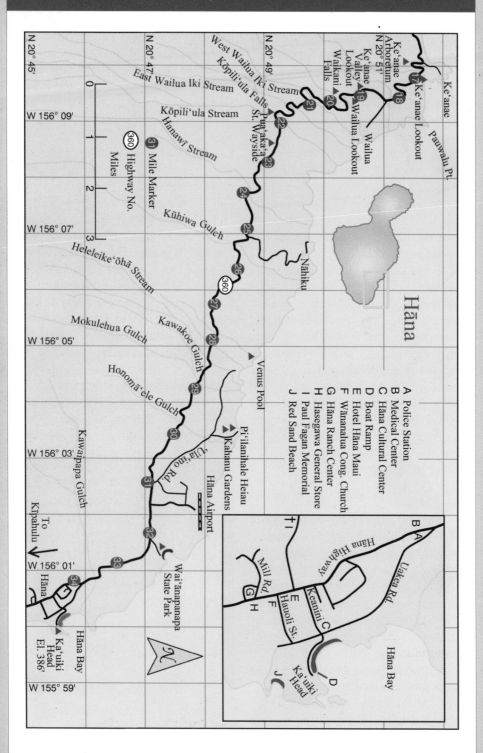

Ke'anae
Arboretum
Ke'anae
Valley
Lookout
Waikani
Falls

N 20° 51'

Wailua Lookout

Wailua

West Wailua Iki Stream

Kōpili'ula Falls

East Wailua Iki Stream

Kōpili'ula Stream

Pua'aka'a
St. Wayside

Hanawī Stream

Kūhiwa Gulch

Nāhiku

Heleleike'ōhā Stream

Mokulehua Gulch

Hononā'ele Gulch

Kawakoe Gulch

Kawaipapa Gulch

'Ula'ino Rd.

360 Highway No.

31 Mile Marker

Miles

N 20° 45'

W 156° 09'

W 156° 07'

W 156° 05'

W 156° 03'

W 156° 01'

W 155° 59'

N 20° 47'

N 20° 49'

Ke'anae

Pauwalu Pt.

Ke'anae Lookout

Venus Pool

Pi'ilanihale Heiau

Kahanu Gardens

Hāna Airport

Wai'ānapanapa
State Park

To
Kipahulu

Hāna

Ka'uiki
Head
El. 386'

Hāna Bay

Hāna

A   Police Station
B   Medical Center
C   Hāna Cultural Center
D   Boat Ramp
E   Hotel Hāna Maui
F   Wānanalua Cong. Church
G   Hāna Ranch Center
H   Hasegawa General Store
I   Paul Fagan Memorial
J   Red Sand Beach

Hāna Highway

Uakea Rd.

Mill Rd.

Keanini C

Hauoli St.

Ka'uiki
Head

Hāna Bay

Kamehameha's campaign to unify the islands under his reign. Marking the south end of Hāna Bay, Ka'uiki Head once housed a cave purported to be the **birthplace of Queen Ka'ahumanu** in 1773. A war between rival chiefs at the time of her birth forced the future Queen's mother to hide in the cave. Kamehameha first saw Ka'ahumanu near Hāna when she was seven years old. When she was sixteen, she married Kamehameha and became his favorite wife. A cinder trail sheltered by ironwood trees starts at the right side of Hāna Bay and follows the base of Ka'uiki Head to a plaque marking her birthplace.

Missionaries Daniel Conde and Mark Ives estimated Hāna's population at 3,000 when they arrived in 1837. When George Wilfong started a sugar plantation in 1851, immigrants from other countries were added to the ethnic mix. Sugar production became the mainstay of East Maui's economy until the middle of the twentieth century. In 1946 Paul Fagan, a San Francisco industrialist, bought thousands of acres surrounding Hāna and developed them into the **Hāna Ranch**. Descendants of the Hereford cattle he brought in graze in the pastures above Hāna. Hawaiian cowhands work the ranch today. When cattle are ready for O'ahu stockyards, they are trucked along the Hāna Highway (at night to avoid traffic) to Kahului Harbor.

Fagan loved Hāna so much that he decided to live out the rest of his life here. He built the exclusive **Hotel Hāna Maui**, planning to use it as a spring training site for the baseball team he owned and as a place for his well-to-do friends to stay when they visited. The first year his Pacific Coast League champion San Francisco Seals came to train, dozens of sportswriters reported home about the beauty of Hāna. The word got out about "Heavenly Hāna" and visitors started to come in force.

When Paul Fagan died in 1959, his family erected a huge lava-rock cross, across from the Hotel Hāna Maui, atop the camel-backed hill, Pu'u o Kahaula. For a magnificent view of the town and bay, you can hike or drive the short road through a pasture to the **Paul Fagan Memorial**. Ask at the front desk of the Hotel to borrow a gate key (deposit required).

At the corner of Uakea Road and Keanini Drive is **Hāna Cultural Center and Museum**. The three-acre grounds have three attractions. In the small museum building, artifacts such as primitive stone tools, fishhooks made from shells, poi pounders and boards, old photographs and elaborate quilts are displayed. Next door is the old Courthouse and Police Station, built in 1871 to be the seat of legal authority for Hāna. A circuit judge stills hold court there on the first Tuesday of each month. You can tour a replica Hawaiian village on the site with grass huts used for living, cooking and canoe-building. The museum is staffed with friendly volunteers. Open daily from 10:00 a.m. to 4:00 p.m., $2.00 donation. Phone 248-8622, website <www.planet-hawaii.com/hana>.

On the National Register of Historic Places, **Wānanalua Congregational Church** is a lovely chapel built in 1838 with lava-rock walls. It sits with its small cemetery where Hauʻoli Street intersects with the Hāna Highway. Early missionaries had it built atop an ancient heiau, symbolically expressing the time when Christianity was displacing the old Hawaiian beliefs.

At Mill Road and the Hāna Highway is the **Hāna Ranch Center,** the closest thing Hāna has to a commercial center. It has a post office, a tiny branch of the Bank of Hawaiʻi, the Hāna Ranch general store and the Hāna Ranch Restaurant. Across the highway is **Hasegawa's General Store** which stocks a cluttered array of wares.

Hāna residents like to frequent **Hāna Beach Park**, which lies on the sandy shore of half-moon-shaped Hāna Bay (see Beaches). The park has a recreation center, Tutu's Snack Bar and picnic benches. Impromptu music-making often happens here.

Beyond Hāna

Most of the people who make it to Hāna continue on the road to **ʻOheʻo**, part of Haleakalā National Park, which reaches to the sea via **Kīpahulu Valley**. The road changes its name to the Piʻilani Highway from here on. It's an extraordinarily lush stretch. The road from Hāna to ʻOheʻo is narrow and winding, dotted with one-lane bridges and congested with drivers wanting to take in all the sights. Allow a half hour to drive the 10 miles. A few celebrities own homes and estates along this road, but almost all of the large houses are built back from the road—safely hidden from curious tourists.

Traffic usually slows down or stops 7.8 miles from the Hotel Hāna Maui for **Wailua Falls**. The cascade drops 95 feet to the pool at its base. If

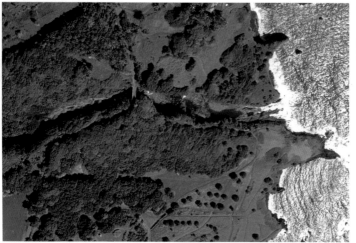

The Pools at ʻOheʻo Gulch are part of Haleakalā National Park

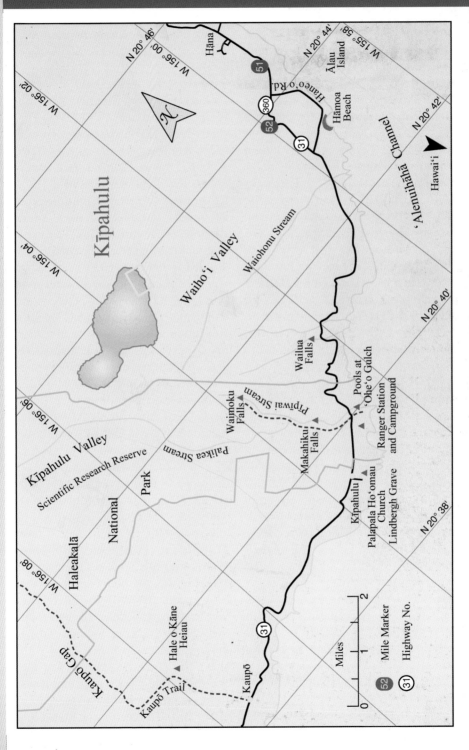

you are able to park, take the trail just before the bridge to get a closer look or for a swim in the pool.

At 'Ohe'o Gulch, 10 miles from Hāna and just inside the boundary of Haleakalā National Park (no entrance fee), a bridge bisects a series of small waterfalls and pools, each tumbling into the one below. The parking lot for the **Pools at 'Ohe'o** and Ranger Station (248-7375) is just ahead on the left. Toilets are the only amenity found here. A 15-minute walk leads down to the lower pools and then loops back with interpretive signs along the way. The terraced pools connected by rushing white water present a beautiful sight, framed by the verdant mountain behind and the blue Pacific below. When the weather is nice, the pools can be crowded with swimmers. The two pools closest to the ocean are connected by an underwater tunnel about 8 feet below the surface. Park rangers may prohibit swimming if heavy rains have raised the waters to an unsafe level. Years ago the pools were dubbed the "Seven Sacred Pools" as a promotional scam. There is actually a chain of 24 pools leading up the mountain and they were never sacred. This area is beautiful enough without the need for window-dressed nomenclature.

The National Park allows camping in an open pasture between the ranger station and the ocean. It probably has the most stunning scenery of any place you can pitch a tent on the island. The campground has minimal development, some pit toilets and picnic benches, but no potable water. Permits are not required and stays are limited to three nights each month.

In 1969, Haleakalā National Park added the wet Kīpahulu Valley to bring its total acreage to 28,655. The funds needed to purchase the land that includes the 'Ohe'o pools were provided by the Nature Conservancy Group. Kīpahulu Valley descends from the summit of Haleakalā, a subalpine area with frequent frosts, to a subtropical rain forest in just 7.6 miles. Four streams drain the valley of the 250 inches of rain it receives annually. Upper Kīpahulu Valley is a reserve providing sanctuary for native flora and fauna. The steep uplands are still cloaked in rare native koa and 'ōhi'a rain forest. No one is permitted to enter except on closely supervised scientific expeditions. Since 1967, scientists studying the area have found more than 200 species of plants indigenous or endemic to Hawai'i; of these, 15 were previously unknown.

Palikea is the most accessible of the valley's four streams and a trail parallels it up to two of Maui's largest waterfalls. The rewards of hiking this one-and-a-half mile trail are 200-foot **Makahiku Falls** and 400-foot **Waimoku Falls**. This is a spectacular hike and the two hours spent for the return trip are well worth it. The trailhead begins across the road from the 'Ohe'o parking lot, ascending through grasslands interspersed with guava and Christmas berry. Near the one-third-mile point a spur trail leads right, around some hala trees, to a safety railing protecting the Makahiku

Above:
The trail to
Waimoku Falls
leads through a
bamboo forest

Right:
Waimoku Falls

Previous Page:
Pools at 'Ohe'o
National Parks Service

Within earshot of Waimoku's crashing water, you must hopscotch across the stream's slippery rocks. The falls create a filigree of water, embraced by an amphitheater of sheer rock walls with mosses and ferns clinging to it. You have to crane your neck as far as it will go to see the top of the pali. Spray cools and dampens everything. The pool at the bottom is too shallow for swimming, having been partially filled by falling rocks.

One mile past the 'Ohe'o parking lot a dirt entrance road on the left side leads two-tenths of a mile to Pāpala Ho'omau Congregational Church. Built in 1857, it has thick stone walls, simple wooden pews and a window painting of a Polynesian Christ dressed in a red and yellow feather cape. The small cemetery behind the church is the **burial place of Charles Lindbergh**. The first aviator to cross the Atlantic lived the last years of his life in a home he built in the Kīpahulu district in 1968. He died of cancer in 1974 and was buried in a simple grave surrounded by a chain and marked with little US flags. The epitaph on the grave marker

Falls viewpoint. Back on the main trail, you pass through a livestock gate and around a large banyan tree. Watch your head as you pass through a thick grove of guava trees that relentlessly drop their fruit. The trail bends onto a footbridge across Palikea Stream where the first of three bamboo forests awaits. Breezes bend and sway the flexible bamboo stalks providing a percussive accompaniment to the rustling leaves. The path is lined with fragrant yellow ginger as you walk out of the first grove of bamboo and the long ribbon of Waimoku Falls appears in the distance. The trail is perpetually damp and muddy. Wood walkways help you through the boggy spots. Sunlight is obliterated by the towering bamboo growing in the last grove.

Charles Lindbergh's grave at Kīpahulu

reads: "If I take the wings of the morning And dwell in the uttermost parts of the sea." Next to the cemetery is Kīpahulu Park. It has a few picnic tables and sits on a cliff overlooking the coastline.

Those returning via the Hāna Highway should turn back at this point. The Piʻilani Highway (Highway 31) continues to follow Maui's southeast coastline, rising to transverse Haleakalā's southwest rift and cross Maui's "Upcountry" before returning to Kahului. There is no shortcut route to Kīhei or West Maui. The road through this nearly unpopulated region of stark beauty is treacherous in places and designated off-limits by most car rental companies. If your car breaks down, you're a long way from help and will most likely be held responsible for repair and towing costs. A stretch of the road is unpaved and deeply rutted when it isn't washed out. Check with the ranger station at ʻOheʻo for the latest road conditions.

It's six miles of slow driving on a narrow road to get to **Kaupō**. Along the route you will see a few houses belonging to people who appreciate isolation. The only structure at Kaupō is a small store that is as likely to be closed as open. Looking up, you can see **Kaupō Gap**, one of Haleakalā's major lava escape points. A trail leads from here, along the west side of **Manawainui Gulch**, past the **Hale o**

Kāne heiau and through the gap to **Palikū cabin**, where it connects with a trail that crosses the crater floor. This rugged hike is extremely difficult and is more often attempted by hikers from the top who have stayed overnight at the cabin.

Once you get to Kaupō, the lush vegetation stops suddenly and the landscape becomes barren and arid. The harsh dirt road improves in a couple of miles. Watch out for free-range cattle. Heiau and house sites provide evidence that in ancient times this area was abundantly populated. The economy of the area would have depended upon agriculture, probably sweet potatoes, which did not require extensive terracing or irrigation. Reefs are limited, so inshore fishing would have provided scanty results. When La Pérouse became the first European to set foot on Maui he wasn't very impressed with this area, referring to it as a "dismal coast."

At Mile Marker 29 start looking for the natural arch at **Pākōwai Point**, formed by an ancient lava flow and sculpted by waves. From here the road turns away from the sea and gradually climbs the southern slope of Haleakalā. You are more than 1,700 feet high when the black shores of La Pérouse Bay appear directly below. Now the road is bordered by the old ʻUlupalakua Ranch, the last destination in the "Upcountry Sights" chapter.

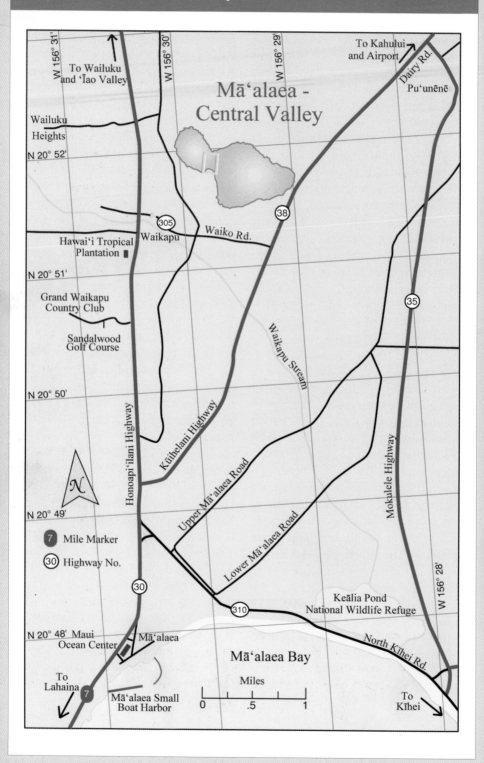

Sunset on Maui's South Coast

SOUTH MAUI SIGHTS

Māʻalaea

South Maui includes the sunny and dry 18-mile stretch of coast on Haleakalā's leeward side, from Māʻalaea Bay on the north end to La Pérouse Bay at the south. Because of a chain of beautiful beaches, faithfully good weather and an abundance of accommodations, South Maui has developed into a popular visitor destination.

Māʻalaea Bay runs in a gentle arc along the south side of the isthmus that joins the two mountain masses of west and east Maui. The prevailing trade winds gain speed as they funnel between the mountains and release over Māʻalaea. Blowing sand can make beach-going uninviting, but the bay is popular with windsurfers.

Māʻalaea Harbor served as an active shipping point until 1906. Now it is busy as the launching place for pleasure craft and charter boats. Most of the snorkel and dive cruises headed for South Maui and Molokini originate here.

Sightseers returning to Māʻalaea Harbor

Maui's newest village is under construction at Māʻalaea. The centerpiece of this housing and business development is the new **Maui Ocean Center**, which bills itself as a world-class Hawaiian aquarium. Nearly all of its occupants were captured in Hawaiian waters. The aquarium circulates filtered sea water from the bay without adding chemicals.

The first thing a visitor will see at the Ocean Center is the surge pool. Waves strike the rocks in this shallow setting for marine life such as spiny urchins and cauliflower coral. Next door is the Reef building, where local coral and fish live in tanks. Visitors descend into the building to view various coral communities and habitats. Large tanks showcase an expanse of coral while small tanks focus on small fishes and rarely seen creatures. Outside is a turtle pool, a touch pool with starfish and urchins and a pool featuring spotted eagle rays, with views from the top and underwater. A 13,500-square-foot building hosts, on one side, the **Whale Discovery Center**. Although not containing a live whale, it houses interactive displays featuring humpback behavior, life cycle and migration. In addition to displays featuring mahimahi, jellyfish and plankton, the other side of the building contains a 100-foot-long main tank holding 600,000 gallons of seawater— the state's largest aquarium tank. Showcased here are some of Hawaiʻi's ocean predators, the tiger shark, gray and whitetip sharks, jack and yellowfin tunas, as well as surgeonfish, triggerfish and puffers. Visitors can walk though the middle of the tank via a 57-foot-long acrylic tunnel. Also on the aquarium grounds are two restaurants and a well-stocked gift shop. Admission is $17.50 for adults, $12.00 for children 3–12 years. Audio guides can be rented for $4.00. Open 9:00 a.m. to 5:00 p.m. daily. Phone: 270-7000. Website: <www.coralworld.com/moc>

Turtles return to Māʻalaea to lay their eggs

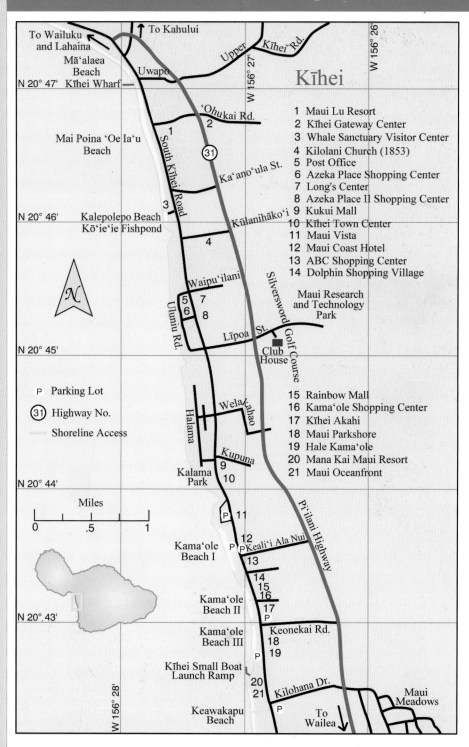

To Wailuku and Lahaina
To Kahului
Māʻalaea Beach
Upper Kīhei Rd.
Uwapo
N 20° 47' Kīhei Wharf
W 156° 27'
W 156° 26'
Kīhei

Mai Poina ʻOe Iaʻu Beach
ʻOhukai Rd.
2
1
South Kīhei Road
(31)
Kaʻanoʻula St.
3
N 20° 46' Kalepolepo Beach
Kōʻieʻie Fishpond
Kūlanihākoʻi
4

1 Maui Lu Resort
2 Kīhei Gateway Center
3 Whale Sanctuary Visitor Center
4 Kilolani Church (1853)
5 Post Office
6 Azeka Place Shopping Center
7 Long's Center
8 Azeka Place II Shopping Center
9 Kukui Mall
10 Kīhei Town Center
11 Maui Vista
12 Maui Coast Hotel
13 ABC Shopping Center
14 Dolphin Shopping Village

Waipuʻilani
5
7
6
8
Uluniu Rd.
Līpoa St.
Silversword Golf Course
Maui Research and Technology Park
N 20° 45'
Club House

P Parking Lot
(31) Highway No.
Shoreline Access

Halama
Welakahao
Kupuna
9
10
Kalama Park

15 Rainbow Mall
16 Kamaʻole Shopping Center
17 Kīhei Akahi
18 Maui Parkshore
19 Hale Kamaʻole
20 Mana Kai Maui Resort
21 Maui Oceanfront

N 20° 44'

Miles
0   .5   1

Piʻilani Highway

P 11
12
Kamaʻole Beach I
P Kealiʻi Ala Nui
13
14
15
16
Kamaʻole Beach II
17
N 20° 43'
Keonekai Rd.
Kamaʻole Beach III
18
19
P
Kīhei Small Boat Launch Ramp
20
21
Kilohana Dr.
Maui Meadows
Keawakapu Beach
P
To Wailea
W 156° 28'

Keālia Pond Bird Sanctuary, lying across North Kīhei Road from Māʻalaea Bay, is a saltwater marsh and 691-acre bird sanctuary. From the side of the road, you can usually spot Hawaiian stilts, Hawaiian coots and herons wading in the shallow water. The best place to observe wildlife is from the roadside berm and on the mudflats at the pond outlet, between Mile Markers 1 and 2.

During the winter months, the **Pacific Whale Foundation** offers a free lecture Monday through Friday at 12:15 p.m. and viewing from their Ocean Observatory Deck in the **Keālia Beach Shopping Plaza** (next to Margarita's Beach Cantina) at 101 North Kīhei Road. Attendees receive a free color whale-watching guide and tips for whale watching from shore.

Canoe paddlers return to Kīhei at day's end

Kīhei

A narrow strip of a town, extending six miles south of Māʻalaea Bay to the exclusive resort area of Wailea to the south, Kīhei's key attractions are its nearly uninterrupted string of sandy beaches. From the beaches you have views of Lānaʻi, Kahoʻolawe, and Molokini, as well as West Maui, which, because of the deep indentation of Māʻalaea Bay, appears from here to be a separate island.

Kīhei's development has followed a haphazard plan. South Kīhei Road, which runs the full length of town, is lined with condos, shopping centers, vacant lots, and fast-food restaurants. There is no place that can be pinpointed as a town center. Nearly every visitor here stays in a condo. A flurry of building in the 1970s created an abundance of units, which keeps rates the lowest on the island. Inland, the Piʻilani Highway (Highway 31) runs parallel to South Kīhei Road and bypasses much of the traffic congestion. Several crossroads connect the two routes.

Kīhei makes an excellent base for a Maui visit. Every convenience is nearby; the weather is the sunniest and driest on Maui (average annual rainfall is 13 inches) and beautiful beaches are just across the street. Many people who live here are making attempts to beautify their town. Recently, a weed-infested plot of land along South Kīhei Road was planted with flowering Singapore plumeria trees, Manila palms and beach naupaka groundcover.

In 1930, only 350 people lived in Kīhei. This arid area did not garner much interest until World War II. Ruins of cement pillboxes strategically situated on the beaches are remnants of the army's reaction to the threat of Japanese invasion.

The **Hawaiian Islands Humpback Whale National Marine Sanctuary Visitor Center** (879-2818) is located in a white, wood-sided building on Kalepolepo Beach at 726 South Kīhei Road. It is one of 12 marine sanctuaries administered by the National Oceanic and Atmospheric Administration (NOAA). Established in 1972, the marine sanctuary program balances protection of natural and cultural marine resources with their human use and enjoyment. Here you can find information on Hawai'i's favorite returning visitor. During whale season (December to May) you can use their telescope for spotting whales breaching in the waters offshore. When the humpbacks are not in Hawai'i, the sanctuary administers research projects such as water quality and coral reef monitoring as well as educational programs. Their hours are 9:00 a.m. to 3:00 p.m., Monday to Friday, phone 879-2818, website <www.t-link.net/~whale/>. See the South Maui Beaches chapter for the **Kō'ie'ie fishpond** next to the visitor center on Kalepolepo Beach.

Kalama Park, located across from Foodland, is 36 acres of grass, pavilions, picnic tables and recreation facilities. There are public restrooms, pay telephones and a children's playground. There are no beaches here, but it is a good place for family activities and to enjoy watching the sun set over the ocean.

Wailea

Wailea lies south of Kīhei, the genteel antithesis to its unrefined neighbor. What was 1,450 acres of kiawe scrubland owned by Alexander and Baldwin Co. is now a carefully planned, precisely manicured destination resort. A chain of small crescent-shaped sandy beaches link the coastline, backed by five world-class resorts. The resorts are connected by Wailea Alanui Drive, which separates them from three golf courses. Nothing in Kā'anapali or Kapalua can surpass the luxury and exclusiveness of the Wailea resorts. The careful planning that put the resorts on the oceanfront also caused them to block the view of the ocean from the road. Public access to each beach is assured by law, although parking at times is hard to find (see South Maui Beaches). The resorts' facilities such as bathrooms, showers and a mile-and-a-half-long paved ocean walkway are there for all beach visitors to use.

There are condo developments interspersed throughout the area, but this community is not a town. The **Wailea Shopping Center** sits next to the main road; however, it is scheduled to be torn down and replaced with even greater upscale shops.

Mākena

When you pass the white, exotic-looking Kea Lani resort you have left Wailea and entered Mākena. The name of the road changes from

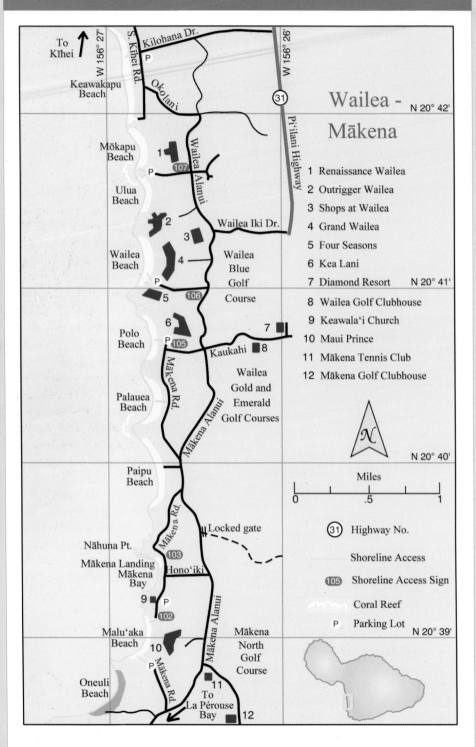

To Kīhei

W 156° 27'

S. Kīhei Rd.

Kilohana Dr.

P

Keawakapu Beach

Oko'lan'i

W 156° 26'

31

Wailea - Mākena

N 20° 42'

Mōkapu Beach

1

P

107

Wailea Alanui

Ulua Beach

2

Wailea Iki Dr.

3

Wailea Beach

4

Wailea Blue Golf Course

P

106

5

Polo Beach

6

P

105

Kaukahi

7

8

Pi'ilani Highway

1 Renaissance Wailea
2 Outrigger Wailea
3 Shops at Wailea
4 Grand Wailea
5 Four Seasons
6 Kea Lani
7 Diamond Resort   N 20° 41'

8 Wailea Golf Clubhouse
9 Keawala'i Church
10 Maui Prince
11 Mākena Tennis Club
12 Mākena Golf Clubhouse

Palauea Beach

Makena Rd.

Makena Alanui

Wailea Gold and Emerald Golf Courses

N 20° 40'

Paipu Beach

Miles

0   .5   1

Nāhuna Pt.

Makena Rd.

103

Locked gate

31 Highway No.

Mākena Landing Mākena Bay

Hono'iki

Shoreline Access

9

P

102

105 Shoreline Access Sign

Coral Reef

P   Parking Lot   N 20° 39'

Malu'aka Beach

10

P

Makena Rd.

Makena Alanui

Mākena North Golf Course

Oneuli Beach

11

To La Pérouse Bay

12

Wailea Alanui Drive to Mākena Alanui Drive. Mākena is less developed than Wailea with two golf courses and one resort, the **Maui Prince**. The road continues south for seven miles, past several beaches and some large oceanfront houses before degrading into a bumpy trail at **La Pérouse Bay**.

In the 19th century, the bustling port of Mākena ranked behind only Lahaina in economic importance to Maui. Cargo ships carried Maui's fresh produce and cattle from the 'Ulupalakua Ranch to markets on the other islands. With the building of the Kahului Harbor, commercial traffic bypassed **Mākena Landing**.

On Mākena Road, south of Honoiki Street, is the **Keawala'i Congregational Church**, which was established in 1832 and built in 1855. Services, in a mix of Hawaiian and English, are held each Sunday at 9:30 a.m. inside the three-foot-thick stone walls. Many of the gravestones in the cemetery display ceramic pictures of the deceased.

Most prominent among geographical features along this coast is the 360-foot cone, **Pu'u 'Ōla'i**. The hill, covered with red cinders and kiawe trees, juts upwards from the slopes of Haleakalā at the coastline, three-quarters of a mile south of the Maui Prince, and is visible 12 miles away at Mā'alaea.

Pressing south from Pu'u 'Ōla'i the road gets a little rougher as you pass by some large houses facing **'Āhihi Bay**. A couple of roadside turnouts allow you to stop and take in the scenery. Behind is the long stretch

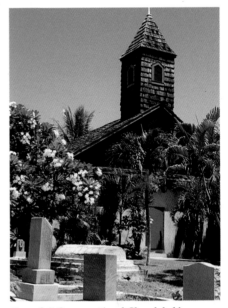

Keawala'i Congregational Church holds services in Hawaiian and English

of sand making up Big Beach and ahead is the black-lava point of **Cape Kīna'u**. The last lava flow on Maui created Cape Kīna'u, and to the southeast, **Cape Hanamanioa**, leaving a one-mile gap between the capes. In an area called Keone'ō'io, La Pérouse Bay was created on what was previously a straight shoreline.

The last eruption of Haleakalā was generally thought to have occurred around 1790. This was assumed from two things: old maps by the legendary explorers Jean Francois La Pérouse and George Vancouver and from the oral history gathered from Maui residents in the 1840s. La Pérouse prepared a map in 1786 that showed a large bay carved out between points on the coast of southwest Maui. When British mariner George Vancouver

A lava wall re-radiates the sun's heat onto Big Beach

visited the same coast in 1793 he mapped an outcropping of land, now called Cape Kīna'u, in the middle of the wide bay. The date of 1790 was arbitrarily given as a likely date for the lava flow. In addition, Maui residents in the 1840s told missionary Edward Bailey that their grandparents had witnessed the eruption. According to radiocarbon testing done recently by researchers at the U.S. Geological Survey, Haleakalā might have last erupted 300 years earlier than assumed. The agency reported that charcoal samplings taken from beneath the lava flow indicate that the lava flowed between 1480 and 1600. More research is being done; the oral history will need to be given weight as well.

La Pérouse was a student of the French Enlightenment. He was unlike most explorers of his time who made it a practice to claim new lands in the name of their king or country. La Pérouse wrote in his journal, "Although the French were the first in these latest times to land on Maui, I did not think it was my right to take possession of it in the name of the King. The customs of Europeans in this respect are completely ridiculous."

The road carves its way through the tormented landscape of the lava flow to La Pérouse Bay. Cape Kīna'u and part of La Pérouse Bay make up the 2,045-acre **'Āhihi-Kīna'u Natural Area Reserve**, so designated because of its distinctive marine life habitat and its unique geological features, including kīpukas (areas of land spared when lava flows around it).

From La Pérouse Bay you can look up directly along Haleakalā's southwest rift, which sharply divides its southern from its western flanks. The rift leads to Red Hill, Haleakalā's summit, 10,023 feet above your vantage point. The western flank takes a gentle six-degree slope, ending at the isthmus. The southern flank drops off toward Kaupō at 17 degrees, continuing its plunge into the abyssal depths of the ocean.

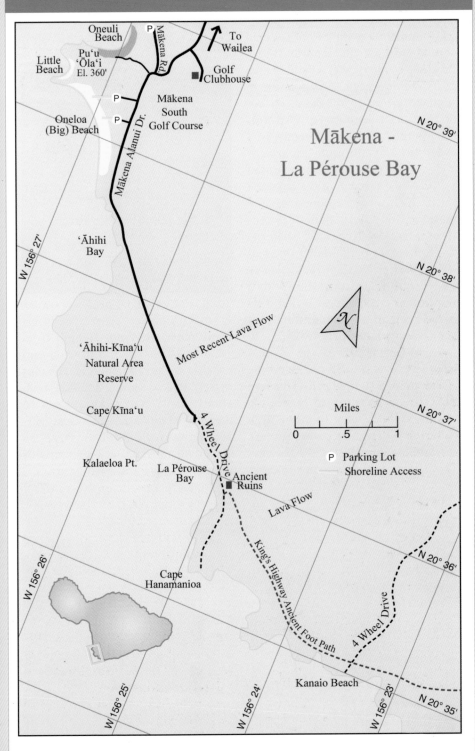

Oneuli Beach

Little Beach

Pu'u 'Ōla'i El. 360'

Oneloa (Big) Beach

P

Mākena Rd.

To Wailea

Golf Clubhouse

Mākena South Golf Course

Mākena Alanui Dr.

P

P

N 20° 39'

Mākena - La Pérouse Bay

'Āhihi Bay

W 156° 27'

'Āhihi-Kīna'u Natural Area Reserve

Cape Kīna'u

Most Recent Lava Flow

N 20° 38'

N

N 20° 37'

Miles

0   .5   1

Kalaeloa Pt.

La Pérouse Bay

4 Wheel Drive

Ancient Ruins

P Parking Lot
____ Shoreline Access

Lava Flow

W 156° 26'

Cape Hanamanioa

King's Highway Ancient Foot Path

4 Wheel Drive

N 20° 36'

N 20° 35'

Kanaio Beach

W 156° 25'   W 156° 24'   W 156° 23'

A marker at the end of the road commemorates the landing of La Pérouse. To the right is a parking area at the water's edge. It is possible to continue on the very rough trail on foot or by four-wheel drive. The trail follows the bay for eight-tenths of a mile, winding through thickets of kiawe trees and over large exposed rocks. At the far side of the bay look to the left, under a tangle of tree branches, for a heiau built of lichen-speckled rocks. Just past the heiau, the trail forks to the right, leading one-half mile to the light on Cape Hanamanioa. Past the fork, a stone wall with a vehicle barrier appears on the left. This is the beginning of the ancient trail known as the **King's Highway**.

The King's Highway cuts across the lava flow

This portion of the King's Highway, which once encircled the island, transits straight across the lava flow. It was constructed before the arrival of Westerners to allow high chiefs, royalty and tax collectors easy accessibility to homesteads in the area. The "Highway" was built in its present form under Governor Hoapili from 1824 to 1840. The 6-foot-wide trail consists of fitted boulders and chunks of lava laid to form a trailbed, with small rocks wedged between to provide stability and a smooth surface. Mortar was not used. Flat rock slabs and boulders were stacked to provide raised borders.

Right: A man fishes off the lava flow that separates Mākena's Big Beach and Little Beach

Opposite page: Maui's south coast has become a popular visitor destination

Hawai'i State Archives

Keawakapu Beach and Kama'ole Beach III await development in the 1950's

You can walk the King's Highway just as the ali'i did, but you should bring sturdy hiking footwear. The lava is rough and abrasive and wobbles a bit under each footstep. It's a good idea to tackle this walk early in the day and bring plenty of drinking water. The dark lava re-radiates the sun's heat and there is neither shade nor shelter along the path.

A mile and a half from its start, the King's Highway descends to a cove known as **Kanaio**. It's a picturesque area, marred slightly by the trash littered about. If you make it this far, it's usually best to turn back now. The trail continues for four miles, but becomes more difficult to traverse and ends on private property.

UPCOUNTRY SIGHTS

Horses graze amid cacti on Haleakalā's slopes

Upcountry is the western slope of Haleakalā that overlooks Maui's Central Valley. It presents spectacular views of sugarcane fields, the ocean on both sides of the isthmus and the West Maui Mountains. With altitudes between 2,000 and 4,000 feet, the air is cooler in Upcountry and rainfall is ample enough to keep the countryside green. You must pass through Upcountry to get to Haleakalā National Park, but it is worth visiting for its own sake. Its sparse population consists of cowboys who work the cattle ranches, farmers, artists and well-to-do commuters who work at lower elevations. Horses grazing in the green pastures and vegetable farms add to the rural ambiance. Exotic proteas bloom in a palette of colors and in the spring, jacaranda trees punctuate the landscape with purple blossoms.

The neighboring towns of Pukalani and Makawao lie at the entrance to Upcountry. Pukalani is six

The Kula Highway cuts across Upcountry

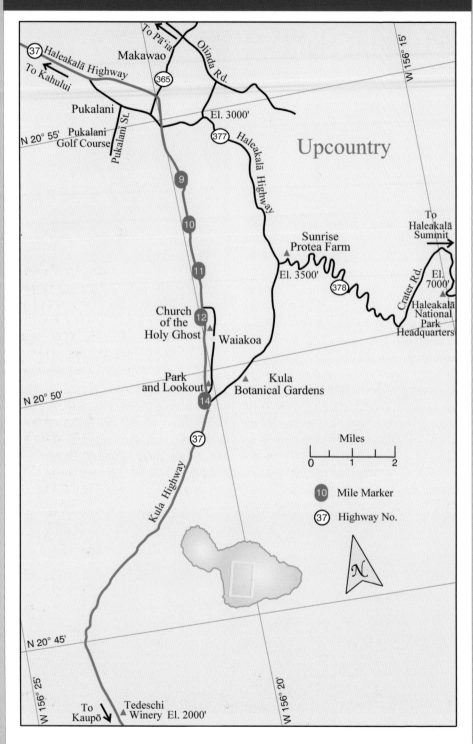

miles up Highway 37 (Haleakalā Highway) from Kahului and Makawao is six miles up Highway 390 from Pā'ia. Makawao has been cowboy country since the 1820s when whaling ships' cooks started asking for meat. Mexican and Portuguese immigrants were brought in to teach the Hawaiians cattle ranching. The town retains an Old West flavor with many worn, wooden buildings that retain weathered false fronts. Cowboy culture is celebrated each year on the fourth of July at the Makawao rodeo.

It was in Makawao that King Kamehameha III ushered in the era of private land ownership and broke down the feudal land system of the ali'i. Bowing to the pressure of Westeners, the king announced an experiment whereby commoners could purchase land throughout the area for one dollar an acre. One hundred Hawaiians scraped together enough money to buy a total of 900 acres. This led three years later to the Great Mahele, a government policy permitting land ownership by Hawaiians and foreigners.

Octagon-shaped Church of the Holy Ghost

Makawao is evolving. Behind the false fronts, no-nonsense supply stores have given way to boutiques, art galleries and health food emporia. While on Maui, this is the place to go if you need shiatsu massage, herbs, crystals, hemp clothing or naturopathic treatment.

Just past Pukalani, Highway 37 continues to the right and the road to Haleakalā (Highway 377) forks to the left. To explore Upcountry stay on Highway 37, which is now called the Kula Highway. In this area, because of

M.V.B./Ron Dahlquist

Sunset from the 'Ulupalakua Ranch

Hang glider takes off into Upcountry clouds

agreeable climate and soil conditions, agriculture is probably at its most diversified in Hawai'i. Potato farms date from 1840 and the delectable, extra-sweet Maui onion is harvested here.

Turn left onto Lower Kula Road, 4.2 miles from the Pukalani junction and drive another half mile to the **Church of the Holy Ghost** in the village of Waiakoa. The octagonal church's silver roof can often be seen glistening in the sun from the valley below. Built in 1894 and restored in 1992, this landmark continues the traditions of Maui's Portuguese community. Its pink interior is decorated with 14 stations of the cross and a hand-carved altar.

From the church, follow Lower Kula Road 1.3 miles to the vantage point of **Rice Memorial Park**. This park has picnic tables, bathrooms and at an altitude of 3,000 feet, a stunning view. There are great photo opportunities here of West Maui and the long gentle curve of Mā'alaea Bay. Lower Kula Road returns to the Kula

Highway just beyond the park. In two-tenths of a mile, Highway 377 connects again on your left. Remember this intersection if you want to visit the sights along Highway 377 on the return trip.

From this intersection the Kula Highway cuts across Haleakalā, losing 1,200 feet in elevation as it passes through the **'Ulupalakua Ranch**. Originally a sugarcane plantation and a potato farm, the land was sold to Honolulu businessman and former whaling captain James Makee, who proceeded to import cattle. Makee planted roses, a flower rarely seen in the tropics, in the formal gardens of his estate and even along the roadside. He named his estate the Rose Ranch. The deep pink roses gained such notoriety that the Lokelani variety was chosen as the island's official flower and pink as its official color.

Seven miles from the Highway 377 junction you pass above Hawai'i's only vineyard. Just past the vineyard, on the left is the **Tedeschi Winery** (878-6058). Established in 1974, its first vintage was Maui Blanc pineapple wine. Since then they have used grapes to produce red, white, rosé and sparkling wines. The tasting room, open daily from 9–5, is in an old jailhouse built in 1857 of lava and coral. Free tours of the winery and its historic grounds are given once each hour on the half hour, from 9:30 to 2:30 (878-6058).

The Kula Highway continues past the winery, traversing Haleakalā's southwest rift and dropping to the arid and rugged southeast coast to Kaupō (see East Maui Sights). Although you can see Wailea and Mākena just three miles down the slope there is no road or shortcut to take you there. Some maps may show a trail but it is on private land and behind locked gates. Turn around and take the right fork back at the junction onto Highway 377.

In three quarters of a mile, on the right side, is **Kula Botanical Gardens** (878-1715). The landscaped slopes of the gardens range over a five-acre hillside site. Terraces overflow with more than 1,700 types of plants, shrubs and trees flourishing in the mild climate at 3,200 feet above the sea. Most unusual is the "Taboo Garden," filled with poisonous plants. Open daily, 9:00–4:00. Admission is $4.00 adults and $1.00 children 6–12 years.

It's another 2.2 miles along Highway 377 until the intersection of Highway 378 and its 32 switchbacks to the summit. Just two tenths of a mile up 378, on the left side, is the **Sunrise Protea Farm**. Proteas are exotic, otherworldly looking plants

Upcountry homes and ranches cling to the slopes of Haleakalā

biologically related to the macadamia nut. Native to Australia and South Africa, Upcountry Maui's sunshine and cool nights have been perfect for raising proteas since they were introduced here in 1975. Sunrise is the largest of several Upcountry farms commercially growing proteas for a worldwide market. They have a small, walk-through garden with several varieties on display and a gift shop where they can arrange to ship plants nearly anywhere. Open daily, 8:00–4:00, free.

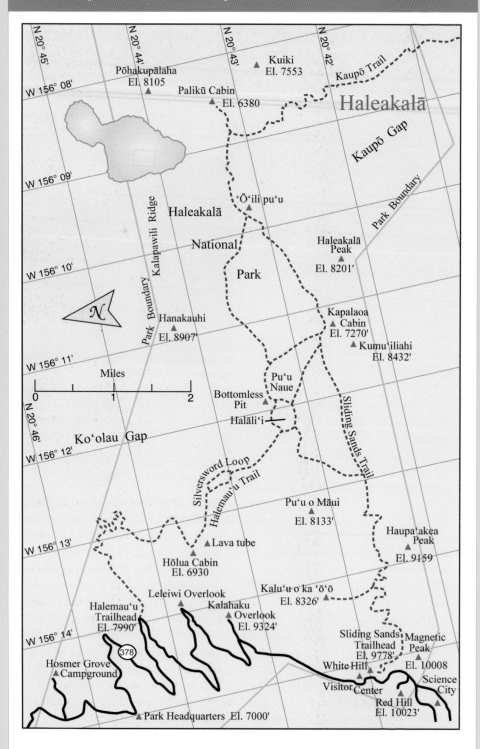

Colors abound in Haleakalā's crater

HALEAKALĀ SIGHTS

If there is a "don't miss" attraction on Maui, it is the trip to the summit of Haleakalā. Each year, 1.6 million visitors travel to **Haleakalā National Park**, driving the only paved road in the world that ascends from sea level to 10,023 feet in just under 38 miles. The centerpiece of the 28,665-acre park is a gaping chasm, 7.5 miles long and 2.5 miles wide, crowning the apex of this dormant volcano.

Haleakalā means "house of the sun." According to Hawaiian legend, the sun rose from Haleakalā every morning and then would race across the sky. The sun would disappear before crops ripened and people did not have light long enough to finish all their work. The island's namesake, the demigod Māui, saw that his mother, Hina, could not dry her kapa cloth without the sun's heat, so Māui devised a plan to lengthen the day. He noticed that the sun thrust long sunbeams, first one then another, over the rim of Haleakalā, much as a spider would climb over a rock. Using some strong 'ie'ie vines that grow in Hāna, Māui wove 16 snares and carried them up Kaupō Gap to the summit where he hid in a cave. When the first of the sun's legs crept over the crater's edge, Māui lassoed it. He did this with each leg in turn before the sun could race away.

White Hill and the start of the Sliding Sands Trail are in the center of the western rim

Threatening to slay the sun with a jawbone given to him by Hina, Māui forced the sun into striking a deal. The sun would slow down half the year—causing summer, and speed up for the other half—causing winter. Even today, the sun is wary of Māui and his snares, slowly and deliberately rising over Haleakalā before filling its chasm with light and warmth.

Sunrise is a favored time for a summit pilgrimage. The sun, as it rises over the summit crater, infuses the clouds below you with streaks and flares of pastels while at the same time silhouetting the crater, backlighting it in radiant reds and yellows. While observing a Haleakalā sunrise, Mark Twain was quoted as exclaiming, "I felt like the last man, neglected of the judgment, and left pinnacled in mid-heaven, a forgotten relic of a vanished world….It was the sublimest spectacle I ever witnessed, and I think the memory of it will remain with me always."

Plan on taking a minimum of one-and-one-half hours to make the drive from Kahului. The best light show occurs in the half hour before sunrise. Expect it to be cold at the top, even near freezing. It's a good idea to bring a blanket from your room. Call 572-7749 for a recorded view/weather report before making the drive. Viewing conditions change throughout the day. The crater is generally clearest in the morning. Clouds formed by mid-morning heat rising push upward to spill through gaps in the crater's rim. Photographic light is best in the afternoon. Late afternoon and evening can be clear; sunset can be just as beautiful as sunrise—and warmer.

Add **silverswords** to the list of reasons to visit Haleakalā. A member of the sunflower family, the silversword has stiff, stiletto-shaped leaves and a brilliant flower stalk. Found nowhere else in the world, the silversword descended from ancestral seeds carried via trade winds and birds from the Americas. In Hawaiian, it's called 'ahinahina because hina means

Silversword in bloom

Ron Dahlquist

Haleakalā Crater

gray and the silversword has a reputation as a plant sacred to the goddess Hina. Hawaiians at the time had not been introduced to metals from foreigners so they could not have given its color a metallic description. After growing anywhere from four to twenty years, the flower stalk will reach up to six feet in height, then in a brilliant burst it will produce hundreds of purple, sunflower-like blooms. The silversword flowers once; then it dies, leaving its seeds to reproduce. Hikers should not tread too close to live plants as their fragile roots can be destroyed by trampling.

Today silverswords are scattered sparsely about Haleakalā's higher elevations, but a century ago there were thousands of them clustered in large groves. Some of the depredation of the plant came from cattle and feral goats grazing on them. Introduced Argentine ants are believed to prey on the plant's pollinators—the native yellow-faced bee. Hikers made leis from the leaves and vandals uprooted the young plants just to watch them tumble like snowballs down the crater slope.

Ancient Hawaiians traveled to Haleakalā's summit to hunt birds, conduct religious ceremonies and to gather ankaramite, a dense rock used for making adzes. The crater was a desirable burial site to the Hawaiians, who often ventured to isolated and distant regions to inter their dead. The coast of East Maui was so rugged and the rain forest so thick that Hawaiians used Haleakalā as a shortcut when traveling north and south. They created a footpath across the summit and out through Kaupō Gap by laying out smooth rocks.

The first written account of an ascent of the mountain came from a party of three missionaries in 1828. Charles Wilkes of the United States Exploring Expedition reconnoitered the area 13 years later. Nineteenth-century visitors shortsightedly maltreated the landscape that was theirs to enjoy, often plucking silversword leaves to use as hat decorations or uprooting the plant entirely. With the goal of protecting the summit's once plentiful endemic plant, Haleakalā was awarded National Park status in 1916. President Woodrow Wilson signed a bill submitted by Hawaiian congressional delegate Prince Jonah Kūhiō Kalaniana'ole and created Hawai'i National Park, comprised of Kīlauea and Mauna Loa Volcanoes on the Big Island and Haleakalā summit on Maui. Congress allocated $750 for the new park. In 1961, Hawai'i National Park was divided into two parks—Hawai'i Volcanoes National Park on the Big Island and Haleakalā National Park on Maui. Haleakalā National Park expanded in 1969 to include the Kīpahulu Valley, an eight-mile corridor of land from the summit down the southeastern flank of the mountain to the ocean. By 1986, the daunting task of fencing in part of Haleakalā was completed. A 32-mile perimeter fence keeps feral goats and pigs out of the crater and controls animals within the park.

The Road to the Summit

Before starting your drive be prepared to spend the better part of a day on your outing. According to the National Parks Service, the average visitor's stay at the summit is only half an hour—a sadly short time for three or four hours of driving. Pack a lunch, bring plenty of water and start off with a full tank of gas. Even if good weather is predicted, expect a drastic drop in temperature from your sea-level resort. High winds and rain can blow in quickly.

The **Haleakalā Highway** begins on the east side of Kahului as Highway 37. From here the drive to the summit takes about one-and-one-half hours. If you're traveling after sunrise, add on time to stop at viewpoints along the way. Follow the highway for 8.5 miles to the clearly marked intersection with Highway 377 and turn left. You probably will encounter caravans of bicyclists rapidly coasting down the road. Use caution, as some of them clearly have not been on a bicycle in many years. Be patient if you're stuck behind them on the way down. Tour guides pull the cyclists over frequently to allow motorists to pass.

By now, you have risen past the sugarcane and pineapple fields into Upcountry with cattle and horses grazing among eucalyptus trees and cacti. After six miles, turn left onto Highway 378. The grade steepens as the road snakes up the mountain's slope. In the next 10.5 miles to the

The Haleakalā Highway takes motorists to the clouds and above

park's boundary you'll drive through an undulating alpine desert clustered with lava boulders, where billows of cloud sweep over wide vistas.

At an elevation of 6,800 feet, just inside Haleakalā National Park's boundary, is a turnoff to the left to **Hosmer Grove Campground**. Here, you'll find a picnic area, a campground, and the trailhead for a half-mile nature trail loop that winds through a dark, misty forest of introduced trees. In 1910 Ralph Hosmer planted groves of eucalyptus trees from Australia, sugi pine from Japan, deodar from India, Douglas fir and several species of pine from the mainland U.S. Hosmer, Hawai'i's first territorial forester, planted the trees in an attempt to improve Maui's watershed, which had been severely damaged through the removal of native forests, and to provide building lumber and fuel for the sugarcane mills. The trail is half a mile long and takes about 30 minutes. The picnic area has tables, fireplaces, a cooking shelter with barbecue grills, drinking water and chemical toilets. Camping is limited to three nights per month and no permit is required. The campground's limit of 25 persons is often filled, especially on weekends. Guided three-mile hikes into the **Nature Conservancy's**

Waikamoi Preserve leave Hosmer Grove at 9:00 a.m. on Mondays and Thursdays. Reservations are not required, but a hike may be canceled because of inclement weather or if a ranger is unavailable. Call 572-9306 to confirm scheduling of guided hikes.

About a mile inside the park boundary, at an elevation of 7,000 feet, is the park's entrance gate and park headquarters. A National Parks fee of $10.00 per vehicle is collected at the entrance gate and is good for seven days. The headquarters building has bathrooms and drinking water. Inside there are pamphlets, maps and nature books for sale and outside is probably your first opportunity to see specimens of silversword plants. The headquarters building is open 7:30 a.m. to 4:00 p.m. daily.

Continuing up the road for three miles you will see to the left the turnoff for the parking lot and trailhead for the **Halemau'u Trail** into the crater. There isn't a view into the crater from the parking lot but a group of Hawai'i's state bird, the nēnē, often frequents the area. Your first good view into the crater comes at the **Leleiwi Overlook**, at an elevation of 8,800 feet. The view is to the southeast with the Ko'olau Gap to the left. To put the size of the depression into scale, Manhattan Island could fit into the crater and you would be looking down onto the skyscrapers. The scene is often likened to a moonscape because of the barren rocks and volcanic cones. But the colors—shades of purple, gray, rust and yellow—add beauty to the barrenness. Sunlight dappled by swirling clouds changes the hues and patterns on the crater's floor and walls.

One mile up the road, at an elevation of 9,423 feet, is another viewpoint, **Kalahaku Overlook**. Save this stop for the return trip as an uphill

The peak of Hanakauhi stands above the east side of the Ko'olau Gap

turn onto the highway is not allowed when exiting its parking lot. You'll be treated to another spectacular view of the crater, dotted with a chain of cinder cones. While they look like bumps on the landscape, the largest of the cinder cones, **Pu'u o Māui,** rises 600 feet above the crater floor. Downslope from the parking lot is a geology exhibit and a protected area of silverswords.

Haleakalā Visitor Center, located near the summit at the 9,745-foot elevation, is a popular spot with the sunrise and sunset watchers. The visitor center offers exhibits on geology, ecology, archeology and the wilderness protection program. It has bathrooms and is open sunrise to 3:00 p.m. If you journeyed here for the sunrise, you can join the huddled, shivering masses in their pre-dawn vigil. A short hike from the parking lot up **White Hill**, a volcanic plug composed primarily of gray-white andesite, will give you a panoramic view. Step carefully and slowly over the rocky trail—you're in rarified atmosphere at nearly 10,000 feet.

Behind White Hill is the start of the **Sliding Sands Trail** into the crater. Even if you didn't plan on a long hike it's worthwhile to walk the trail for a short distance. You get a different perspective of the crater when you are in it. Watch your step as the trail's name is a literal description. The trail and surrounding area are covered with cinders and ash that were expelled from vents during eruptions and were carried by the wind to line the volcano. As the volcanic debris rolls underfoot it makes a glassy, chinking sound. It

Top: Haleakalā Crater from the summit, Red Hill, elevation 10,023'

Bottom: A chain of cinder cones traverses the crater. The Big Island can be seen in the distance

will be the only sound you hear besides your own breath. Even tour helicopters are prohibited from flying directly over the crater. Soon after descending into the crater a vast openness stretches before you and you feel isolated from the rest of the world. Keep in mind that your return trip is uphill. A two-hour, ranger-guided hike on Sliding Sands Trail is conducted at 10:00 a.m. on Tuesdays and Fridays. Call 572-9306 for more information.

It took about a million years for this masterpiece to be created from molten rock and to be shaped and defined by earthquakes, rain, gravity, ice and wind. Taking into account slow island subsidence from its own weight, rapid caldera collapse and thousands of years of erosion, it can be inferred that almost 3,000 feet has worn away from the summit of Haleakalā. Stream erosion from the valleys of Ke'anae and Kaupō cut deep canyons into the mountain's flanks. The heads of those deep canyons almost merged near the volcano's summit and carved out the

Moon over Haleakalā

crater to a depth even greater than today's. Later eruptions covered much of the floor with lava and created the chain of nine cinder cones. The volcano has erupted 20 times in the last 2,500 years. The erosional cut into the crater's rim coming from the **Ke'anae Valley** is **Ko'olau Gap**, to the left of your view. **Kaupō Gap** is to the right, on the crater's southeast corner. The peak in front of Kaupō Gap is **Haleakalā**, the place the ancient Hawaiians called the "house of the sun." Stone shelters, platforms and a heiau are here at what must have been a significant place.

The highest point on Maui is just a short distance up the road. **Pu'u 'Ula'ula** or **Red Hill** caps off the mountain at 10,023 feet. A glassed-in shelter protects you while you take in the 360° view. Guided naturalist programs start each day at the summit shelter at 9:30, 10:30 and 11:30 a.m. Three hundred yards to the southeast

is **Magnetic Peak**, so named for the effects it exerts on a compass. More than 80 miles to the southeast are the Big Island's snow-capped peaks of Mauna Kea and Mauna Loa, each over 13,000 feet in elevation. Scanning west and northwest, you can spot the islands of Kaho'olawe, Lāna'i, and Moloka'i when conditions are clear. When it is exceptionally clear even O'ahu is visible.

Separating the western from the southern flank of Haleakalā is the southwest rift. Following the rift down fourteen miles from the summit to La Pérouse Bay is a series of cinder cones, including the origin of the latest lava flow. The last visible evidence of the rift is the tiny islet of Molokini, a tuff cone formed three miles offshore.

The summit parking lot is built in a shallow crater among examples of volcanic bombs—pieces of once-molten lava that were launched from

TIMES OF SUNRISE AND SUNSET

AND HOURS OF DAYLIGHT AT HALEAKALĀ

	SUNRISE	SUNSET	HOURS OF DAYLIGHT
JANUARY 1	6:56	6:00	11:04
FEBRUARY 1	6:56	6:21	11:25
MARCH 1	6:39	6:35	11:56
APRIL 1	6:12	6:46	12:34
MAY 1	5:50	6:55	13:05
JUNE 1	5:38	7:08	13:30
JULY 1	5:41	7:16	13:35
AUGUST 1	5:52	7:09	13:17
SEPTEMBER 1	6:02	6:52	12:50
OCTOBER 1	6:10	6:14	12:04
NOVEMBER 1	6:20	5:55	11:35
DECEMBER 1	6:38	5:47	11:09

a vent and hardened as they soared through the air. A few good specimens of silverswords brave the elements at the summit parking lot as well.

A few hundred yards from the summit and just outside the park is a collection of metal, white-domed buildings known as **Science City**. It's a research and communication center, including a Department of Defense satellite tracking station and University of Hawai'i solar/lunar observatory. The space surveillance facilities receive daily instructions from Space Command about what to look for in the space above Maui's horizons. The Air Force installation is one of the worldwide data-gathering tentacles that provide data to Space Command in Colorado. Objects as small as a baseball to the Mir Space Station are under the watchful eye of the nine optical Cassegrain telescopes inside the domes. Public tours are held on the last Friday of each month and are booked months in advance (874-1601).

Hiking Haleakalā

There are two trailheads that hikers can use to access the 30 miles of trails in the lunar-looking crater. The **Halemau'u Trailhead** starts at 7,990 feet, two miles from the park entrance. **Sliding Sands Trail** begins next to the parking lot at the Visitor Center at an elevation of 9,778 feet. A series of trails connects the two trailheads with each other as well as with points of interest in the crater, three cabins and two campsites. Hikes range from moderate to strenuous, from one day to an arduous three days.

There are three cabins that can be reserved for parties of up to 12 hikers. The three cabins are: **Hōlua Cabin**, which is accessed by the Halemau'u Trail, **Kapalaoa Cabin,** which is on Sliding Sands Trail, and **Palikū Cabin** at the eastern edge of the crater, 1.4 miles past the convergence of both trails. Cabins have tables, benches, bare bunkbeds (you supply the sleeping bag), a kitchen with water that needs to be treated and a wood stove with wood. To reserve a cabin you must write to the Park Superintendent at least ninety days in advance specifying your first and alternate choices of dates and cabins preferred. Send your request to: Haleakalā National Park, Box 369, Makawao, Maui, HI 96768. Successful applicants are picked by lottery and notified by mail. Call (808) 572-9177 for a recording of camping and cabin information.

There are two tent campgrounds in the crater, one next to Hōlua Cabin and the other near Palikū Cabin. Permits are required for tent camping and are issued only in person at Park Headquarters and only on the day you begin your trip. There is no fee for camping but there is a limit to the number of permits issued each day. Day hikers need not register for their hike.

Day hikes can begin at either trailhead and return to the starting spot or start at one trailhead and finish at the other. In that case two vehicles are needed or arrangements made for the hikers to be picked up. A popular choice is to begin by descending into the crater

Sunrise from the summit of Haleakalā

on the Sliding Sands Trail, traversing the crater floor to Hōlua Cabin and exiting via the Halemau'u Trail. You need to be in good shape for this and allow about twelve hours. Day hikes can also be made on Sliding Sands Trail with a two-way trip to the Kapalaoa Cabin. Hikers that are overnighting here must have a reservation for Kapalaoa Cabin as it has is no adjoining campground. The next day, hikers can continue to Palikū Cabin to the east, cut across the crater and take the Halemau'u Trail to Hōlua Cabin or return on the Sliding Sands Trail.

Advance preparation for a crater hike is essential. Trails are covered in sharp lava, often with uneven surfaces. Sturdy footwear is needed; boots with ankle support are recommended. Sunscreen and lip protection with an SPF of at least 30 and a wide-brimmed hat will ward off an assault of intense ultraviolet radiation. Weather conditions can change rapidly. Be prepared for wind and cold rain, even if fair weather is forecast. Carry first aid supplies and food and water. There is no potable water in the crater and open fires are not permitted. Hikers should not wander off the maintained trails.

Sliding Sands Trail

The Sliding Sands trailhead begins just south of the parking lot at the Visitor Center. If you are using a GPS receiver its position is N20° 42.75', W156° 14.99'. More than 100 years ago, author Charles Warren Stoddard, recounting his experiences on the very same trail, wrote, "and while we crept slowly onward toward the rim of the crater, the sun rose, and we forgot all else save his glory. We had reached the mouth of the chasm. Below us yawned a gulf whose farther walls seemed the outlines of some distant island, within whose depths a sea of cloud was satisfied to ebb and flow, whose billows broke noiselessly at the base of the somber walls among whose battlements we clung like insects."

The trail descends in a series of switchbacks into a vast bowl of gray and rust cinders. To the left, the **Ko'olau Gap** appears as a wide notch in the crater wall with a dark lava flow that solidified as it spilled out. Ahead, the trail stretches out, zig-zagging as if it were connecting dots until it dwindles away. Distant, light-colored specks contrasted against the crater floor are fellow hikers. As you descend farther, distant cones grow in size; spires, ridges, jagged rocks, pits and craters surround you. Long graceful curves of talus sweep down from the summit, engulfing the landmarks. If you are taking photographs in the crater, you will probably get better results metering off the dark ground than the bright sky.

Although the crater is at first devoid of any vegetation, plant life becomes more abundant the deeper you go into the crater. After walking 1.8 miles and losing 1,400 feet in elevation, clumps of silverswords mark the junction with the spur path on your left, to the cinder cone, **Kalu'u o ka 'ō'ō**. The position here is N20° 42.69', W156° 14.00'. The one-mile roundtrip will take you to the top of the cone where the trail circles a steep-sided depression at its center. The crater's tallest cinder cone, Pu'u o Māui, sits in repose one mile to the east.

When you return to Sliding Sands Trail you may decide to return to the Visitor Center now or continue hiking into the crater. Another 1.8 miles along Sliding Sands brings you to a junction positioned at N20° 42.59', W156° 12.95'. Turning left will take you to the **Halemau'u Trail** and **Hōlua Cabin**, which is described later starting at the **Halemau'u Trailhead**.

The trail straight ahead is visible for the 1.9 miles to Kapalaoa Cabin. Plants appear more frequently as you near the cabin. Mountain pili, a native bunchgrass, adds a touch of green to the black cinders. You can also find the mountain pilo, a shrub with orange-colored berries belonging to the coffee family. Evening primrose, a bright yellow flower, carpets the crater floor. Although attractive, the plant is host to the Argentine ant, which is suspected of preying upon pollinators of the silversword. High on the cliffs near the rim above you, dark-rumped petrels have built nests. Each night at dusk as this bird returns home from the sea it emits a strange call somewhat like that of a small dog barking. Shortly before you reach the cabin two trails branch to the north to join the Halemau'u Trail. **Kapalaoa Cabin** is perched on a small grassy platform, backdropped by the scrub-covered pali rising 1,200 feet behind it. Its position is N20° 42.48', W156° 11.23'. This is a great place to rest and enjoy the views and eat your lunch. Solicitous nēnē will beg for food but you should resist the temptation to feed them; they can find all the food they need on their own. If you are backtracking to the Visitor Center your return hike is nearly six miles with a nasty incline at the end. Those with cabin reservations can prepare their bunks and head for either Hōlua or Palikū Cabin in the morning. If you are camping or staying in Hōlua Cabin you will take the trail you just passed across the crater floor to Halemauʻu Trail. That route will cover 4.3 miles. Continuing along Sliding Sands Trail for 3.4 miles will bring you to Palikū Cabin and campground.

After leaving Kapalaoa Cabin you begin a gentle descent. Palikū's meadow becomes visible to the east then is hidden by the scrub-covered hill, ʻŌʻili puʻu. Kaupō Gap opens to your right with the peak of Haleakalā guarding its western wall. You will walk across a congealed river of rough ʻaʻā that once moved slowly across the crater floor, then accelerated as it poured through the gap and down the steep slope to the ocean. At ʻŌʻili puʻu, two miles after leaving Kapalaoa Cabin, the Sliding Sands Trail meets with the Halemauʻu Trail. Your position now is N20° 43.27', W156° 09.75'. The trail traces over a field of pāhoeohoe, solid as pavement and comfortable to walk on. Your next landmark is 1.1 miles later where the Kaupō Trail splits to the right. From there, **Palikū Cabin** is just three-tenths of a mile ahead at a position of N20° 43.29', W156° 08.66'. The Kaupō Trail descends sharply for nine grueling miles, leaving the park and ending at Highway 31 on Maui's southern coast.

Palikū Cabin is a 9.8-mile trek from the Sliding Sands trailhead. The elevation here is 6,380 feet—the lowest encountered in the crater.

Shrubland has given way to green meadows, and trees dot the landscape. Most of the crater receives only about 20 inches of rain per year but Palikū receives ten times that amount. From the pali behind Palikū Cabin you can hear waterfalls.

Three-quarters of a mile to the north is a high point on the ridge called **Pōhakupālaha**. This was the point where all the boundary lines of the ahupuaʻa or ancient land divisions of East Maui met, radiating like spokes from the hub of a wheel. The boundary lines extended from the highlands to the ocean, assuring the people living within them access to both sea and mountain for sustenance.

Halemauʻu Trail

The other route into the crater begins in the northwest corner with the **Halemauʻu Trail**. You can find the trailhead clearly marked from the highway, about three miles uphill from the park entrance. The trailhead's position is N20° 45.38', W156° 13.93'. The trail is described here from the trailhead to Palikū Cabin, but it can be traveled in the other direction to exit the crater from Palikū. An interesting day hike can begin at Halemauʻu and return there. Longer overnight trips to Palikū and Kapalaoa Cabins are possible, exiting on the Sliding Sands Trail. Hikers generally prefer to exit at Halemauʻu, though, because its elevation is 1,800 feet lower than the Sliding Sands trailhead.

Ko'olau Gap and the cinder cones, Kaoma'ali'i and Pu'u o Māui

The start of the Halemau'u Trail heads east for three-quarters of a mile to **Leleiwi Pali** at the western edge of the Ko'olau Gap. If the gap is not socked in with clouds, you'll be treated to a view of the Ke'anae Valley down to the sea on your left and Haleakalā's crater to your right as you descend through 1,100 vertical feet of switchbacks. Erosion of the pali has revealed many layers of volcanic ash that settled after each eruption. Varying chemical compositions have given them red, gray, brown and yellow colors. The trail cuts under a circular yellow outcropping of rock that is a filled-in lava tube.

At the end of the switchbacks the trail passes through a stock gate and cuts through a meadow of tall grass fed by the moisture that sweeps in through the gap. The hike down from the trailhead takes about one-and-one-half hours and the walk through the meadow to **Hōlua Cabin** will take an additional half-hour. The cabin sits on a small grassy plateau about 120 feet north of the campground. Its position is N20° 44.71', W156° 13.26' and its altitude is 6,930 feet. There are picnic tables and toilets here and water that needs to be treated before drinking.

An information sign at the trailhead claims that Haleakalā is home to 150 of the 600 nēnē that live in the wild. It would appear that most of Haleakalā's nēnē reside here at Hōlua. They will curiously walk quite close to you, giving you a chance to observe how they adapted anatomically to their environment. Having survived on rugged lava flows far from water, these descendents of Canada geese lost most of the webbing between their toes, giving them feet better suited to terrestrial life.

Close to the cabin is an interesting side trip that only takes about 30 minutes. It's not, however, for the claustrophobic. An underground lava tube, about 200 yards long, has a separate entrance and exit near the trail. You will need a powerful flashlight for each person in the party. Don't explore the tube by yourself. To find the entrance, continue on the trail about 150 yards past the cabin where you will find a circular pit on the left. About 25 yards past that, watch for a faint trail on the right. Take this trail over the lava for about 150 yards until it reaches a depression at the tube's entrance. A metal ladder with 16 steps leads down into the tube. Once you negotiate the low entry there is room to stand upright. Give yourself a few minutes for your eyes to adjust to the darkness. After a short distance you will need to negotiate around the right side of a big rock. The faint light from the entrance will have disappeared by now and the crushing darkness seems to drain every bit of light out of the flashlight. The floor is uneven with large rocks, and water drips from a ceiling covered with an icing of razorlike serrate stone. Continue carefully, and at the first fork take the path to the left. At the next fork take the left option again. The tube continues to cant uphill until you see the light marking the exit. When you climb out of the tube you will be in another depression south of the cabin's campsite.

Halemauʻu Trail ascends gradually when you leave Hōlua Cabin through low ridges of jagged brown lava. A bank of clouds usually buttresses the lower flanks of Hanakauhi, the prominent peak on the eastern edge of Koʻolau Gap. Three-quarters of a mile from the cabin, at a position of N20° 44.17', W156° 12.71', you can take a short diversion off the trail at **Silversword Loop**. The loop takes you through the most prolific outcropping of silverswords in the crater.

Back on Halemauʻu Trail you soon come upon a junction; the fork on the right connects with the Sliding Sands Trail while Halemauʻu continues on the left, running parallel to Sliding Sands a mile to its south. The trail winds, rises and falls through the long slopes of varicolored cones. On your right is Halāliʻi cone,

streaked in pink, gold and red; on your left, fiery red stands out against the orange, brown and charcoal grey colors. This area is called **Pele's Paint Pot**. Iron in the rocks oxidizes to the red colors, sulphur compounds create shades of yellow. Some would believe that this is where Pele discarded her paints after she colorfully decorated her volcano home.

Next you come upon a fenced vent rimmed with a colorful, jagged rampart of lava spatter. A posted sign calls it the **Bottomless Pit** and then discloses the vent's depth to be a fathomable 65 feet. At one time blobs of molten lava and superheated gases spewed out of it. Later, Hawaiians placed umbilical cords in it, believing it would ensure safety and strength for the newborn child.

Another trail heads south from here, cutting through the saddle of **Halāliʻi** and **Puʻu Naue** to become the middle spur trail connecting with Sliding Sands. This trail also circles Halāliʻi. On the east side of Puʻu Naue, the third connector trail to Sliding Sands will take you to Kapalaoa Cabin. The position here is N20° 43.40', W156° 11.95'. Halemauʻu continues eastward, closely following the crater's northern rim for two miles until it joins with the Sliding Sands Trail. The trail ends at the Palikū Cabin, 10.2 miles from the Halemauʻu Trailhead.

Following page:
Kapalua Beach

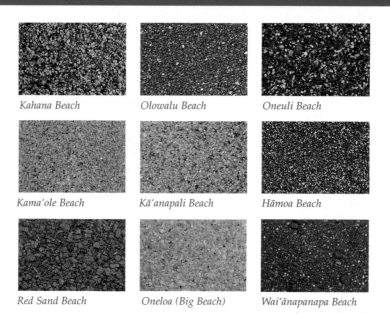

Kahana Beach

Olowalu Beach

Oneuli Beach

Kama'ole Beach

Kā'anapali Beach

Hāmoa Beach

Red Sand Beach

Oneloa (Big Beach)

Wai'ānapanapa Beach

BEACHES

Maui offers beaches as good as any in Hawai'i and with more diversity than any other island can claim. Sand can be as soft as sugar or as coarse as gravel and cover colors from light gold to red to black. Some beaches are perfect for lying on motionless and others invite beachgoers to swim, snorkel, SCUBA dive, surf, sail or windsurf. You may find your favorite beach is right in front of your resort, a few steps from a roadside parking lot or secluded at the end of an unmarked trail. All beaches are there for everyone to use. Hawaiian law prevents private ownership of any beach below the upper reaches of the waves as evidenced by the vegetation line. Even the most exclusive resorts provide public access to their beaches.

Beach Safety

Only a handful of beaches on Maui provide lifeguard service. Understanding the behavior of the ocean, heeding posted hazards and using common sense are all that's needed to safely enjoy the beach and the ocean.

The Sun

Spending too much time in the sun can spoil your entire vacation. The tropical sun is higher in the sky than most visitors are used to and therefore less of the burning ultraviolet rays are filtered by the atmosphere. Water also intensifies the effect by reflecting UV rays. Sunblocks of every factor are readily available everywhere on Maui. Remember that sunblock takes 20 to 30 minutes to take effect, so it should be applied before going outside.

Shorebreaks

Places where waves break directly on or near the shore with downward force have shorebreaks. They occur where a deep ocean bottom changes abruptly to a shallow bottom and the incoming wave is forced upwards. Swimmers could be injured if they try to jump through or over a large shorebreak; instead they should take a breath and swim under the wave. Be aware of the potential danger even if you are not in the ocean. Typical waves can be interrupted by an occasional large freak wave that could knock down someone on the shore. Each year in Hawai'i unsuspecting people drown by being swept away by such waves. Never turn your back on the ocean.

Backwash

After a wave has washed up on shore the water must return to the sea. Backwash is the spent wave rushing back down the beach. On a steep beach the backwash may be powerful enough to sweep you off your feet and out into deeper water.

Rip Current

Because waves generally come in sets, with short lulls between sets, the backwash is partially prevented from returning by the next wave coming in. As a larger volume of water builds up, it moves along the shore looking for a point of release, usually a trough in the sand or a channel in the reef. This riverlike movement of water out to sea is a rip current. A swimmer who gets caught in a rip current should try to flow along with it or swim sideways to it until it diminishes. Trying to swim against a rip current will cause exhaustion.

Undertow

Sometimes the returning water has no channel of escape and must travel under the incoming wave. This creates the condition known as undertow. A swimmer caught in an undertow will be pulled under an incoming wave and released as the wave passes. It only lasts a few seconds, but will certainly seem longer.

Tsunami

A tsunami is a series of waves set into motion by great disturbances such as earthquakes or landslides, capable of traveling across the ocean at high speed. When the possibility exists of a tsunami reaching Hawai'i the public is warned by the sounding of sirens located along the coastlines. If the sirens sound, immediately evacuate coastal areas. An elevation of 50 feet has been arbitrarily set as safe ground. Turn on a radio and listen for information and instructions from civil defense agencies. The sirens are tested at 11:45 a.m. on the first working day of each month.

Marine Life

Jellyfish and the Portuguese man-of-war live in Hawaiian waters. The man-of-war has a translucent, bubble-shaped body usually less than six inches long. As it generally drifts with winds and currents, the man-of-war is more of a problem on beaches where there is a strong onshore wind. Their tentacles are capable of delivering a severe sting and cause a red welt on the skin. The affected area should immediately be cleaned with fresh water and a solution of household ammonia or baking soda. Some people may develop allergic reactions and should seek immediate medical treatment.

Coral is very abrasive and can cause cuts that are susceptible to infections and slow to heal.

Eels are found in nearly every reef in Hawai'i, hiding in holes and crevices. They are not aggressive unless they are threatened. Armed with powerful jaws lined with sharp teeth, eels are best left alone.

Sharks are more likely to be met in open water than close to beaches. If a swimmer or diver encounters a shark, he or she should remain calm until the curious shark moves on.

If a sea urchin is stepped on or brushed against, the needle-like spines break off and can become embedded in the skin. The spines are difficult to remove but will dissolve after about a week. A common folk remedy is to apply urine to the afflicted area. The uric acid is said to hasten the dissolution of the spines.

West Maui Beaches

Pāpalaua State Wayside Park

Location: West of Honoapiʻilani Highway tunnel at Mile Marker 11.

Coordinates: N20° 47.80', W156° 34.47'
Length: 0.5 mile

Facilities: None

The east end of the beach has excellent snorkeling and diving. Locally, the area is called **Thousand Peaks** because of the many breaks formed by the shallow reef. Parking is along the roadside.

Olowalu (Kaʻiliʻili Beach)

Location: Between the 13- and 14-mile markers of Honoapiʻilani Highway.

Coordinates: N20° 48.67', W156° 36.36'

Length: 0.6 mile

Facilities: None

This is one of Maui's favorite spots for snorkelers, particularly beginners. The coral heads nearly reach the surface of the especially calm water. A mixture of black, white and red sand covers the narrow beach that has a row of kiawe trees on it. It is a good idea to wear sandals around the trees because they drop sharp thorns. There is no parking lot; just park off the road. Look behind you at the **West Maui Mountains** to view the results of the heavy erosion that caused the **Olowalu Gap**.

Ukumehame Beach

Location: West of Honoapiʻilani Highway tunnel at Mile Marker 12.

Coordinates: N20° 47.67', W156° 34.89'

Length: 0.5 mile

Facilities: Picnic tables, paved parking lot.

This narrow strip of beach is covered with light gray sand, scattered with some rocks and backed by ironwood trees. The offshore's rocky bottom makes swimming difficult.

Young surfers gather at Launiupoko Beach

Launiupoko State Wayside Park

Location: One mile south of Lahaina.

Coordinates: N20° 50.96', W156° 40.56'

Length: 100 yards

Facilities: Bathrooms, shower, telephone, drinking water, picnic tables.

This is a popular spot for family activities. Rock walls built in the water create a safe wading area for children. The park has picnic tables and shade trees. Surfing is good on the shorebreak, about 100 yards out from the gray, sandy beach. The entrance, between Mile Markers 18 and 19, is indicated with a sign.

Puamana Beach

Location: South end of Lahaina, next to the tsunami siren.

Coordinates: N20° 51.48', W156° 40.00'

Length: 100 feet

Facilities: Portable toilets, picnic tables.

Sand- and rock-covered, this small beach is rarely used for recreation.

Wahikuli State Wayside Park

Location: Between Kā'anapali and Lahaina.

Coordinates: N20° 54.51', W156° 41.34'

Length: 0.1 mile

Facilities: Bathrooms, telephone, shower, picnic tables.

The Hawaiians prophetically named this stretch of coastline Wahikuli, meaning "noisy place." Often crowded due to its proximity to Lahaina, the beach and park back onto the Honoapi'ilani Highway.
Of the three entrances from the highway, the middle one, across from the Lahaina Post Office, is closest to the beach. The beach is

composed of gray sand and the usually calm waters provide for good swimming. Sheltered picnic tables and shade trees make the park a popular place for locals and visitors alike.

Hanaka'ō'ō Beach

Location: South of Kā'anapali Beach near the Hyatt Regency.

Coordinates: N20° 54.80', W156° 41.53'

Length: 0.4 mile

Facilities: Bathrooms, telephone, showers, lifeguard, picnic tables.

This beach adjoins Kā'anapali Beach to the south and is a popular spot for launching canoes and kayaks. A reef lies offshore, creating small breaks for bodyboarders.

Kā'anapali Beach

Location: Two miles north of Lahaina on Maui's westernmost shore.

Coordinates: N20° 55.56', W156° 41.91'

Length: 1.3 miles

Facilities: Showers, telephone, rental booths, restaurants.

West Maui's most popular beach has a close-up view of Moloka'i and Lāna'i in front of it and an even closer view of the large resorts behind it. This is a great beach for the active visitor. You can windsurf, snorkel, parasail, jet ski and kayak—or watch others do it. Weak swimmers should exercise caution as the steep foreshore creates a strong backwash and the bottom drops off quickly offshore. Public access is provided for anyone not staying at one of the beach resorts, but parking is a problem. Pay parking is available at Whalers Village ($1.00 for the first two hours). Free parking, with 50 spaces for beach users, is available at Public Access 212, south of Whalers Village. The parking attendant will give you a free pass if space is available. More free parking is available by turning off Kā'anapali Parkway onto Nohea Kai Drive. Public Accesses 209 and 210 each have a few stalls. The largest free lot is behind the Hyatt Regency at the south end of the beach. Take the hotel entrance road and turn left at the Lū'au parking sign.

Airport Beach (Kā'anapali Beach)

Location: North side of Kā'anapali in front of Royal Lahaina resort.

Coordinates: N20° 56.24', W156° 41.74'

Length: 0.6 mile

Facilities: Pavilion, bathrooms, showers, telephone, picnic tables.

The beach of the Kā'anapali resorts is divided into two sections by **Pu'u Keka'a** or

Black Rock. North of this volcanic cinder cone is commonly called Airport Beach. Winter surf creates a fairly steep shore, which is covered with fine-grained sand. At the north end of the beach is **Kahekili Park** with a lawn, picnic shelter and a large parking lot that closes 30 minutes after sunset. Access from the highway is on Kai Ala Drive, which is across the highway from Pu'ukoli'i Road and the north depot of the **Sugar Cane Train**. Booths have been set up for kayak, windsurfer and small catamaran rentals.

There is no reef in front of this beach but excellent snorkeling can be found along the walls of **Black Rock**. An amazing number of fish species can be spotted here, probably due to people feeding them.

Honokōwai Beach

Location: On Lower Honoapi'ilani Road between Kahana and Kā'anapali.

Coordinates: N20° 57.47', W156° 41.40'

Length: 0.1 mile

Facilities: None

The lava shelf a few feet offshore provides a shallow swimming area safe for children. The beach is very narrow and is backed by a county park, which is open 5:00 a.m. to 8:00 p.m. The parking lot is across the street from historic **Kā'anapali Congregational Church** (built in 1850).

Kahana Beach

Location: Off Lower Honoapi'ilani Road between Nāpili Bay and Honokōwai and in front of the Kahana Beach Resort.

Coordinates: N20° 58.08', W156° 40.87' (south end)

Length: 1.0 miles

Facilities: Portable toilets and picnic tables at the parking lot, showers at resort.

This deep and level beach stretches nearly a mile. The sand is a little coarse by Maui standards with salt and pepper colors. Swimming is good here with a shallow bottom offshore. The parking lot at **Pōhaku Park** is at the south end of the beach off of Lower Honoapi'ilani Road. Akahele Road is just south of the parking lot and accesses Highway 30.

Length: 0.2 mile

Facilities: None

Nāpili Bay is just south of Kapalua Beach and is about twice as long. The surf breaks harder on shore here than Kapalua, making it a good spot for surfing novices. The bay, backed by wall-to-wall condos, has two public accesses but no parking lot. The north access is from Hui Drive and the south access is from Nāpili Place. Both roads connect with Lower Honoapi'ilani Road, which in turn connects with Highway 30 at the Nāpili Plaza shopping center.

Keonenui Beach

Location: Kahana district just south of Nāpili Bay.

Coordinates: N20° 59.13', W156° 40.59'

Length: 0.1 mile

Facilities: None

Keonenui Beach has a steep foreshore which carries into the ocean. The sharp drop-off in the water can be a hazard to children and weak swimmers. Public access no. 217 from Hui Road E. is cut off by a private fence, leaving use of the beach to guests of the **Kahana Sunset Resort**, which backs the beach, or those who choose to cross their property.

Nāpili Bay

Location: South of Kapalua, off Lower Honoapi'ilani Road.

Coordinates: N20° 59.94', W156° 40.14'

Kapalua Beach

Location: On Kapalua Bay off Lower Honoapi'ilani Road.

Coordinates: N21° 00.18', W156° 40.17'

Length: 0.1 mile

Facilities: Bathrooms, showers, concession shop.

This little beach was voted by *Condé Nast* magazine as the best beach in the world. Covered with nearly white sand, the beach is protected by rocky points at either end that frame the view of Moloka'i. Behind the crescent-shaped beach is a line of coconut palm trees and the 194-room **Kapalua Bay Hotel**. A well-formed reef protects the shore from surf and provides excellent snorkeling. Exposed rocks in the water make wading and swimming uncomfortable. The paved public parking lot south of the beach is woefully small. Your chances of finding a parking spot are better in the morning. A well-stocked concession stand at the north end sells drinks and snacks and rents snorkeling equipment. The entrance to the parking lot is on Lower Honoapi'ilani Road next to the Nāpili Lani Beach Club. From the parking lot, take the pathway under the golf cart overpass.

Oneloa Beach or Ironwood Beach

Location: Behind the Kapalua Development on Ironwoods Lane.

Coordinates: N21° 00.44', W156° 39.71'

Length: 0.3 mile

Facilities: None

This beautiful beach is not well known and is a good bet for avoiding crowds. It's a third of a mile long and covered in fine, nearly white sand. To the right are the cliffs of Makāluapuna Point, which provide some protection for swimming, but watch for the occasional errant golf ball. With high surf, the beach experiences backwash and rip currents. Turn into Kapalua's main entrance and left at the stop sign that has a chapel next to it. Turn into the parking lot at Ironwood Lane. Erosion has caused a ledge with a high step at the beach entrance. The parking lot is

not visible from the beach, so don't leave valuables in your car.

D. T. Fleming Beach Park

Location: On Highway 30 across from Kapulua Golf Course.

Coordinates: N21° 00.49', W156° 39.23'

Length: 0.3 mile

Facilities: Lifeguard, bathrooms, showers, telephone, picnic tables.

The beach and park are named after the Scottish-born manager of Honolua Ranch. Situated on Honokahua Bay, this fairly steep beach is covered in fine-grained, light-colored sand. The north-facing beach is backed with shade trees, so it's not a good spot in the winter for suntanning. In winter the beach is subject to pounding from high surf. Snorkeling is fair, but the waves break well for bodyboarding. Parts of this beach experience rip currents. There is a grassy park behind the beach and a paved parking lot. The back end of the parking lot is not visible from the park and is subject to car break-ins. Next to the beach is the **Ritz-Carlton resort**. The short entrance road is Lower Honoapi'ilani Road, which exits Highway 30 across from the road to Kapalua Golf Course and has a "No Outlet" sign and Emergency Call Box 15.

Mokulē'ia Beach or Slaughterhouse Beach

Location: Just past the 32-mile marker of Highway 30.

Coordinates: N21° 00.86', W156° 38.64'

Length: 0.1 mile

Facilities: None

Locally, this beach is better known as Slaughterhouse Beach because the Honolua Ranch built a slaughterhouse on the cliffs above. Snorkeling is excellent in this **Marine Life Conservation District**. The reefs are on the sides of the bay. As with Honolua, the winter surf may be too high for safe water activities. The sand covering the beach in the summer is often lost to erosion during winter. Park in the roadside pullout next to the chain link fence and descend the newly constructed stairway 100 feet to the beach. Do not leave valuables in your car.

Honolua Bay

Location: 8/10 of a mile past the 32-mile marker on Highway 30.

Coordinates: N21° 01.00', W156° 38.45'

Length: 0.1 mile

Facilities: None

Honolua means "two harbors." Combined with neighboring Mokulē'ia Bay, the area is designated a **Marine Life Conservation District**. Possession of fishing gear or the taking of any marine life is unlawful here. A beautiful reef on both the left and right sides of the bay provides for good snorkeling unless the winter surf is too high. According to state aquatic officials, the waters teem with damselfish, aholehole, manini, saddleback wrasse, nenue and tangs. Dive shops that rent equipment recommend Honolua Bay and

many excursion boats stop here. Close to shore, the water is often murky, but visibility improves farther out. The beach is unattractive, covered with boulders, patches of sand and a deteriorating boat ramp. A dirt road with a locked gate leads to the beach. Park next to the road, remove all valuables from your car and walk the 200 yards to the beach.

Punalau or Windmill Beach

Location: Just past Mile Marker 34 on Highway 30.

Coordinates: N21° 01.52', W156° 37.86'

Length: 0.1 mile

Facilities: None

Steep rocky slopes conceal this secluded beach. The sand is a mixture of white and black grains of all sizes. Strong currents and high surf make this a poor choice for swimmers. The surrounding land is owned by the Maui Land and Pineapple Co. which will allow people to camp at the beach if they register first by calling 669-6201. As part of Honolua Ranch, a windmill was used here for drawing water for cattle, hence its name. The entrance road to the beach is marked by a yellow and black sign that reads "Private Property, Keep Out, Maui Land & Pineapple Co."

Honokōhau Bay

Location: Just past Mile Marker 36 on Highway 30, 8.8 miles north of West Maui Airport turnoff.

Coordinates: N21° 01.49', W156° 36.71'

Length: 0.2 mile

Facilities: None

This is a rocky beach bordered by high cliffs on either side. Honokōhau Stream empties into the bay at the middle of the beach. Since the bay faces north, the beach is subject to large storm surf. Swimming, snorkeling and boat launching are possible only on calm days.

South Maui Beaches

Māʻalaea Beach

Location: The south coast of the isthmus, from Māʻalaea Harbor to North Kīhei.

Coordinates: N20° 46.87', W156° 27.77' (south end)

Length: 3.0 mile

Facilities: None

Miles of windswept sand gently curving around Māʻalaea Bay make up the longest beach in Maui. Hugging the beach is North Kīhei Road and behind that is **Keālia Pond Bird Sanctuary**. Persistent winds funneling through the isthmus make the waters here a windsurfer's paradise, but poor for swimming and snorkeling. The hard-packed sand is good for long walks. The south end of the beach abuts the road. It is possible to park your car off the road and keep an eye on it while you're on the beach. The southernmost point is **Kīhei wharf,** which is a good place for shore fishing.

A project designed by U.S. Fish and Wildlife to rebuild the sand dunes across from **Keālia Pond** is aimed at reversing beach loss and dune erosion while building up the nesting area of the endangered hawksbill sea turtle. A wood-slat fence a mile and a half long was erected to trap the windblown sand and act as a temporary barrier to keep the turtles from wandering onto North Kīhei Road. Openings in the fence allow pedestrians to access the beach. Off-road vehicles are not allowed onto the sand.

Mai Poina ʻOe Iaʻu Beach

Location: South of Kīhei wharf and across from the Maui Lu hotel.

Coordinates: N20° 46.45', W156° 27.62'

Length: 1.1 miles

Facilities: Bathrooms, shelter, telephone, picnic tables.

In Hawaiian, Mai Poina ʻOe Iaʻu means "forget me not" and the park is dedicated to Maui veterans who died in combat. This sandy beach stretches one mile south of the **Kīhei Wharf**. There is a shelter and small parking area with additional parking available along the roadside. The offshore bottom is shallow and sandy. It's a good beach for launching a kayak or for the family to play in the surf.

Kalepolepo Beach

Location: Across from Kīhei Bay Surf, 715 South Kīhei Road.

Coordinates: N20° 45.83', W156° 27.55'

Length: 100 feet

Facilities: Shower, picnic tables, parking lot.

This tiny beach is a good place for canoe launching. The beach is the site of **Kōʻieʻie fishpond**, which means "rapid current of rushing water." Kōʻieʻie was likely built in the late 1500's by Umi, a ruling chief of the island of Hawaiʻi. Along the seaward wall of the fishpond was a wooden sluice gate. At high tide the water and fish would surge into the fishpond, and as the water receded, the narrow slats in the gate would allow small fish to return to the sea and trap the larger fish inside. Next door is the **Hawaiian Islands Humpback Whale Marine Sanctuary Visitors Center** (see South Maui Sights).

Waiohuli Beach

Location: One block west of South Kīhei Road on Waipuʻilani Street.

Coordinates: N20° 45.31', W156° 27.57'

Length: 0.1 mile

Facilities: Bathrooms.

Behind this narrow beach is a grassy area and very nice condos. The beach, frequented by undesirable characters, is not a recommended visit.

Kawililīpoa Beach

Location: End of Līpoa Street at Shoreline Access 118.

Coordinates: N20° 44.86', W156° 27.47'

Length: 100 yards

Facilities: None

This narrow beach, strewn with seaweed, is not a recommended visit.

Kamaʻole Beach I

Location: 2300 block of South Kīhei Road.

Coordinates: N20° 43.55', W156° 27.04'

Length: 0.4 mile

Facilities: Lifeguard, bathrooms, shower, picnic tables, volleyball net.

Kamaʻole means "childless" and is the name carried by three beach parks, simply called Kamaʻole I, II and III. The parks and the string of three beaches divided by rocky points are Kīhei's best attractions. The largest and most northerly of the three is Kamaʻole I. The beach is an uninterrupted stretch of fine-grained golden sand and has a full range of facilities in the park behind it. The parking lot is off South Kīhei Road across from Kīhei Plaza. On weekends the lot is often full so an additional lot was built on the north end of the beach across from the Maui Vista. The north end of the beach is sometimes called **Charley Young beach**, named after the long-time Kīhei resident and civic leader who died in 1974.

The sun almost always shines in Kīhei and this beach is the perfect place to relax and enjoy the sunshine, the warm Pacific waters and views of the West Maui Mountains, Lānaʻi, Kahoʻolawe and Molokini rising out of the water and Haleakalā looming behind. The surf is usually gentle and the shallow sandy bottom offshore is perfect for wading and swimming.

Kamaʻole Beach II

Location: South Kīhei Road across from the Kamaʻole Shopping Center.

Coordinates: N20° 43.18', W156° 26.97'

Length: 0.2 mile

Facilities: Lifeguard, bathrooms, shower, picnic tables.

There is no parking lot for this beach so parking must be made along South Kīhei Road. This beach is particularly popular with seniors, many of whom are staying at the condos across the road. There is good swimming at this beach and snorkeling along the rocks on the south end.

Kama'ole Beach III

Location: On South Kīhei Road across from the Kama'ole Sands.

Coordinates: N20° 42.94', W156° 26.95'

Length: 0.2 mile

Facilities: Lifeguard, bathrooms, shower, picnic tables, volleyball net, playground.

Even though this is the smallest of the Kama'ole beaches, it is often the busiest. This is probably because its park is the biggest and has a playground. The beach has good swimming but there are rock outcroppings in the water and on the beach. Snorkeling is good along the rocky point between Kama'ole II and III.

Keawakapu Beach

Location: South end of Kīhei.

Coordinates: N20° 41.84', W156° 26.67'

Length: 0.6 mile

Facilities: Showers

There's lots of room on this long beach that gets visited less often than the Kīhei beaches

to the north. The sand here is as soft as sugar and extends into the water to create a shallow bottom for swimming. Snorkeling and spearfishing are good at the south end of the beach. There is a large parking lot at the north beach entrance where South Kīhei Road intersects with Kilohana Drive. The parking lot at the south end of South Kīhei Road is closer to the beach but it only has 22 stalls. To the north of the beach is a public boat ramp.

Mōkapu Beach

Ulua Beach

Mōkapu and Ulua Beaches

Location: Wailea, in front of Renaissance Wailea Beach Resort.

Coordinates: Mōkapu N20° 41.79', W156° 26.81', Ulua N20° 41.63', W156° 26.79'

Length: 0.2 mile each

Facilities: Bathrooms, shower.

The twin beaches of Mōkapu and Ulua are separated by a rock outcropping and are joined by a boardwalk running behind them.

Both crescent-shaped beaches are about 200 yards long. Mōkapu, which is north of Ulua, has exposed beach rock. Ulua offers more protection in windy conditions. The reef around the rock outcropping provides some of the best snorkeling on Maui. An outer reef, with a maximum depth of 35 feet awaits SCUBA divers. A parking lot is provided for the public, but it is often full for those who don't arrive early. Turn off Wailea Alanui Drive at Shoreline Access No. 107 sign south of the Renaissance Wailea Beach Resort.

Wailea Beach

Location: In front of Grand Hyatt Wailea and Four Seasons Resorts.

Coordinates: N20° 41.18', W156° 26.66'

Length: 0.3 mile

Facilities: Bathrooms, shower.

This attractive crescent of golden sand is used mostly by the guests of the very exclusive resorts backing it. Very popular among walkers and joggers is the paved, elevated pathway along the rocky point to the south of the beach. Below the rocky point is the best spot for snorkeling at this beach. The bottom offshore is sandy and shallow and the shorebreak is mild except during storms. If the wind is blowing directly onshore, watch for jellyfish. From Wailea Alanui Drive, turn at the Shoreline Access No. 106 sign south of Grand Wailea Resort. The public parking lot has only 20 stalls.

Polo Beach

Location: In front of Kea Lani Resort.

Coordinates: N20° 40.72', W156° 26.69'

Length: 0.2 mile

Facilities: Bathrooms, shower.

More impressive than this half-moon-shaped beach is the Kea Lani Resort that borders it. Private villas of the resort overlook the beach and behind them, glistening in the sun, is the whitewashed hotel, punctuated with the spires and towers that give the hotel a Mediterranean flavor. Situated in the lee of Haleakalā, Polo Beach can have glass-still water, particularly in the morning. The best snorkeling is at the north end of the beach. The Kea Lani has provided an especially nice bathroom building for beachgoers to use. In the shaded area next to it are barbecue pits and seven picnic tables. Turn seaward off of Wailea Alanui Drive just south of the Kea Lani Resort, and follow Kaukahi St. to Shoreline Access No. 105 sign at the public parking lot, which has room for 90 vehicles.

Palauea Beach

Location: Off Mākena Road between Polo Beach and Hāloa Point.

Coordinates: N20° 40.44', W156° 26.66'

Length: 0.2 mile

Facilities: None

Palauea Beach is worth seeking out if you want a secluded, undeveloped place to swim, suntan and snorkel. The beach is a flat, wide crescent of golden sand. Snorkeling and diving are especially interesting around **Hāloa Point** at the south end of the beach. Underwater await shallow caves and crevices, lava arches, all kinds of reef fish and occasionally, white-tipped reef sharks. The back of the beach is lined with beach morning glory, kiawe and undeveloped land that is the subject of local controversy. The property, covering nearly five acres, is owned by an Oʻahu-based land development company, which has set up fences and no trespassing signs on the only access the public has to the beach. Backed by petitions and public support, the Maui County Council has passed a resolution to acquire the land for a public park using its power of eminent domain. Until those protracted negotiations conclude, you can get to the beach by turning off Wailea Alanui Drive south of the Kea Lani onto Kaukahi Street and then left onto Mākena Road. Follow the road two-tenths of a mile to a widening by a fire hydrant and park along the road. A trail through the trees leads to the beach 100 feet away. Leave nothing in your car; this is a particularly high-risk area for property crime.

Paipu Beach Park (Poʻolenalena Beach, Chang's Beach)

Location: Across from Wailea Orange Golf Course.

Coordinates: N20° 39.96', W156° 26.66'

Length: 0.5 mile

Facilities: Portable toilets.

Undeveloped Paipu Beach is also known as Poʻolenalena, meaning "yellow head," or

Chang's Beach, after the family that has long owned land in the area. The beach, which has rock outcroppings at the south end, is suitable for swimming. Snorkeling is best at **Hāloa Point** on the north end of the beach. The entrance road is off Wailea Alanui Drive, one-tenth of a mile south of the fork from Mākena Road, and is marked with a sign. From the parking area, the north end of the beach is out of sight, but can be reached by walking over the small hill to the right.

Nāhuna Point (Five Graves)

Location: Just south of Mākena Surf on Mākena Road.

Coordinates: N20° 39.55', W156° 26.74'

Length: 100 feet

Facilities: None

A rocky cove at Nāhuna Point is the entry point for one of the best dives in Maui. Look for underwater caves, sea turtles, spiny lobsters and maybe a white-tipped reef shark. Use caution when the entrance is awash and frothy; the offshore current can be strong here. At the Mākena Surf Hotel, take Mākena Road off of Mākena Alanui Drive two-tenths of a mile to the small graveyard next to a low lava-stone fence and park in the lot. A short path leads to the cove.

Mākena Landing County Park

Location: North end of Mākena Bay, 3/10ths of a mile north of Maui Prince Hotel.

Coordinates: N20° 39.42', W156° 26.63'

Length: 0.1 mile

Facilities: Bathrooms, shower.

At one time Mākena Bay was a busy port, shipping sugar and cattle by interisland steamer. In the 1920s, improvements to Kahului Harbor focused the shipping and commerce there and the community at Mākena died out. The pier was torn down during World War II. The bay has two small pockets of sand that can be used as entry points for the excellent diving and snorkeling found here. Many commercial boats bring snorkelers and divers here each day from Māʻalaea and Kīhei. Mākena Landing is two-tenths of a mile south of the Five Graves site at Shoreline Access No. 103 on Mākena Road. Or, from Mākena Alanui Drive, turn makai (towards ocean) at Honoiki Street and right at Mākena Road.

Maluʻaka Beach

Location: In front of the Maui Prince Hotel.

Coordinates: N20° 39.03', W156° 26.73'

Length: 0.2 mile

Facilities: Bathrooms, shower.

This quarter-mile-long beach is excellent for swimming but don't go too far out as the current can be strong. Behind Maluʻaka Beach is the Mākena Golf Course and the Maui Prince Hotel, the last of a string of large resorts from Wailea to Mākena—hence its nickname—"The Last Resort." Even with its proximity to a large resort, this beach is never crowded. The north entrance to the beach is at Shoreline Access No. 102 and can be reached by parking at the lot for beach users across from the historic Keawalaʻi Church, 200 yards north of the beach on Mākena Road. Bathrooms and showers are situated at the parking lot. The south entrance can be reached by traveling south on Mākena Alanui Drive past the Maui Prince Hotel and making a hard right onto Mākena Road (which has a "Dead End" sign) and driving back to the parking lot by the Gold Course. From here follow the stone-covered pathway to the beach.

Oneuli Beach (Little Black Sand Beach)

Location: Immediately north of the cinder cone, Puʻu ʻŌlaʻi (Red Hill).

Coordinates: N20° 38.38', W156° 26.82'

Length: 0.3 mile

Facilities: None

Situated at the base of 360-foot-high Puʻu ʻŌlaʻi, this is an interesting beach to see. The sand isn't pure black, but more like pepper and salt, and finer textured than the black-sand beaches on the Big Island. On a sunny day the sand will be pretty hot so foot protection is needed. The sea can be rough here and swimming is dangerous around the point of Puʻu ʻŌlaʻi, where the current is strong. Turn off Mākena Alanui Drive, eight-tenths of a mile south of the Maui Prince Hotel, onto the entrance road on the north side of the hill. An orange metal gate closes the road from 8:00 p.m. to 7:00 a.m. each night. The deeply rutted trail leads to a gravel parking lot.

Oneloa Beach

Oneloa Beach
(Big Beach, Mākena Beach)

Location: Last sandy beach in Mākena, just south of Red Hill.

Coordinates: N20° 38.16', W156° 27.08'

Length: 0.7 mile

Facilities: Bathrooms.

Appropriately, Oneloa means "long sand," which is why it is often called "Big Beach." There is over half a mile of nearly white sand covering the gentle arch of this exquisite beach of magnificent scale. Kahoʻolawe and Molokini are in view in front of the beach, the red and black lava outcropping of the cinder cone, Puʻu ʻŌlaʻi, anchors the north end and Haleakalā rises above the kiawe forest behind. Nowhere is there development of any kind in sight. The turquoise water is clearer here than elsewhere on Maui, probably because of naturally formed ponds in the forest behind the beach which trap runoff from heavy rains.

Mākena, appearing as a decorous family beach, belies its checkered recent history. From 1968 to 1972, as many as one hundred hippies made the beach their counterculture home. The majority of Maui's kamaʻaina population wanted what they saw as bead-wearing, pot-smoking interlopers off the island. In April 1972, authorities evicted the squatters on public health grounds.

The kiawe forest backing the beach used to be owned by developers who planned a hotel complex on the site. Public outcry resulted in the state purchasing the land to create a beach park. Ironically, the people of Maui find themselves having to conduct campaigns to preserve beaches that they themselves can use. Fortunately, the excesses of new resort development of the 1970s and 1980s have subsided and the focus has been on improving and renovating existing resorts.

Exposed to open ocean, the beach here is noted for having "killer breaks." Unless the water is calm, only experienced bodysurfers should test them. The sandy bottom offshore drops off quickly and the current that flows around the point of **Red Hill** is very strong so swimmers should stay close in. Snorkeling is good in the clear water among the rocks at the north end of the beach.

There are two parking lots for the beach park. The first is one mile south of the Maui Prince Hotel turnoff on Mākena Alanui Drive and the second is just south of that. On weekends both lots can be full by 11:00 a.m. The gates are closed from 9:00 p.m. to 5:00 a.m. because of escalating crime and vandalism. The days of unofficial camping at "Big Beach" are over, although state park officials have proposed construction of an enforcement officer's residence at the park as a way of dealing with after-hours crime and allowing the park to stay open at night.

Le Pérouse Bay

Pu'u Ōla'i Beach (Little Beach)

Location: Seaward side of the cinder cone Pu'u 'Ōla'i (Red Hill).

Coordinates: N20° 38.27', W156° 27.26'

Length: 0.1 mile

Facilities: None

Little Beach is located northwest of Big Beach in a cove under the cinder cone, Pu'u Ōla'i. The only land access to Little Beach is found by turning right when you get to Big Beach and following the trail over the lava bluff. This isolated beach is only 400 feet long but a lot of people use it. And most of those people are naked. Technically, nude sunbathing is illegal on Maui, but it's rarely enforced. Swimming, snorkeling and body-surfing are good here but don't go too far out or you'll be caught in the strong current.

La Pérouse Bay

Location: 3-1/2 miles south of Big Beach at the end of the road.

Coordinates: N20° 36.14', W156° 25.34'

Length: 0.7 mile

Facilities: None

The rocky shoreline and offshore bottom of La Pérouse Bay are not friendly to swimmers but this is a good spot for snorkeling and diving. Set amidst the stark lava landscape created by Maui's last volcanic eruption, the bay contains an intriguing lava bottom often visited by large fish. The waters in the bay are generally safe, being protected from the current. Stormy weather can cause turbulent water in the bay, making entry over the rocks treacherous. The waters next to Cape Kīna'u on the north side of the bay are part of a nature reserve and shore fishing or spearfishing are not allowed. Follow Mākena Alanui Drive south across the lava flow to the bay named after the first European to set foot on Maui. This is as far as you can go on this road by passenger car.

Central Maui Beaches

generally gentle here. It is also the home of the **Outrigger Canoe Club**. Behind the park is the Kahului Airport and an industrial area. You can find more attractive, visitor-friendly beaches than this.

Waiheʻe Beach County Park

Location: 2-1/2 miles northwest of Wailuku on Highway 340.

Coordinates: N20° 56.13', W156° 30.14'

Length: 0.4 mile

Facilities: Bathrooms, shower, picnic tables.

This narrow beach of coarse salt and pepper sand is strewn with coral rubble and seaweed and is used mostly by local residents. Offshore is one of Maui's longest and widest reefs. It's a good area for beachcombing and picnicking. Follow highway 340 two-and-one-half miles northwest of Wailuku to the golfcourse sign and turn right on Halewai Road. The park is one-half mile down the road, behind the golf driving range.

Kanahā Beach County Park

Location: In front of Kahului Airport.

Coordinates: N20° 54.25', W156° 26.56'

Length: 0.6 mile

Facilities: Lifeguard, bathrooms, telephone, picnic shelter.

This is a good place for inexperienced sailboarders to practice. The wind and surf are

H. A. Baldwin County Park

Location: Three miles east of the intersection of the Hāna and Haleakalā highways.

Coordinates: N20° 55.05', W156° 23.80'

Length: 0.7 mile

Facilities: Lifeguard, bathrooms, telephone, covered shelter, picnic tables.

The consistent shorebreak here is a favorite with the young bodysurfers of the area. This can be a busy park because of its proximity to Kahului and Pāʻia. The park contains sports fields and a pavilion that is sometimes the scene of loud parties. Crime has also been a problem here. Cars in the parking lot are hidden from view of the beach by a sand berm. There was a campground here but the county closed it due to safety and health concerns. The entrance road is at Mile Marker 6 of the Hāna Highway.

Pā'ia Bay

Location: At the town of Lower Pā'ia on the Hāna Highway.

Coordinates: N20° 55.19', W156° 23.13'

Length: 0.2 mile

Facilities: None

The beach on the bay by the funky town of Lower Pā'ia is narrow and sloping. Swimming is safe in the summer when the water is calm but not recommended when the surf is up. Because the water tends to be murky, snorkeling is not recommended. Access is gained by walking east from H. A. Baldwin Park or by walking two blocks north of the Shoreline Access sign on the west side of Lower Pā'ia.

Ho'okipa Beach County Park

Location: Six miles from the intersection of the Hāna and Haleakalā highways.

Coordinates: N20° 56.07', W156° 21.50'

Length: 0.3 mile

Facilities: Portable toilets, picnic shelter.

Ho'okipa was the birthplace of contemporary surfing on Maui in the 1930s. Windsurfing was introduced in the 1970s and soon Ho'okipa was recognized the world over as a premier boardsailing site. Numerous international windsurfing competitions are held here. Waves can reach 20 feet, there's a powerful current offshore and razor-sharp coral under the surface—only the adept should enter this water. It's an entertaining place for spectators though. Above the beach, next to the upper parking lot, is an excellent vantage point. Bring your binoculars and a telephoto lens for your camera. Surfers are out primarily in the morning and the windsurfers show up in the afternoon when the wind picks up. The park is just under two miles past Pā'ia on the Hāna Highway at Mile Marker 9. Drive past the park and turn left into the upper parking lot. On busy days the lower parking lot will be filled by the surfers and windsurfers.

Windsurfing at Ho'okipa Beach

East Maui Beaches

Honomanū Bay

Location: On the Hāna Highway, 2 miles west of the Keʻanae peninsula.

Coordinates: N20° 51.84', W156° 10.14'

Length: 0.1 mile

Facilities: None

Erosion from rain and the sea have cut a deep V into the cliffs of northeast Maui at Honomanū Bay. The highway enters the bay high on the cliffs from either side and drops to sea level at the mouth of Honomanū Stream. The dirt road on the Hāna side of the stream, at Mile Marker 14, leads to the beach. Rocks and boulders cover the beach and the bottom offshore, making wading or swimming unappealing. Surfers sometimes use this beach but the rocky bottom makes it a risky venture. The bay is subject to extremely high and dangerous surf, particularly in the winter when storms in the North Pacific send large swells down to the north shores of all the Hawaiian Islands.

Waiʻānapanapa State Park

Location: Just off Highway 360, two miles before Hāna.

Coordinates: N20° 47.45', W156° 00.38'

Length: 0.1 mile

Facilities: Bathrooms, picnic tables.

Waiʻānapanapa, meaning "glistening water," is Maui's true black-sand beach and presents a striking scene. The sand is black lava eroded into small pieces by the wave action of the sea. Black-sand beaches have a coarser texture than most coral beaches. Snorkeling is possible on a very calm day—it's best around the natural lava arch to the right. Do not enter the water except when it is very calm as there is a heavy rip current when the surf is up. Waiʻānapanapa Park has cabins that can be rented and caves to explore (see Sights). The entrance road is clearly marked, just past the 32-mile marker.

Hāna Bay Beach

Location: Below the village of Hāna on Ua Kea Road.

Coordinates: N20° 45.49', W155° 59.18'

Length: 0.2 mile

Facilities: Bathrooms, change rooms, shower, picnic shelter.

North of the center of the village, Hāna Bay Beach Park is a popular local destination. The south end of the park, below the cinder cone, Kaʻuiki Head, is a pier that is used by small craft, but is no longer used for inter-island shipping. Just beyond the pier is Puʻu Kiʻi island and its lighthouse. A lava point and the pilings of the old Hāna Landing border the park on the north. It has a long, broad stretch of dark gray sand and faces one of the area's safest swimming spots. Even during periods of heavy surf, only a gentle shorebreak forms in the bay. Snorkeling is

volcanic cinder beach, the cinders originating from the erosion of Ka'uiki Head. Iron oxide in the cinders gives the sand its red color. A narrow trail leads to either a lookout point on the cliffs above the beach or follows a precarious route down to the beach. From the Hāna Highway, turn towards the ocean at Hau'oli Road. At the end of the road, park in front of the open field between the Community Center and the Hāna Hotel cottages. Cut diagonally across the field to the large ironwood tree on the right. At the tree take the left fork in the trail, which will pass a Japanese cemetery, to reach the viewpoint. Take the right fork for the trail to the beach, but do so at your own peril. There are large signs here warning people to stay off the trail because of the danger. The narrow trail skirts around a steep cone covered with loose cinders. A slip off the trail here would send you over a cliff and into the rocks and ocean below.

Heavy surf washes into the cove but most of it is stopped by the natural lava barrier protecting the beach. Swimmers should stay away from the north side of the beach where a rip current develops from the water returning to the ocean.

good between the pier and Pu'u Ki'i but don't venture past the protection of the island. This is a great spot for a family picnic, or lunch can be purchased at Tutu's Snack Shop located at the park's community center. When approaching Hāna from Highway 360, turn left at the hospital and follow Ua Kea Road down to the park.

Red Sand Beach (Kaihalulu Beach)

Location: The opposite side of Ka'uiki Head from Hana Bay.

Coordinates: N20° 45.36', W155° 59.08'

Length: 100 yards

Facilities: None

Red Sand Beach is located in a cove enclosed by the high cliffs of Ka'uiki Head on the opposite side of Hāna Bay. It is a

Hāmoa Beach

Location: 2 1/2 miles south of Hāna.

Coordinates: N20° 43.35', W155° 59.43'

Length: 0.1 mile

Facilities: Bathrooms, shower and dining pavilion for guests of the Hotel Hāna Maui.

Hāmoa Beach is defined by sea cliffs on

Kāʻanapaliʻs Airport Beach.

either end and covered with salt and pepper sand. Situated at the head of Mōkae Cove, it is unprotected from the surf breaking onshore. Surfers reach the water by jumping off the rocks on the north point of the beach.

The Hotel Hāna Maui owns the land surrounding the beach and treats the beach as a semi-private reserve. Shuttle buses run guests of the hotel back and forth between the beach and the hotel. The hotel provides a private lifeguard and holds a weekly lūʻau at the pavilion.

Access for the public is from the walkway leading down from the north cliff. Haneoʻo Road connects the beach with the Hāna Highway at two spots. The intersection farther from Hāna is closer to the beach.

FLORA AND FAUNA

So dire has the plight of endemic species on the Hawaiian Islands become that conservationists have bestowed the Islands with the unhappy distinction of being the endangered-species capital of the country. Already, Hawai'i has lost hundreds of original life forms while hundreds more teeter on the brink of oblivion. The U.S. has 526 plants and 88 birds on the endangered and threatened species list; more than a third are found in Hawai'i. Three-quarters of the United States' extinct plants and birds once lived only in Hawai'i even though its islands represent just two-tenths of one percent of the nation's total land area.

Creatures and plants have been vanishing ever since Polynesian voyagers—and later European explorers—first set foot on the Islands about 1,500 years ago. Having evolved on the most remote group of islands on earth, native species were not equipped to survive the onslaught of predators and competitors that accompanied human arrival. Twenty species of flightless birds—easy prey for the hunter—were among the first decimated.

The original Hawaiians' presence was not as benign as was once thought. The settlers brought with them breadfruit, bananas, sugarcane and taro, clearing lowland forests to cultivate them. They brought small pigs that escaped to become feral. The first humans on Hawai'i caused the extinction of 35 species of birds. Later, in the several decades following the arrival of Captain James Cook in 1778, outsiders introduced cattle, goats, sheep and large European pigs. Many of these animals escaped and flourished. Settlers introduced guavas, Java plum, lantana, bamboo and ginger which pushed aside and destroyed

Above: Protea blooms take on many forms

Following page: Torch ginger

numerous indigenous species and native flora in the wild.

Most of the threatened and endangered species in Hawai'i find refuge among uplands too steep for development. More than a quarter of Hawai'i's land remains unspoiled, giving conservationists cause for hope. By restoring and maintaining healthy ecosystems, conservationists hope to give native species the respite and protection they need to survive. Their work crews kill feral animals, erect fences to keep ungulates away from fragile plants, breed birds in captivity, pollinate flowers by hand, and destroy nonindigenous plants.

On Maui, the upper reaches of Haleakalā National Park's Kīpahulu Valley hold a wealth of native plants and birds. The National Park Service has declared much of the valley off-limits to visitors while conservationists work to save endangered species and reclaim the land from alien plants and animals. In the battle to save and restore Maui's native flora and fauna, alien plants are uprooted or sprayed with herbicides, locations of endangered species are recorded and fence lines are checked for gaps that pigs can squeeze through.

Plants and Trees

There are more than 2,500 kinds of plants that occur only in the Hawaiian Islands. Native plants are common today only in such remote places as the headwalls of deep valleys, on steep cliffs, and on mountain ridges and peaks. The coconuts, orchids,

sugarcane and pineapples that visitors associate with Hawai'i are neither native nor unique. Native plants have evolved from about 275 species of successful natural immigrants that arrived in Hawai'i on the average of once every 100,000 years since the time when the Islands emerged from the sea.

Silversword

Maui's most famous indigenous plant, the silversword, descends from ancestors whose seeds were carried across the Pacific from the Americas by air currents. The silversword, known as 'āhinahina in Hawaiian, matures for up to 20 years, then it blooms, releases its seeds, and dies. Before it blooms the plant emerges as a globe of silvery-gray lanceolate leaves starkly contrasted against Haleakalā's dark lava cinders. Its inwardly curved leaves catch water and funnel it to a central root. Water loss is minimized through narrow leaf surfaces, which are covered with thick layers of silvery hairs that create a reflective surface to shield the plant

The silversword plant before it blooms

from the sun's ultraviolet radiation. During summer months a flower stalk develops, sometimes reaching six feet high. A torchlike cluster of 100–500 yellow and magenta flowers adorns the stalk. Once flourishing on Haleakalā's slopes and summit, the plant suffered destruction from unthinking tourists who uprooted plants and rolled them down the crater's slope. Grazing cattle and goats trampled the plants. Haleakalā's signature plant was nearly extinct before the national park was established to protect it in 1916. Recently the silversword has made a remarkable comeback with more than 2,500 plants blooming each year.

Protea

These exotic and captivating flowers are originally from South Africa. Proteas are shrubs that bloom into more than 40 flower types that can resemble anything from pincushions to a bouquet of feathers. The Kula district of Maui has perfect growing conditions for proteas, which thrive on warm days, cool nights, ample rainfall and well-drained volcanic soil.

Bird of Paradise

This African native has become a trademark of Hawai'i. Their orange and blue flowers nestle in green bracts, looking somewhat like birds in flight. Birds of paradise seem to be most abundant in the gardens of vacation resorts and in cut-flower arrangements in hotel lobbies.

Bird of paradise

Above: *Protea blooms take on many forms*

Opposite Page: *Yellow ginger*

Gingers

Some of Hawai'i's most fragrant flowers are white and yellow gingers. They are usually found growing four to seven feet high in areas blessed with a lot of rain. Their flowers are three inches wide and composed of three dainty, petal-like stamens and three long, thin petals. White and yellow gingers were introduced in the nineteenth century from Malaysia. More exotic-looking is the torch ginger. The red flower stalks are about six inches long and resemble the fire of a lighted torch.

Hibiscus

The yellow hibiscus is Hawai'i's official state flower. Hibiscuses grow on hedges up to 15 feet high. The four- to six-inch flowers, which resemble crepe paper, bloom in colors from white to deep red, with stamens and pistils protruding from the center. Because it shrivels quickly, it is unsuitable for use in a lei but it is a favored flower to tuck behind the ear. Tradition says that a flower behind the left ear means the lady's heart is committed and behind the right ear means that she is available.

Red hibiscus

Taro

Originally from Sri Lanka, taro is a food crop planted in flooded patches and found growing wild around pools and streams. The plants, with their large, heart-shaped leaves, are grown and harvested by Hawaiians on the Ke'anae Peninsula of east Maui.

'Ōhi'a Tree

The 'ōhi'a is the most abundant of the native Hawaiian trees and is usually the first life to appear in new lava flows. 'Ōhi'a can grow as a miniature tree in wet bogs or as an 80-foot giant on cool slopes at high elevations. Its petal-less flowers, lehua blossoms, are composed of a large mass of brightly colored stamens, usually red but sometimes orange, yellow or white. The flowers are also an important source of nectar for rare endemic birds.

Koa Tree

The beautifully grained wood of the koa is prized for the making of canoes, paddles, bowls, furniture and even surfboards. Its beauty and diverse uses has resulted in the harvest of nearly all the large trees. A native tree, the koa is frequently mentioned in Hawaiian legends and songs.

Kukui Tree

Early Polynesians imported the kukui because of its many uses. Kukui nuts are rich in oil and were used as candles or made into leis. When baked, the kernels are edible. The roots and shell of the fruit yield a black dye.

Jacaranda Tree

From March until May, the upcountry of Maui is colored with the purple blossoms of the jacaranda. The large trees bear fern-like leaves and bountiful clusters of bell-shaped flowers. It is an introduced tree, native to Peru.

Jacaranda tree

African Tulip Trees

The flaming red flowers on these large trees provide a welcome contrast to the multihued greens of the rain forests they live in. The trees produce globes of frilly, tulip-shaped flowers on branch tips. Watch for African tulip trees brightening the nature trail at Maui's Ke'anae Arboretum.

Birds

Because of Hawai'i's isolated location in the middle of the Pacific Ocean, the first birds to arrive probably were blown off course or floated in clutching driftwood. Here, with abundant food and no predators, they were free to evolve into 67 species particularly suited to their environment. Human settlement of Hawai'i caused the demise of 40 percent of native bird species and endangered another 40 percent. Early Polynesians cleared lowland vegetation and replaced it with introduced plants that were used for food and fiber. As a result, when foreigners from many lands made a new home in Hawai'i during the nineteenth century, there were no songbirds in the lowlands. It was natural for them to want to import familiar birds from their homelands. When sugarcane, pineapple and cattle became economically important, settlers introduced foreign birds that would feed upon the insect pests of the crops and cattle. Since 1796 when the first pigeons or rock doves were released, 170 different kinds of exotic birds have gained their freedom in Hawai'i.

Just as the Hawaiian people had never developed resistance to measles, Hawaiian birds had no resistance to avian malaria. Common among mainland birds, avian malaria is caused by a microscopic parasite in their blood. Caged pet birds and foreign birds introduced by the early colonists likely carried this parasite. An incident that occurred in the port of Lahaina in 1826 led to the spread of this disease to the native bird population. In that year the ship *Wellington* put in at Lahaina to fill its water casks, having last filled them on the west coast of Mexico. Released from those casks into a clear Maui stream were the larvae of a particular mosquito, *Culex pipiens fatigans*, which inhabits tropical and subtropical regions. It is now found on all the main Hawaiian Islands from sea level to an elevation of 3,000 feet. These mosquitoes were the carriers that transmitted blood parasites and viruses from migratory birds and domestic poultry to Hawaii's endemic birds. Birds that lived above the level of the mosquito infestation but migrated to lower levels during winter storms were also bitten and mortally infected. Today it is only in the highlands that Hawai'i's rare endemic birds are found.

Nēnē

The endangered nēnē is Hawai'i's state bird. It is believed to be a descendant of the Canada goose, which it still resembles. The large, colorful bird grows to weigh five pounds and measure 28 inches in length. Nēnē can only be found in and near the crater of Haleakalā on Maui, on the slopes of Mauna Kea and Mauna Loa on the Big Island, and just

recently has been released near Līhu'e and Kīlauea, Kaua'i. Predation of their nests by mongooses, rats and feral cats, coupled with overhunting, nearly drove the nēnē to extinction. By 1951 only 33 individuals were known, half of which were in captivity.

Much of the reason that the nēnē survives today can be credited to the work of the late Sir Peter Scott, who founded the Wildfowl and Wetlands Trust in England. Just after the trust's formation in 1946, its officers suggested to the territorial government of Hawai'i that steps be taken to save the nēnē. At the time only 50 of the birds were left, none of them on Maui. The International Union for the Protection of Nature, a United Nations–sponsored organization, placed the nēnē on a list of 13 most threatened bird species in the world. In 1949 a rancher on the Big Island, who was keeping many of the surviving nēnē, shipped a breeding pair to England. Nine goslings were hatched from them in the following year. That same year the Hawaiian government started its own breeding project on the Big Island with the help of the Trust's curator. Slowly, the population of nēnē in England grew, and in 1962, 30 were returned to the Islands and released, with 5 going to Haleakalā Crater. Over the years, breeding projects have returned more than 2,000 birds to the wild. Maui's wild population now numbers between 200 and 250.

Nēnē

Pueo

The Hawaiian short-eared owl, or pueo, has brown and white markings and heavily feathered legs. It grows to 13–17 inches long. Unlike most owls, the pueo is often active at midday. As it soars at high altitudes, watchful for its prey of mice and rats, some observers mistake it for the 'io, or Hawaiian hawk. Pueo build their nests on the ground, usually in grass, which leaves their eggs vulnerable to rapacious feral cats and mongooses. The pueo can be found from sea level to 8,000 feet in elevation on all the main Hawaiian islands, in areas dominated by both native and alien vegetation and from pastures and grasslands to dry and wet forest. Many Hawaiians consider the pueo to be an ancestor spirit and spotting one a good omen.

'Io

The 'Io, or Hawaiian hawk, lives in the forests of Hawai'i, where it preys on rats and spiders. Adults grow to 18 inches in length and have a light brown color. Regally circling the Hawaiian skies, the endangered bird is esteemed by some as an ancestor spirit. Its name honors the 'Iolani Palace in Honolulu.

'I'iwi

The 'i'iwi is one of over fifty species of honeycreepers that evolved from a single ancestral species that colonized the Islands millions of years ago. It is easily distinguished from other Hawaiian forest birds by its bright red feathers, pink curved bill and black wings and tail. In the mountains, where it lives, its presence can be detected by the sounds its wings make as it flutters from tree to tree. The movements of the 'i'iwi are also unique as it spends much of its time hanging upside down poking its long, curved bill into flowers. The lehua blossom is one if its favorites. Hawaiians prized the 'i'iwi's bright red feathers for adorning capes, helmets and other ornaments for the ali'i. Some large cloaks required the sacrifice of 8,000 birds to make them.

Maui Parrotbill

One of Maui's most distinctive birds, the Maui parrotbill is easily recognized by its large, compressed, parrot-like beak. Males are olive-green with a yellow belly, while females are drab and smaller-billed. The endangered Maui parrotbill is found on the east slopes of Haleakalā, from Ke'anae Valley to Kīpahulu, between 3,700–6,500 feet in elevation. The birds forage for insects along trunks and branches of koa and 'ōhi'a trees. Their powerful bills are adapted for wrenching away chunks of bark and crushing twigs while searching for caterpillars and the grubs and pupae of beetles.

Mammals

Because of their geographic isolation, only two land mammals arrived on the Hawaiian Islands through natural dispersal and became established. They are the hoary bat and the Hawaiian monk seal. Marine mammals such as whales and dolphins, widely distributed throughout the world and of ancient origin, likely have been in Hawaiian waters since very early times. Seafaring Polynesians brought with them dogs and pigs (both for eating) and stowaway rats. Most of the land mammals found in Hawai'i today were introduced after Captain Cook's landing in 1778. These aggressive, transplanted species have profoundly affected Hawaiian wildlife.

Hawaiian monk seal

Hoary Bat

Theirs is a remarkable example of wayward migration. The hoary bats of North and South America are strongly migratory and regularly reach the Farallon Islands off California, the Galàpagos and Bermuda. Flights that brought bats to Hawai'i may have been rare. The local bats have formed their own subspecies after probably being isolated from their progenitors for tens of thousands of years. Even now, the reddish-brown Hawaiian bat lays on a reserve of body fat late in summer in preparation for a migration it no longer takes. Their principal breeding ground is on the island of Hawai'i but bats can be spotted on all the Islands. It is not known if they are resident there or move regularly between the islands.

Hawaiian Monk Seal

It may be their monk-like preference for solitude or the loose skin around their necks that resembles the hood of a monk's robe that gave these seals their name. Monk seals are sometimes referred to as "living fossils" because as the oldest living members of the pinniped order they have remained virtually unchanged for 15 million years.

There have been three known species of monk seals: Hawaiian, Caribbean and Mediterranean. Last sighted in 1952, Caribbean monk seals are thought to be extinct. Mediterranean monk seals survive in small numbers in isolated caves and beaches rarely visited by humans. The Hawaiian monk seal is considered an endangered species with its population currently estimated to be between 1,200 and 1,500 individuals.

Hawaiian monk seals breed in the remote Northwestern Hawaiian Islands, which stretch 1,200 miles northwest from Kaua'i. Occasionally, seals rest on beaches on the main islands, particularly on Kaua'i and O'ahu. A pair of monk seals was released on a remote beach of East Maui's north coast with the hope they can become established there. Their exact location is kept secret from the public.

Adults measure about seven feet in length and weigh between 400 and 600 pounds. Because Hawaiian monk seals have evolved free of terrestrial enemies, they did not develop the need or the instinct to flee from predators. Being easily approached by humans has proven to be one of the major factors leading to the population decline of the species. In the early 19th century, Hawaiian monk seals were taken by sealers for their oil and pelts. Within a few years, the population had been drastically culled to a point where hunting the seals commercially was no longer worthwhile.

Hawaiian monk seals are extremely sensitive to human activity. Mothers will abandon preferred pupping areas and even their pups when disturbed by human visitors. It is illegal in Hawai'i to approach the seals.

Pig

Without hesitation, conservation biologists would indict the feral pig as the most significant threat to native Hawaiian rain forest species today. Pigs uproot shrubs and rototill the soil with their snouts in search of grubs and worms. They sow the seeds of alien plants in their droppings. Those seeds grow into tangles of vines like the South American banana poka and small trees like the Brazilian strawberry guava, which form dense thickets that crowd out native trees. More than 100,000 pigs roam the Islands.

The pig that the Polynesians brought with them was much smaller than the tusked troublemakers roaming the forests now. When Captain Cook bartered with the Hawaiians for larder for his ships he complained that the largest of their pigs weighed only 50 to 60 pounds. After many generations, the Polynesian pigs have bred with imported domestic breeds and the resulting feral pig is large in size, resembling the European wild boar.

Mongoose

The mongoose in Hawai'i is a classic case of biocontrol gone wrong. The small, weasel-like flesh-eater was imported from India in the nineteenth century to rid sugarcane fields of rats. The nocturnal rat rarely encounters the diurnal predator, which feasts instead on nēnē and other ground-nesting birds and their eggs.

Humpback Whale

Warm Hawaiian waters provide the winter habitat for humpback whales migrating from Alaska and the Bering Sea. Fifth-largest of the great whales, humpbacks feed all summer in the plankton-rich northern waters to develop the layer of blubber they will need to sustain them through the winter. Humpbacks screen small schooling fish such as herring, mackerel, pollock and haddock, and crustaceans such as krill through balleen in their mouths. From their summer feeding grounds the whales migrate more than 3,500 miles to the warm tropical waters of Hawai'i to mate and give birth. They don't eat for the six months that they are migrating and living in Hawaiian waters. The favorite area in the Islands for their winter habitat is the shallow water between Maui, Moloka'i, Lāna'i and Kaho'olawe. Migrating humpback whales don't arrive at or depart Hawai'i en masse but begin filtering in each year around November and start heading back north around May. The North Pacific population of humpbacks is estimated at between 2,000 and 3,000 with approximately two-thirds of them migrating to Hawai'i and the rest traveling to Mexico.

On average, adults grow to 45 feet long and 45 tons in weight. They have long flippers, reaching one-third of body length. A newborn calf weighs in at 1.5 tons and can range in size from 10 to 16 feet. In five to nine years the humpback will reach sexual maturity and can expect to live for 30 to 40 years. Their gestation period is 10 to 12 months. Females calve every second or third year, although some have been known to calve every year for several successive years. Births usually occur between January and April. Mothers and calves are often accompanied by a third whale called an escort whale. The escort whale, assumed to be a sexually active male, only remains with the pair for less than a day.

Generally, humpback whales have dark blue or gray backs with white marking on their fins, sides and ventral surfaces. Individuals can be identified by the unique markings on

the underside of their tails, or flukes. Researchers catalog photographs of humpback whale flukes to study the movements and social interactions of individuals.

There is little evidence of when the humpbacks first began wintering in waters around the Hawaiian Islands. Narrative reports documenting their appearance go back to the 1840s. The whale doesn't seem to figure prominently in Hawaiian folklore. Whales appear in native Hawaiian chants but they have only one generic word for whale, koholā, which translates to mean hump dorsal. A whale carcass was called palaoa. The kohalā was kapu to common people. Ali'i valued the ivory teeth and bones. A palaoa that drifted ashore became the property of a chief. Native Hawaiians believed that a whale breaching and blowing foreshadowed a storm.

Lahaina was a major port for the Pacific whaling fleet during the early and mid-nineteenth century. Initially, whalers hunted the larger sperm, blue and white whales. Humpback whales were faster swimmers and had less whale oil than the other great whales— giving a smaller return for the greater effort it took to kill and process them. Whalers eventually depleted the other whale populations, subjecting the humpbacks to intense whaling in the first half of the 20th century. Between 1905 and 1965 whalers reduced the North Pacific humpback whale numbers from 15,000 to about 1,000. Since 1965, when commercial whale hunting was substantially curtailed globally, the humpback whale has slowly made a comeback, however it remains on the endangered epecies list.

Humpback whales are noted for their long and highly complex vocalizations, called songs. Singers are usually lone males or males escorting cow-calf pairs. A song generally lasts between six and eighteen minutes and may be repeated many times. Singing only occurs during the breeding/birthing season. As the season progresses, small changes in the song may occur. Humpbacks breeding off the coast of Mexico sing virtually the same songs as Hawai'i's humpbacks.

A humpback calf rests its head on its mother's back

ACTIVITIES

Biking

Coasting down the paved roads that snake across Haleakalā's slopes on a mountain bike is an exhilarating way to experience the volcano and the views that its high elevations offer. Imagine riding a bike for 38 miles from mountaintop to sea level and never having to pedal. Several bicycle tour companies make this unique Maui experience possible and easy. They drive a group of riders and specially equipped mountain bikes up Haleakalā in a van and let you coast back down to a pickup spot. Most companies have tours that take you to the summit crater to watch the sun rise before starting the downhill trek. Some tours ride in organized groups where everyone pulls over at the same time to rest while others are less structured and each rider sets his or her own pace. Riders need to be able to direct a bicycle down steep grades on a twisting road while negotiating traffic—this is no place for beginners to learn how to ride. Riders should wear closed shoes and clothing in layers that can be shed as the temperature warms on the descent. Tour companies will provide waterproof windbreakers, gloves and helmets. Reservations are required by all the bike tour companies. If you are planning a sunrise tour, a good idea is to take it on your first or second morning on the island when you are still on mainland time and will be waking up early anyway.

Aloha Bicycle Tours

Phone: (808) 249-0911
(800) 749-1564
Website: www.maui.net/~bikemaui

This family-run business begins their Volcano Bike Adventure Tour with a continental breakfast at Rice Park in Kula. Riders are transported to the entrance of Haleakalā National Park where you begin your descent. Throughout the tour, riders set their own pace and stop as often as they like. The road is smoothed by new bikes with front shocks and rear suspension seatposts. The final stop is the Tedeschi Winery, for lunch, a tour of the winery and a visit to the tasting room. Non-riders and young children may ride in the tour van. Rates are $89 per rider and $40 for non-riders. Aloha Bicycle Tours operates Monday to Friday and recommends making reservations one to three months in advance.

Chris' Adventures

Phone: (808) 871-2453

The Haleakalā Wine Trek is Chris' Adventures' most popular tour. Their tours from the summit crater to the Tedeschi Winery and beyond to the lava fields above La Pérouse Bay have morning and afternoon starts. Morning tours take six to eight hours, are 34 miles long and cost $77; afternoon tours cover 22 miles in four hours and cost $59. Breakfast and lunch are provided for the morning tour and afternoon tours include snacks. The "Wilder Side of Haleakalā" tour continues around to the south slope of the volcano for a total of 46 miles. It costs $99 with off-road options available. Tour group size is limited to eight riders.

Haleakalā Bike Co.
Phone: (808) 575-9575
(888) 922-2453
Website: www.bikemaui.com/t_tour.html

Tours from the Haleakalā Bike Company begin at its store at 810 Ha'ikū Rd., Ha'ikū. They let you ride down at your own pace and don't provide meals. Kids as young as eight can ride on smaller bikes and trailers for kids that don't cycle are available. The Sunrise Special Tour leaves their store two hours before sunrise, includes a van tour of the park and costs $69. The Summit Tour leaves at 9:00 a.m., includes a van tour and costs $59. You can save money on the Express Tour, which excludes a tour of the crater. It leaves at 9:00 a.m. and costs $49.

Maui Downhill
Phone: (808) 871-2155
(800) 535-2453

Maui Downhill offers five tours each day including sunrise-watching trips. They also feature hotel pickup with some tours. Reservations are taken 24 hours a day. Prices range from $60 to $115.

Maui Mountain Cruisers
Phone: (808) 871-6014
(800) 232-6284

Riders can keep warm with the Windstopper Gore jackets and Gore gloves that are provided. Their sunrise and midday tours offer hotel pickup. The sunrise tour has two meals, the latter being breakfast in Pā'ia. Rates are $120 for the sunrise tour and $110 for the midday tour. A ten-percent discount is offered to customers who book directly with Maui Mountain Cruisers.

Mountain Riders Bike Tours
Phone: (808) 242-9739, (800) 706-7700

Riders that want a sunrise tour can be picked up at their hotel by Mountain Riders at 2:00 a.m. The tour includes a continental breakfast at the summit and full breakfast in Makawao. Its cost is $115. You can get a little more sleep if you take the morning tour. Hotel pickup is at 7:00 a.m. and breakfast is provided before the trip up to the summit. The cost for this tour is $110.

Upcountry Cycles
Phone: (808) 573-2888

Tours meet at Upcountry Cycles store at 81 Makawao Ave., Pukalani. On the $45 morning-departure tour, a van takes you to the staging area at the park's boundary at the 6,500-foot elevation. Their sunrise tour takes the riders to the crater for viewing the sunrise and then back down to the staging area for the start of the bike ride. It costs $68. Riders can cycle to the Tedseschi Winery and then back to Pukalani or they can call for a pick-up at the winery for a $10 charge. No meals are provided on the tours.

Caving

Maui Cave Adventures
Phone: (808) 248-7308
Website: www.maui.net/~Hanacave

Hāna's Ka'elekū Caverns have been a secret to most visitors until tours conducted by Maui Cave Adventures opened them to anyone who wants to try spelunking. Prices are $25 for the beginner 50-minute hike, $50 for the two-hour tour, $100 for the four-hour tour and $175 for the six-hour tour, which is restricted to 18-year-olds and up. The two-hour tour of the cave follows the lava tube to a rain-forest skylight for snacks and photography. The lava cinders that line the cave floor to this point make for easy walking. On the longer tours, the trail becomes more difficult. You can look forward to climbing a rope ladder over a frozen lava fall and crawling through a couple of tight squeezes as you make your way through the 8,000-foot-long tube. All hikes are led by experienced guides educated in the geology of this area. Tours begin at 11:00 a.m and 1:30 p.m. at the cave entrance, in 'Ula'ino Road, the first left turn after Hāna Highway marker 31. Hikers must wear long pants and closed-toe shoes, be in good physical condition and weigh less than 230 pounds. Maui Cave Adventures supplies hardhats, gloves, flashlights and water. Reservations are required.

Diving

Maui was ranked the 11th most popular SCUBA diving destination in the world in the sixth annual Rodale's SCUBA Diving Magazine Reader Choice Awards for 1999. Maui was also ranked the ninth-best destination overall in the Pacific and Indian Oceans, fourth-best destination for visibility (water clarity), second-best destination for snorkeling, best destination for shore diving and best destination for beginner diving. Molokini crater was voted eighth most popular dive site in the world.

Visitors to Maui who want to go SCUBA diving usually choose a boat dive. There is a good variety of shore diving available but generally the visibility is better on boat dives. The best spots for shore diving in West Maui are Honolua Bay, Slaughterhouse Beach, Black Rock at Kā'anapali Beach and the area known as Thousand Peaks at Pāpalaua Beach. Along the south coast, shore diving is best at Mōkapu Beach, Palauea Beach, Mākena Landing and La Pérouse Bay. Look in the Beaches chapter for descriptions of diving conditions in these areas.

Several operators teach beginner SCUBA lessons and offer certification programs while some take only certified divers. Their destinations may vary according to weather and ocean conditions.

Ed Robinson's Diving Adventures

Phone: (808) 879-3584, (800) 635-1273
Website: mauiscuba.com/erd1.html
Charters for certified divers only. Ranked as the seventh-best dive operator in the Pacific and Indian Oceans by the readers of Rodale's *SCUBA Diving* magazine.

Extended Horizons Scuba

Phone: (808) 667-0611
Website: www.playmaui.com/exthorizons.html

Hawaiian Rafting

Phone: (808) 661-7333
Website: www.maui.net/~hra/homepage.html

Lahaina Divers

Phone: (808) 667-7496, (800) 998-3483

Charters for certified divers only. Readers of Rodale's *SCUBA Diving* magazine picked Lahaina Divers as the sixth-best dive operator in the Pacific and Indian oceans.

Mākena Coast Charters

Phone: (808) 874-1273, (800) 833-6483
Website: www.maui.net/~diving/frame.html

Maui Diamond Seasports

Phone: (808) 667-0633, (800) 959-7319
Website: www.mauidiving.com/maui-boat.html

Maui Dive Shop

Phone: (808) 879-3388, (800) 542-3483
Website: www.mauidiveshop.com

MOLOKINI

THREE MILES TO the west of the Mākena coastline 19 acres of solidified volcanic eruption protrude 80 feet above the 'Alalākeiki Channel. Molokini (meaning "many ties") is a tuff cone which formed when molten rock worked its way toward the surface and superheated water trapped within porous rock. Pressure built as the trapped water's temperature exceeded its boiling point. Suddenly, the burden of overlying rock exploded away as the water burst into steam. The explosion blasted outward at a low angle from the crater, hurling water, rock, ash and dust into the air. The mound of ash and dust settled in a wide ring, hardening into a buff-colored stone called volcanic tuff.

Molokini is designated a Marine Life Conservation District and a bird sanctuary. Every day, dozens of tour boats bring snorkelers and SCUBA divers to the calm waters inside its crescent. Marine life, being protected and fed, is bounteous. Divers will usually see reef sharks, trumpetfish, tangs, surgeonfish, parrotfish, Moorish idols, moray eels and manta rays. The backside of Molokini has the only wall dive in Maui. Molokini is a 20-minute boat ride from Mā'alaea Harbor and about 40 minutes from Lahaina.

Maui Diving Snorkel Shop

Phone: (808) 667-0633, (800) 959-7319
Website:
www.maui.net/~dive4me/scuba.dive.html

Maui Scuba Diving Center

Phone: (808) 667-0633, (800) 959-7319
Website: www.mauiactivities.net/forms/mall/
mauidiving.html

Maui Sun Divers

Phone: (808) 879-3337
Website: www.maui.net/~sundiver/home.html

Mike Severns Diving

Phone: (808) 879-6596
Website: www.severns.maui.hi.us/index.html

Charters for certified divers only. Dives are
guided by an experienced Hawai'i biologist
or naturalist.

Prodiver Maui

Phone: (808) 875-4004

Scuba Shack

Phone: (808) 891-0500, (877) 213-4488
Website: www.scubashack.com

Tropical Divers Maui

Phone: (808) 669-6284, (800) 994-6284
Website: www.mauiactivities.net/
tropicaldivers.html

Golf

Maui is a golfer's paradise.
Spectacular views surround
challenging holes at all of Maui's 16
resort, public and private golf courses.
Golf courses anchor four major resort
developments on Maui's west and
south coasts. Visitors may tee off at
America's most expensive private golf
club or enjoy the tropical sun on
reasonably priced public courses.

Kapalua Resort

West Maui's Kapalua resort has become a
Hawaiian golf mecca. Backdropped by the
green West Maui Mountains, the three courses
roll down to black lava ocean cliffs and
panoramic views of Moloka'i and Lāna'i.
Kapalua Resort's golf courses are certified by
Audubon International as Audubon Cooperative
Sanctuaries for their role in environmental
protection. Golf services include: video golf
instruction, daily clinics, private lessons, two
practice ranges, rental equipment and caddies.
Reservations may be made four days in
advance; 30 days in advance for resort guests.
Green fees include golf cart.

Phone: (808) 669-8044
Reservations: (877) 527-2584
Website:
www.kapaluamaui.com/kapaluagolf2.html

Kapalua Bay Course

Par: 72
Yardage: Championship 6,600, Regular
6,051, Front 5,124
Designers: Arnold Palmer and Francis Duane
Opened: 1975
Green Fees: Standard $160, Resort Guests
$100, Twilight $75
Course Record: 62, Mike Sullivan, 1995
Lincoln-Mercury Kapalua International

Kapalua Village Course

Par: 71
Yardage: Championship 6,632, Regular
6,001, Front 5,134
Designers: Arnold Palmer and Ed Seay
Opened: 1980
Green Fees: Standard $160, Resort Guest
$110, Twilight $75
Course Record: 64, Marty Keiter, 1995
Kapalua Clam Bake

Kapalua Plantation Course

Par: 73
Yardage: Championship 7,263,
Regular 6,547, Front 5,627

Designers: Bill Coore and Ben Crenshaw
Opened: 1991
Green Fees: High Season, 12/20–3/31:
   Standard $175, Resort Guest $110,
   Twilight $80. Low Season, 04/01-12/19:
   Standard $155, Resort Guest $110,
   Twilight $75
Course Record: 63, Steve Pate, 1997 Kapalua
   International

Kāʻanapali Resort

The two Kāʻanapali Resort courses stretch
out behind the row of beachfront, high-rise
resorts. The senior PGA tour concludes each
year at Kāʻanapali. Hawaiʻi's string of
hosting tournament championships began
here in 1962. The resort's North Course is
one of only two golf courses in Hawaiʻi
designed by the legendary Robert Trent
Jones, Sr. Golf services include: golf shop,
rental equipment, golf lessons, driving range,
putting greens and restaurant.
Green fees include golf cart.

Reservations: (808) 661-3691
Website: www.maui.net/~kgcgolf/index.html

Kāʻanapali North Course
Par: 71
Yardage: Championship 6,994, Regular
   6,136, Front 5,417
Designer: Robert Trent Jones, Sr.
Green Fees: Standard $130,
   Resort Guests $105, Twilight $65

Kāʻanapali South Course
Par: 71
Yardage: Championship 6,555, Regular
   6,067, Front 5,485
Green Fees: Standard $130,
   Resort Guests $105, Twilight $65

Wailea Resort

Maui's sunny south coast is the setting for three
golf courses at the Wailea Resort. The Blue
Course is Wailea's oldest and consistently ranks
among the top resort courses in the nation by
Golf Digest. Its fairways have 72 bunkers and
three lakes. The Gold Course has unusual
hazards—ancient Hawaiian lava rock walls.
Newest of Wailea's courses, the Emerald Course
was among Golf magazine's top ten new courses

in the U.S. in 1994. Wailea Golf Club has a 12-
acre training facility consisting of two putting
and chipping areas, fairway and greenside
practice bunkers and a driving range sporting
two sets of tee boxes and three built-in target
greens with pins and traps. Dress code requires
soft spikes on golf shoes. Green fees include golf
cart.

Phone: (808) 875-5111, (800) 332-1614
Reservations: (808) 874-7450, (888) 328-6284
Website:
   www.wailea-resort.com/pages/w_golf.html

Wailea Gold Course
Par: 72
Yardage: Gold 7,078, Blue 6,653,
   White 6,152
Designer: Robert Trent Jones, Jr.
Green Fees: Standard $120,
   Resort Guests $95

Wailea Emerald Course
Par: 72
Yardage: Emerald 6,825, Blue 6,407,
   White 5,873
Designer: Robert Trent Jones, Jr.
Green Fees: Standard $120,
   Resort Guests $95

Wailea Blue Course
Par: 72
Yardage: Blue 6,758, White 6,152, Red 5,291
Designer: Arthur Jack Snyder
Green Fees: Standard $110,
   Resort Guests $80

Mākena Resort

Mākena Resort's two golf courses
are south of Wailea under the broad slopes of
Haleakalā. The narrow fairways of the North
Course follow the mountainside, offering
extraordinary panoramas. The par-5, 620-yard
14th hole has a 300-foot elevation drop. On the
South Course, the wide open fairways stay
closer to the ocean, especially the 15th and 16h
holes where the ocean becomes a hazard.
Available are equipment rentals, driving range,
restaurant and showers. Green fees include golf cart.

Phone: (808) 879-3344

Mākena North Course

Par: 72
Yardage: Tournament 6,914, Championship 6,567, Resort 6,151, Forward 5,303
Designer: Robert Trent Jones, Jr.
Green Fees: Standard $120, Resort Guests $80, Twilight $70

Mākena South Course

Par: 72
Yardage: Tournament 7,017, Championship 6,629, Resort 6,168, Forward 5,529
Designer: Robert Trent Jones, Jr.
Green Fees: Standard $120, Resort Guest $80, Twilight $70

Grand Waikapu Resort Country Club

Due to unfavorable economic conditions, the Grand Waikapu closed in 1999. The golf course that boasted the highest green fees in the nation and a clubhouse designed by Frank Lloyd Wright will have to wait for the return of wealthy golfing visitors, particularly from Japan, before re-opening.

The Dunes at Maui Lani Golf Course

The Dunes at Maui Lani Golf Course opened in 1999 to accolades and praise from Maui golfers. Maui's newest golf course is located on the Kūihelani (Highway 38), one-half mile south of Kahului. The Dunes is unique among Hawai'i golf courses because the nature of the sand and the dune effect of the elevation changes enabled the firm of Nelson & Haworth to incorporate architectural concepts not seen before in Hawai'i. The result is an Irish linksland-type course that presents a true test of golf as it winds its way through a secluded kiawe forest. A golf cart is included in green fees and soft-spiked shoes are required.

Phone (808) 873-0422
Par: 72
Yardage: Black 6,841, Blue 6,413, White 5,833
Designer: Robin Nelson
Green Fees: $65, Twilight $35

Sandalwood Golf Course

This public course overlooks Wailuku and the Central Valley. The par-3 17th hole is played entirely over a water hazard. Available are: equipment rentals, driving range, showers and a restaurant. Green fees include golf cart.

Phone: (808) 242-4653
Par: 72
Yardage: Blue 6,469, White 6,011, Red 5,162
Designer: Nelson/Wright
Green Fees: $75 for nonresidents

Silversword Golf Club

Silversword is a public course next to the Pi'ilani Highway, above Kīhei. It has equipment rentals, driving range, night lights and a restaurant. Green fees include golf cart.

Phone: (808) 874-0777
Par: 71
Yardage: Gold 6,801, Blue 6,404, White 6,003, Red 5,265
Green Fees: $69, April–December 17 $57, Twilight $44

Pukalani Country Club

This public golf course is located in Maui's upcountry at 360 Pukalani St., Pukalani. Located at the 1,500-foot level, it is the highest golf course on Maui. It provides equipment rentals, driving range, night lights and a restaurant. Green fees include golf cart.

Phone: (808) 572-1314
Par: 72
Yardage: Championship 6,962, Men's 6,494, Women's 5,574
Green Fees: Jan. 1-Mar. 31 $55, Apr. 1-Dec. 31 $45, Twilight $42

Waiehu Golf Course

The municipal golf couse of Waiehu in Wailuku starts off on the coastline and finishes play coming back through the mountains. It is the only golf course on Maui where the use of carts is not mandatory. A driving range is available.

Phone: (808) 243-7400
Par: 72 Men's, 71 Women's
Yardage: Men's 6,330, Women's 5,511
Green Fees: Weekdays $25, Weekends $30, Golf Cart $15

Golf Club Rentals

**Paradise Maui
Golf Rentals**
Phone: 573-0560

Free delivery and pickup. Daily $18.95, Weekly $79.00, Biweekly $149.00

Golf Club Rentals
Phone: 665-0800

Free delivery. Daily $15.00

Helicopter Tours

The best way to take in Maui's legendary scenery in a short time is with a helicopter tour. If you can afford to spend $150 or more for a hour's flight and accept some of the limitations of helicopter flight, you'll be in for a thrilling time. Most helicopter tour companies have flights to West Maui, Haleakalā, Hāna, Moloka'i or combinations of these destinations. Flight times range from 30 minutes to more than an hour and a half. Flying for less than an hour will just whet your appetite and leave you wanting more. All tour operators are based at the heliport at Kahului airport. A sign at the airport's entrance will direct you to the heliport.

More than ninety percent of helicopter tour passengers on Hawai'i are taking their first ride on a helicopter. Window seats, of course, are the best vantage points on a helicopter, but you can't be guaranteed to sit in one unless you're the pilot. Ask the tour company representative, when you're booking, how they determine the seat designations. Some companies weigh passengers and assign the seats to even the weight distribution on board. People weighing more than 250 pounds are assigned two seats and charged 50 percent extra. Whether assigned a window or inside seat, expect cramped quarters. The trips are of short duration and the sights so splendid that you probably won't notice anyway.

Nearly everyone brings a camera on their helicopter tour. A zoom telephoto lens work best; changing lenses in the close quarters will be difficult. Use fast film to help counteract the vibration from the engines. Wearing dark clothing and using a circular polarizing filter will help eliminate glare and reflection on the inside of the windows. And finally, don't spend your whole trip looking through the camera's viewfinder—put the camera down once in a while and marvel at scenery below you.

A tour of West Maui is especially rewarding. Weather permitting, the pilot can take you into the lush valleys of the West Maui Mountains. Flying into 'Īao Valley, you'll see that the 'Īao Needle is really not a needle at all, but the end of a long, sharp ridge. Below the highest point in West Maui, Pu'u Kukui, is the Weeping Wall. After a rainfall, dozens of waterfalls sprout from the near-vertical vegetation-covered rock wall. Most passengers' jaws will drop as the pilot negotiates the narrow valleys with mountain precipices towering above them.

The view above East Maui's Haleakalā is more open and

panoramic. Flight restrictions are in place to preserve the tranquility of the people enjoying Haleakalā on its surface. Helicopters may not fly over the crater unless safety considerations deem it necessary. When flying along the park's southern boundary, through the Kīpahulu district, pilots must maintain an altitude of at least 500 feet above the ground. Although you can't fly directly over the crater, you get an opportunity to comprehend its immenseness while flying around it. Tall waterfalls abound on Haleakalā's southeast slopes. Your pilot should be willing to turn the helicopter about so everyone gets a good view.

Morning flights are most popular because there is usually less cloud cover. If you are coming to Maui during busy seasons it's best to book a flight before your arrival.

Many waterfalls can be spotted when touring by helicopter

Alex Air

Phone: (808) 871-0792, (888) 418-8455
Website: www.helitour.com/flights.html
Fleet: Four-passenger Hughes 500; six-passenger A-Star. Headsets for passengers that allow two-way communication with pilot.
Video: All tours include videotape of your flight except the West Maui and the Deluxe West Maui.
Tours: West Maui, 20 minutes, $69. Deluxe West Maui, 30 minutes, $105. East Maui Special, 45 minutes, $145. East Maui with ground stop and van tour of Hāna, 55 minutes air/80 minutes ground, $195. Mini Circle Island, 50–55 minutes, $165. Special Circle Island, 65 minutes, $195.

Blue Hawaiian Helicopters

Phone: (808) 871-8844, (800) 745-2583
Website: www.bluehawaiian.com
Fleet: 14 six-passenger A-Stars (four passengers in back row and two passengers in front) equipped with Bose electronic noise-canceling headsets for every passenger.
Video: All tours include videotape of your flight captured on their four-camera video system.
Tours: West Maui, 30 minutes, $105. Hāna/Haleakalā, 45 minutes, $150. Complete Island Special, 65 minutes, $200. Molokaʻi/West Maui, 65 minutes, $200. Sunset Spectacular, landing with refreshments, 95 minutes, $230. Sky Trek, lands in Hāna and joins van tour, 36 minutes, $219. Complete Island, lands on slope of Haleakalā for refreshments, 100 minutes, $240. Discount of 15 percent offered to customers who book seven days in advance on the Internet or by phone.

Hawaiʻi Helicopters

Phone: (800) 994-9099
Website: www.hawaii-helicopters.com
Fleet: Twin-engine Twinstars; 12-passenger, two-pilot, Sikorsky S-76+Universal lift equipment to assist physically challenged and elderly passengers with boarding. Bose electronic noise-canceling headset for every passenger.
Video: Five-camera video system captures your flight with pilot's commentary. Video sales are an extra-cost option.

Tours: Rainbow Special, East Maui, 40–45 minutes, $150. Valley Isle Deluxe, circle island, 55–60 minutes, $200. West Maui and Moloka'i, 55–60 minutes, $179. Heli-Trek, van tour to Hāna and return on helicopter, lunch, $220.

Discount of 15 percent offered to customers who book reservations seven days in advance on the Internet.

Sunshine Helicopters

Phone: (808) 871-0722, (800) 544-2520
Website: www.sunshinehelicopters.com
Fleet: Six-passenger A-Stars
Video: Four-camera video system. Pilot-narrated videotape of your flight sold for $19.95.
Tours: West Maui Deluxe, 30 minutes, $105. Hāna/Haleakalā Special, 45 minutes, $150. Circle Island Tour, 60–70 minutes, $195.

Discount of 15 percent offered to customers who book reservations seven days in advance on the Internet or by phone.

Horseback Riding

Private ranches and stables are located throughout Maui and welcome riders with every level of riding experience. Since most of the horseback tours take place on private property, this is an opportunity for many visitors to get to places that they would otherwise miss. All riding tour companies require reservations. During busy times, they fill up far in advance so book early. Bring your long pants and closed shoes but you can leave your chaps and spurs at home.

Adventures on Horseback

Phone: (808) 242-7445
Area: Ha'ikū Falls, above the Hāna Highway.
Tour: Waterfall Adventure Ride, 10:00 a.m. to 4:00 p.m. Involves riding, some hiking and the option of swimming under waterfalls in freshwater pools. Picnic lunch provided.
Price: $175
Restrictions: A maximum of six guest riders at a time. Riders must be 16 or older. Weight limit of 230 pounds.

Ironwood Ranch

Phone: (808) 669-4991
Area: Nāpili, West Maui
Tours: Four tours available which include pickup at a West Maui hotel or condo. Rides are through a pineapple plantation, lush valley and bamboo forest.
Price: $75–$135.
Restrictions: Maximum six riders per guide. Weight limit of 220 pounds. Minimum age eight years and over four feet tall.

Mākena Stables

Phone: (808) 879-0244
Area: 'Ulupalakua Ranch, overlooking La Pérouse Bay Tours: Introductory two-hour rides, three-hour morning or sunset rides and a once-a-week half-day ride for advanced riders.
Price: $90–$160
Restrictions: Maximum six riders per guide. Weight limit of 205 pounds. Children 12–14 years must have riding experience and be accompanied by an adult.

Maui Mule Ride

Phone: (808) 878-1743
Area: Haleakalā Crater
Tours: Three tours into Haleakalā Crater from the Visitor Center parking lot. From two to six hours.
Price: $90–$170
Restrictions: Minimum age of 10 years for the two-hour and five-hour rides and 16 years for the six-hour ride.

Mendes Ranch and Trail Rides

Phone: (808) 871-5222
Area: Kahakuloa, on West Maui's north shore.
Tours: Morning and afternoon rides along shoreline and to waterfalls of Waihe'e Valley. Trail ride/helicopter tour combo.
Price: $85–$130 for trail rides, $229 for trail ride/helicopter combo.

Restrictions: Six to ten riders. Weight limit of 250 pounds. Minimum age is 11 years.

'Ohe'o Stables

Phone: (808) 667-2222

Area: Twenty-five minutes past Hāna on Highway 31.

Tours: Four-hour ride (two and a half on horseback) into Kīpahulu Valley, with brunch. Five-hour ride (two and three-quarters on horseback) with brunch and lunch.

Price: $119–$139.

Restrictions: Six to ten riders. Children under twelve subject to approval of trail boss. Weight limit of 225 pounds.

Pony Express Tours

Phone: (808) 667-2200

Website: www.maui.net/~ponex

Area: Kula, in Upcountry.

Tours: One- and two-hour rides across Haleakalā Ranch. Half and full day rides into Haleakalā Crater.

Price: $40–$85 for ranch trail rides. $130–$160 for crater rides.

Restrictions: Limited to eight riders.

Seahorse Ranch

Phone: (808) 244-9862

Website: www.mauigateway.com/~seahorse/index.html

Area: Kahakuloa, on West Maui's north shore.

Tours: Three-and-a-half-hour ride in valleys and mountains of West Maui with lunch.

Price: $99.

Restrictions: Limited to eight riders.

Thompson Ranch

Phone: (808) 878-1910

Area: Kula, in Upcountry.

Tours: One-and-a-half-hour and two-hour trail rides through the ranch at the 3,700-foot level of Haleakalā.

Price: $50–$60

Restrictions: Limited to six riders per guide. Weight limit is 230 pounds. Children as young as five are allowed to ride by themselves.

Kayaking

If your balance is good enough to ride a bicycle then you probably can handle a kayak. Sea kayaking on the lee coast of Maui is invigorating and fun, especially during the whale season (December to May). Maui has many beaches and shoreline areas perfect for kayaking, but there are some areas that require special instructions or considerations. Guided kayaking tours will take you to the best spots and keep you out of trouble. Prices range from $55–$99 for guided tours of two and a half to five hours. Generally, kayaking conditions are best in the morning before the wind picks up. Coast Guard regulations require a floatation device for every person on the kayak. Bring a hat, sunglasses with a tie string, sunscreen and water. Tour operators will provide you with snorkeling gear.

Big Kahuna Kayaks

Phone: (808) 875-6395

Launch Site: Mākena Landing

Kelii's Kayak Tours

Phone: (808) 874-7652

Launch Sites: Mākena Landing, Honolua Bay, Olowalu

Mākena Kayak Tours

Phone: (808) 879-8426

Launch Site: Mākena Landing

Maui Sea Kayaking

Phone: (808) 752-6299

Website: www.maui.net/~kayaking

Launch Site: Mākena Landing

South Pacific Kayaks

Phone: (808) 875-4848, (800) 776-2326

Website: www.mauikayak.com

Launch Sites: Mākena, Lahaina

Kayakers launching from the Mākena coastline

Lū'aus

It was the custom in early Hawai'i to celebrate special occasions with a feast. Hawaiians shared their bounty to mark such auspicious occasions as the birth of a child, victory in war, a successful harvest or the completion of a new home or canoe. Originally called 'aha'aina (gathering for a meal), the term lū'au came into use much later and refers to the edible taro leaves that traditionally were used to wrap the food prior to being placed in the imu (underground oven). Today, lū'aus are a time to share traditional foods, enjoy songs and dances of early Hawai'i and other parts of Polynesia.

On the morning of the lū'au, a pit is dug and filled with kiawe branches and rocks. A fire is lit to heat the rocks and then a pig wrapped in banana and ti leaves is placed in the pit. The pit is covered with sand and the pig is left to steam all day. At sunset, the pig is unearthed and presented to the guests at the "imu ceremony." This main dish of the lū'au is called kalua pork and its slow-cooked meat is tender and succulent. The modern lū'au is set up as a buffet, which usually includes mahimahi, lomilomi salmon and poi served along with many traditional American and Asian dishes. Poi is a starchy staple made from taro root and lomilomi is salted salmon with onions and tomatoes. If laulau is available, it is worth trying. It is chicken or pork mixed with butterfish and dark green taro leaf, steamed together in a wrapper of ti leaf. An open bar keeps the party spirit alive.

After the meal, guests continue drinking while entertainers sing and perform hula dances under the stars. Reservations are needed for all of these lū'aus—plan on making them at least a week in advance. Seating begins between 5:00 and 5:30 p.m.

Aston Wailea Lū'au

Phone: (808) 879-1922
When: Monday, Tuesday, Thursday, Friday
Location: Aston Wailea Resort, Wailea
Price: $60 Adults, $27 Children 6-12 years

Grand Wailea Lū'au

Phone: (808) 875-1234, ext. 4900
When: Monday, Wednesday
Location: Grand Wailea Resort, Wailea
Price: Dinner Show $56 Adults, $29 Juniors;
   Cocktail Show $29 Adults, $19 Juniors

Hyatt Regency Maui Lū'au

Phone: (808) 667-4420
When: Daily
Location: Sunset Terrace, Hyatt Regency
   Maui, Kā'anapali
Price: $62 Adults, $39 Juniors 13–20 years,
   $25 Children 6–12 years

Marriott Lū'au

Phone: (808) 661-5828
When: Daily
Website: www.mauigateway.com/rw/luau
Location: Maui Marriott, Kā'anapali
Price: $60 Adults, $27 Children 5–12 years

Old Lahaina Lū'au

Phone: (808) 667-1998
When: Daily
Location: 1251 Front Street, Lahaina (behind the Lahaina Cannery Mall)
Price: $65 Adults, $35 Children under 12

The Old Lahaina Lū'au has earned the reputation of being the best lū'au on Maui. Talented and energetic performers, dressed in beautiful and authentic costumes, present the history of the settling of Hawai'i through chants, songs and dances. Their dancers perform the hula with respect and reverence.

Renaissance Wailea Lū'au

Phone: (808) 879-4900
When: Tuesday, Thursday, Saturday
Location: Renaissance Wailea Beach Resort, Wailea
Price: $58 Adults, $27 Children 5–12 years

Royal Lahaina Lū'au

Phone: (808) 661-3611
When: Daily
Location: Royal Lahaina Resort, Kā'anapali
Price: $62 Adults, $28 Children under 12

Parasailing

Parasailing is being pulled behind a powerful speedboat while you are attached to a parachute canopy. The line attaching you and the parachute to the boat can be as long as 900 feet. The exhilarating result is the strapped-in participant sailing high above the ocean. As with most exciting things, it's over too soon. A parasail flight lasts about ten minutes. Parasail season on Maui is May 16 to December 14—the flip side of whale season. Riding thrillcraft such as jet skis and parasailing are prohibited during the winter when humpback whales are in Maui's waters to calve and breed.

Parasail companies recommend making reservations at least a week in advance.

Lahaina Parasail

Phone: (808) 661-4887, (800) 227-7780
Website: www.maui.net/~letssail
Location: Departures from Māla wharf in Lahaina.
Rates: $31–$52

Parasail Kā'anapali

Phone: (808) 669-6555
Location: Departures from Māla wharf in Lahaina.
Rates: $36 and up

UFO Parasail

Phone: (808) 661-7836, (800) 359-4836
Location: Departures from beach in front of Whaler's Village in Kā'anapali.
Rates: $37–$52

West Maui Parasail

Phone: (808) 661-4060
Location: Departures from Slip #15, Lahaina Harbor.
Rates: $31–$50

Parasailing is a popular summer activity in West Maui

THE HULA

Hula is performed by both women and men

ORIGINALLY THE HULA was a religious dance performed before a king by trained male dancers. At the time there was no written word in Hawai'i and the hula preserved the oral history of the Islands by telling a story through its movements.

According to legend, the hula was given to the people of Hawai'i by Hi'iaka, the sister of the volcano goddess Pele. The privileged olapa (dancers) had to undergo disciplined schooling in the halau (hall of learning dedicated to the hula). Only after intense training were the dancers allowed to perform in public. The dancer's costumes and accessories were made of special flowers and plants gathered from the mountains.

Like other aspects of Hawaiian life, the hula was altered by foreigners coming to Hawai'i in the early 1800s. The New England missionaries found the hula's free movements and expression conflicted with their puritanical morals. They insisted that the female dancers replace their hula skirts with long dresses. Later the Portuguese brought with them a small guitar from which the 'ukulele was developed. The strumming of the four-stringed instrument has been associated with the swaying dance ever since.

Under the reign of King David Kalākaua, the hula became a symbol and expression of Hawaiian identity. The "Merrie Monarch" wrote songs for the hula and changed its perception from a sacred to a popular dance.

In the first half of the twentieth century, the hula turned into entertainment for the tourists. Wearing plastic leis and dancing to amplified music, hula girls performed a light-hearted display. In the 1960s a resurging interest in Hawaiian culture brought regained reverence to the hula. Halaus are busy training new dancers and competitions have become hugely popular.

Today, hula is categorized as ancient or modern. The ancient hulas performed at competitions are accompanied by chants and percussion instruments. Modern hula, which you see performed at lū'aus, incorporates many styles and is often danced to popular melodies.

Whether colorfully modern or dramatically ancient, the beauty, grace and strength of the hula continues to educate and entertain us. The gift given to Hawaiians by a god is their gift to the rest of the world.

Shooting

Sporting clays is a shooting game that simulates small-game hunting. Clay targets are used to mimic flights of different game birds. There's even a clay target that hops across the ground like a rabbit. No experience is necessary and the guns, ammunition and targets are provided. Each customer is fitted with eye and hearing protection.

Papaka Sporting Clays
Phone: (808) 879-5649
Location: 'Ulupalakua Ranch, 25 minutes south of Wailea. Pickup at Maui Prince Hotel.
Rates: $65 for 50 targets, $95 for 75 targets, $120 for 100 targets.

West Side Sporting Clays
Phone: (808) 669-7468
Location: Three and a third miles northeast of Kapalua, just past Honolua Bay on the mauka side.
Rates: $75 for 48 pistol shots, $95 for 75 shots with shotgun and/or pistol.

Submarines and Semisubmersible Boats

Not long ago, touring the exotic world beneath the ocean was limited to SCUBA divers and snorkelers. But now anyone can take a comfortable excursion into Maui's underwater wonderland and never get wet. The Atlantis IV, which runs tours from Lahaina, is one of a fleet of 12 Atlantis passenger subs diving in seven locations around the world. Passengers are shuttled from Lahaina Harbor to the battery-powered submarine tethered in 'Au'au Channel. At the dive site, 48 passengers are taken down over 100 feet to observe the coral reef and its undersea inhabitants during a 45-minute dive.

Semisubmersibles are surface vessels with an underwater viewing cabin. As if riding a half-submerged tour bus, everyone has access to a large window below the surface of the water. When the boat reaches the dive site, professional divers leap overboard and go to work. Immediately, schools of fish appear, looking for the handouts of pellet fish food doled out by the divers.

Atlantis Submarines
Phone: (808) 667-6604, (800) 548-6262
Departs: Lahaina Harbor, Slip #18
Website: www.goatlantis.com
Boat: 65-foot, 80-ton U.S. Coast Guard-approved submarine with thirteen viewports on each side and large front viewport
Price: $69-$79 Adults, $39 Children

Reef Dancer Semi-Submersible
Phone: (808) 667-2133, (888) 667-2133
Departs: Lahaina Harbor, Slip #10
Website: www.galaxymall.com/stores/reefdancer
Boat: 34 passenger, nautilus class semi-submersible with 38 viewing windows
Price: $33-$45 Adults, $19-$25 Children 6-12 years

Sea View Adventure Semi-Submersible
Phone: (808) 661-5550
Departs: Lahaina Harbor
Boat: 64-passenger, 56-foot semi-submersible with catamaran hull design and 22 viewing windows
Price: $44 Adults, $25 Children 5-12 years

Surfing

What is more Hawaiian than surfing? Hawaiians invented the sport and if you think you would like to try it there are two surfing schools on Maui that will teach you how. In fact, they promise to have you surfing in one lesson. Lessons are taught on small, gentle surf with soft surfboards. Rates start at $65 for a two-hour group lesson. Lessons are taught in the surf in front of Lahaina.

Andrea Thomas'
Maui Surfing School
Phone: (808) 875-0625

Nancy Emerson
School of Surfing
Phone: (808) 244-7873
Website: www.maui.net/~ncesurf/ncesurf.html

Walking Tours

Lahaina Ghostly Tales and
Historical Walk
Phone: (808) 662-0871

This walking tour takes you behind the souvenir shops and restaurants of Lahaina to a walk on the dark side, a side of ghosts and legend, of violent endings and supernatural phenomena. Lahaina's rich history from whaling and missionary times combined with a strong Native Hawaiian spirituality and a wealth of Hawaiian myths and legends lends itself perfectly to such a tour. The one-and-a-half-mile guided stroll includes stops at the home of the Rev. Dwight Baldwin, the Brig *Carthaginian*, Hale Aloha Cemetery and Moku'ula, the sacred sanctuary of King Kamehameha III. Tour participants are given a lei made from ti leaves, which according to

Hawaiian legend, helps ward off evil spirits. The tour is held nightly and costs $13 for adults and $6.50 for children. Reservations are required.

Whale Watching

Whale-watching season runs from December to May. Between 1,400 and 2,000 humpback whales migrate each year from the Bering Sea to the waters of Hawai'i to calve and breed. The shallow water in the channels between Maui and the neighboring islands of Moloka'i, Lāna'i and Kaho'olawe is the best place in the Hawaiian Islands for whale watching. Two-thirds of the 370,000 people who go whale watching in Hawai'i depart from Maui.

Each winter, dozens of boats take Maui's human visitors out to sea to watch its whale visitors. Everything from kayaks and inflatables to 100-foot ships are pressed into service. The inflatable rafts are fast and exciting while the large boats are stable and offer higher vantage points. Mornings, when the ocean is calmer, are usually best for whale watching. Binoculars will be helpful if you bring them. Cameras must have a telephoto lens or else the whale will appear as no more than a dark speck in the ocean.

Whales are great performers, one reason whale watching is popular on Maui. Whether on a whale-watching boat or from the shore there are a variety of behaviors you can watch for. A blow is when a whale forcefully exhales at the surface. Humpbacks often slap their pectoral fins or their tails against the surface of the water.

SURFING IN HAWAI'I

FOR CENTURIES HAWAIIANS have enjoyed the exhilaration of surfing, which was originally known as he'e nalu, or wave sliding. Big Island petroglyphs carved by early Polynesians depict board-riding figures, and Hawaiian chants from the fifteenth century narrate tales of surfing contests. Wintertime, the season of storms, was their favorite time to surf. Spectators would gather and wager pigs, dogs and fishing nets on their favorite wave rider.

Ali'i, or chiefs, had their own surfing waters that were kapu to common Hawaiians. Commoners still enjoyed surfing, with both men and women showing off their skills on long, heavy planks of native wood. Even Maui's Queen Ka'ahumanu loved to surf Lahaina's waters. However it was her conversion to Christianity that forebode the decline of surfing. Seen by missionaries as an immoral distraction that brought scantily-clad men and women together, surfing had nearly faded away by the beginning of the 20th century.

Legendary Duke Kahanamoku, Olympic swimmer and acknowledged father of modern surfing, brought surfing back to prominence in Hawai'i. On his 114-pound koa-wood board he rode the surf breaking onto Waikīkī Beach, attracting attention as he performed handstands, surfed with a dog sitting on the front of his board or took women along to ride tandem. Contemporary surfing started on Maui in the 1930s and in 1936 a small group of surfers formed the Ho'okipa Surfriding Club. Soon, surfing competitions were featured as part of Kamehameha Day celebrations.

The era of modern surfing began when new lightweight boards became available around 1959. Designs now have evolved greatly from the days of Kahanamoku's heavy wood board. Surfboard makers, called shapers, produce lightweight boards 8 to 12 feet long, filled with polyurethane foam and a thin strip of wood sandwiched in the center. Skegs (fins) are fitted to the bottom and the boards are laminated with

fiberglass cloth and resin. The surface is sanded and polished to a high gloss and finally a colorful logo is painted on.

In the 1970s a modern Hawaiian legend was being created by the exploits of surfer and lifeguard Eddie Aikau. In addition to saving countless lives, the quiet Hawaiian rose to prominence with his competition victories, including the Duke Kahanamoku Classic on Oʻahu's Sunset Beach in 1977. In March 1978 Eddie Aikau was a crew member on the *Hōkūleʻa*, a re-creation of a double-hulled Polynesian voyaging canoe. The *Hōkūleʻa* was navigated in the ancient way, without instruments, on a trip from Hawaiʻi to Tahiti. Just five hours out of Honolulu the canoe met strong trade winds and high seas. Heavily laden with food and supplies, the swamped craft capsized. The sixteen crew members spent the night clinging to the hulls of the stricken vessel, buffeted by the wind and waves. Commuter aircraft flew overhead but no one saw the *Hōkūleʻa*. With ocean currents pulling the vessel out to sea Eddie decided to go for help by paddling his surfboard to Lānaʻi, about 12 miles distant. A fellow crew member wanted to go too but Eddie would go alone. The rest of the crew members were rescued the next night but Eddie's body was never found. Honoring the hero, many surfers in Hawaiʻi sport bumper stickers on their cars that read, "Eddie Would Go."

Winter storms in the North Pacific create the swells that break into waves up to 20 feet high or more on Maui's north shore. Traditionally, Hoʻokipa Beach is home to Maui's best surfing and best surfers. Depending on where the "surf's up," other good spots on Maui for surfing are Lahaina, Launiupoko Park and an area off Pāpalaua Beach called "Thousand Peaks." Recently recognized as a spot for awesome waves and extreme surfing is an offshore area east of Māliko Bay dubbed Jaws. A few brave and talented surfers have challenged its 50-foot waves rolling toward the shore at 25 miles per hour. When conditions are right, about 12 times a year, large north swells break on a massive underwater ridge, the remnant of an old lava flow that juts straight out into the sea. On either side of the ridge are channels of deep water that cause the waves to reflect inward, focusing much of their energy on the center of the wave crest. Surfers tow each other into the big waves with Wave Runners. After releasing the tow rope the Wave Runner heads for the calmer water of the deep channel. When the surfer finishes a 30-second ride of his life, he is rescued by the Wave Runner before the next wave crashes in with deadly force.

Inquisitive whales may also raise their heads above the water, maintaining an elevation just above their eye level, sometimes called spy-hopping. The most exciting behavior is the breach. That is when the whale propels itself out of the water, exposing two-thirds of its body or more. Federal law prohibits vessels from approaching within 100 yards of a humpback whale. For more information about humpback whales, see the Flora and Fauna chapter.

Almost all the whale-watching cruises are two hours in duration. When making reservations check that the boat is equipped with hydrophones for listening to the whales' "songs" and that they offer a guaranteed whale sighting. A whale sighting, for purposes of their guarantee, does not mean a close encounter, or that everyone on the boat will see a whale. If no whale is spotted during the tour, passengers should get free tickets for another time. Prices for the two-hour cruises range from $29 to $39.

America II Sailing Charters
Phone: (808) 667-2195
Departs: Lahaina Harbor
Boat: 28-passenger, 65-foot sailboat

Blue Water Rafting
Phone: (808) 879-7333
Departs: Kīhei Boat Ramp
Boat: 24-passenger, 27-foot rigid-hulled inflatable

Friendly Charter
Phone: (808) 871-0985
Departs: Māʻalaea Harbor
Boat: 36-passenger, 44-foot powerboat

Frogman Charters
Phone: (808) 669-6700
Departs: Māʻalaea Harbor
Boats: 40-passenger, 44-foot powerboat; 59-passenger, 55-foot powerboat

Hawaiian Rafting Adventure
Phone: (808) 661-7333
Departs: Māla Wharf, Lahaina
Boat: Two 22-passenger, 28-foot rigid-hulled inflatables

Kaulana
Phone: (808) 871-0626
Departs: Lahaina Harbor, Slip #4
Boats: 143-passenger, 65-foot power catamaran, 109-passenger, 62-foot power catamaran

Lahaina Princess and Maui Princess
Phone: (808) 661-8937
Departs: Lahaina Harbor, Slip #3
Boats: Lahaina Princess 120-passenger, 65-foot powerboat; Maui Princess 149-passenger, 118-foot powerboat

Leilani
Phone: (808) 875-0955
Departs: Māʻalaea Harbor, Slip #70
Boat: 35-passenger, 50-foot motor yacht

Maka Kai
Phone: (808) 879-4485
Departs: Māʻalaea Harbor
Boat: 100-passenger, 65-foot powerboat

Maui Classic Charters
Phone: (808) 879-8188, (800) 736-5740
Departs: Māʻalaea Harbor
Boats: *Lavengro*, 30-passenger, 60-foot schooner; *Four Winds*, 112-passenger, 53-foot, glass-bottomed, sailing catamaran

Navatek II
Phone: (808) 873-3475
Departs: Māʻalaea Harbor
Boat: 149-passenger, 83-foot SWATH (Small Waterplane Area Twin Hull)

Ocean Riders

Phone: (808) 661-3586
Departs: Māla Wharf, Lahaina
Boat: 20-passenger, 28-foot rigid-hulled
 inflatable

Pacific Whale Foundation

Phone: (808) 879-8811
Boats: *Manute'a*, 49-passenger, 50-foot
 sailing catamaran.
Departs: Lahaina Harbor, Slip 11

Whale II, 26-passenger, 50-foot sailing yacht.
Departs: Lahaina Harbor, Slip 11

Pacific Whale, 34-passenger, 41-foot
 powerboat
Departs: Māʻalaea Harbor, Slip 76

Ocean Spirit, 125-passenger, 65-foot double-
 deck power catamaran.
Departs: Māʻalaea Harbor, Slip 52

Paragon Sailing Charters

Phone: (808) 244-2087, (800) 441-2087
Departs: Māʻalaea Harbor
Boat: 40-passenger, 47-foot powerboat

Pride of Maui

Phone: (808) 875-0955
Departs: Māʻalaea Harbor
Boat: 110-passenger, 65-foot powerboat

Ultimate Rafting Adventures

Phone: (808) 875-5678
Departs: Lahaina Harbor
Boat: 18-passenger, 30-foot rigid-hulled
 inflatable

Waikea Kai

Phone: (808) 879-4485
Departs: Māʻalaea Harbor
Boat: 75-passenger, 65-foot powerboat

Windjammer Cruises

Phone: (808) 661-8600
Departs: Lahaina Harbor, Slip #1
Boat: 93-passenger, 70-foot schooner

A humpback whale shows the white underside of its pectoral fin before splashing with it

DINING

Cuisine unique to Maui has come to mean more than poi and pineapple. In the early '90s, some of Hawai'i's top chefs started to incorporate the Islands' extensive selection of fresh produce into their dishes, blending classic Asian and Western culinary techniques and starting the trend some call "Hawai'i Regional Cuisine." Using the bounty of fish from the sea, locally raised beef and intensely flavored tropical fruits, these resourceful chefs have created dishes such as: 'ahi carpaccio, breadfruit soufflé and papaya cheesecake.

With visitors coming to Maui from all over the world, but particularly from the Pacific Rim nations, restaurants cater to varied culinary tastes with cosmopolitan fare. For an economical taste of local-style cooking, try a plate lunch in the less-touristy areas, Kahului and Wailuku. With plain white rice and cabbage you'll get a choice of curry stew, teriyaki beef or kalua (roasted) pig, a beverage and change back from a ten-dollar bill.

Casual wear is acceptable at nearly all restaurants on Maui. Expensive restaurants may ask for "aloha wear" which means a shirt with a collar and long pants for men and a dress for women. Price categories are symbolized with $ signs and are the average cost for one diner without alcoholic drinks, tax or tips. Reservations are not required unless noted below. Except for fast-food outlets, major credit cards are accepted at all restaurants.

$	Less than $15
$$	$15 to $25
$$$	$25 to $40
$$$$	Over $40

West Maui Restaurants

Aloha Cantina
839 Front Street, Lahaina, 661-8788, Mexican, **$$**

Open to the sea on one side and the hustle of Front Street on the other, this fun eatery features authentic Mexican cuisine, enthusiastic service and upbeat entertainment. Breakfast specialties include huevos rancheros and macadamia-nut pancakes. For lunch try fish tacos, chicken Caesar tacos or a chicken Baja sandwich. Watch the sun go down from your dinner table on either of the two dining decks. Dinner specials include ceviche, Lahaina fajitas and chile relleno cheese enchiladas. There's often a line for dinner. Patrons can wait in Hurricane McShane's Coconut Bar—so called because the bar was hand-constructed from rare coconut wood and every hour a hurricane, produced with Paramount Studio sound effects, roars through the establishment rocking the swaying hula girls on the walls.

Basil Tomatoes

Royal Lahaina Resort, Kāʻanapali, 662-3210, Italian, $$

Basil Tomatoes is new to the restaurant scene in Kāʻanapali. Their large menu offers authentic Italian cuisine, traditional favorites, pizza and daily specials. Happy Hour is featured twice a day: from 5:30 to 6:30 and again from 9:30 to midnight. Reservations are suggested.

BJ's Chicago Pizzeria

730 Front Street, Lahaina, 661-0700, Italian, $

BJ's has won "Best Pizza" awards from the *LA Times*, *Bon Appetit* and the *Orange County Register*. Appetizers, salads and sandwiches, and tropical drinks round out their menu. Their second-floor location, on Front Street across from the seawall, offers great views for sunset dining. Old plantation decor and historic photos complement live Hawaiian music on their "Ocean Front Stage."

Cheeseburger in Paradise

811 Front Street, Lahaina, 661-4855, Burgers, $

This wildly popular burger joint has two floors of spectacular harbor and ocean views. Live music and the party atmosphere spill out onto Front Street. Their namesake cheesburger is juicy and pretty basic—a large patty with Thousand Island dressing, tomatoes, lettuce, a blend of Jack and Cheddar cheese on a whole-wheat bun with a slice of fresh pineapple on the side. Variations on the theme include chicken, tofu and garden burgers. Expect a line to get in at lunch or dinner. A gift shop with lots of "Cheeseburger in Paradise" logo wear has been thoughtfully placed next to the line.

Chez Paul

Olowalu, 661-3843, French, $$$

This intimate French restaurant with only 14 tables is in a small roadside building four miles south of Lahaina. Chez Paul has enjoyed an envied reputation for many years based on its excellent food and service. The menu, which changes daily, includes veal, fish, duck and beef prepared in rich French sauces. They have two dinner seatings, at 6:30 and 8:30. Reservations are essential.

David Paul's Lahaina Grill

127 Lahainaluna Road, 667-5117, Southwestern, $$$

This trendy restaurant is located in the beautifully restored Lahaina Inn. It was voted "Best Maui Restaurant" by *Honolulu* magazine and was awarded three stars by *Condé Nast Traveler* and by *Food & Wine* magazine. David Paul writes the menu each day after he has gathered the fresh ingredients—a concept he calls "New American Cuisine." There's live entertainment and a late-night bistro menu. Reservations are recommended.

Fish & Game Brewing Company

Kahana Gateway Shopping Center, 669-3474, Microbrewery, $$

Tucked away in a corner of the Kahana Gateway, Fish & Game is a microbrewery, restaurant, oyster bar, cigar bar and fishmarket in one establishment. The brewmaster has eight beers on tap, including a Pilsner brewed with Saaz hops from the Czech Republic and Olde Nut Brown Ale— brewed with eight varieties of barley. The lunch menu includes Caesar Salad with Cajun chicken breast, a "George Foreman" cheeseburger and an Oyster Po' Boy sandwich. Dinner selections feature steaks cooked on a wood-fired kiawe grill and chicken, duckling or pork loin slow-cooked on a wood-fired, stone-hearth rotisserie. Television screens in the bar are tuned to sports events and you can buy fresh fish to take with you. Reservations are accepted for dinner.

The Garden Restaurant

Kapalua Bay Hotel, 669-4650, Asian, $$$$

You can enjoy great views and gourmet food in an extravagant setting in the Kapalua Bay

Hotel. Sunday through Thursday nights, the menu is Mediterranean cuisine with Pacific Rim influence. On Fridays a seafood buffet is presented. An Asian buffet is laid out on Saturday nights. Reservations are recommended.

Gerard's
174 Lahainaluna Road, Lahaina, 661-8939, French, $$$

Gerard's is an elegant restaurant located in the turn-of-the-century atmosphere of the Plantation Inn. French-born chef Gerard Reversade has been cooking since he was ten years old. He began an apprenticeship when he was fourteen and worked under four of France's Master Chefs. The menu is traditional French cuisine: duck confit, quails stuffed with basmati rice, lamb rack grilled with persillade crust. A sommelier is on hand to assist patrons in selecting from the extensive wine list. Reservations are recommended.

Hard Rock Cafe
900 Front Street, Lahaina 667-7400, American, $

Like all the other Hard Rocks—but with a local flair. A 1959 Cadillac woody wagon with surfboards stuffed in the back hangs suspended above the bar. Their food is good and the surfboard T-shirts are one of the worldwide chain's best. Try to get there before 12:00 to beat the lunchtime lines.

Hecocks Italian Restaurant
505 Front Street, Lahaina, 661-8810, Italian, $$

Yet another Lahaina restaurant with a great view. Hecocks is at the south end of Front Street in a small shopping center. Open for breakfast, lunch and dinner. Reservations are recommended.

House of Saimin
888 Front Street, Lahaina, 667-7572, Saimin, $

Find the House of Saimin in the Lahaina Shopping Center. It's probably the only place in West Maui where you can eat at 2:00 a.m. You can get big bowls of saimin, hamburgers and hot dogs.

Hula Grill
Whalers Village, Kā'anapali, 661-3894, Pacific Rim, $$

Great location in the heart of Kā'anapali with both indoor and outdoor tables. The restaurant, which looks like a replica of an old Hawaiian beach house, overlooks the beach, with Moloka'i in the distance. They serve lots of salads and sandwiches, dim sum and pupus.

Jameson's Grill & Bar
200 Kapalua Drive, Kapalua, 669-5653, Continental, $$$

Jameson's is the country club restaurant at the Kapalua golf resort. Features include stuffed shrimp, prawns and chicken, herb roasted chicken, prime rib and baked artichoke. Reservations are recommended.

Kapalua Bay Club
Kapalua Bay Hotel, 669-8008, French, $$$$

Since 1977, this beautiful, award-winning restaurant has sat on a lava-rock promontory above Kapalua Bay. The open-air room, which has richly paneled walls and rattan furniture, is the perfect place for a special candlelit dinner. A piano player performs nightly. Reservations are recommended.

Kimo's Restaurant
845 Front Street, Lahaina, 661-4811, Steak & Seafood, $$

Kimo's is very well-established in the Maui restaurant scene. They dish up everything from cheeseburgers and prime rib to fresh fish. From the outdoor dining room and lounge you get a great view of Lahaina harbor. Their special dessert is hula pie—chocolate mousse encased in a crust of crumbled Oreo cookies.
Reservations are recommended.

Lahaina Coolers

180 Dickenson Street, Lahaina,
661-7082, American, **$$**

Lahaina Coolers serves a lot of unusual
dishes, from chicken azteca pasta to fish
tacos to artichoke heart pizza. They're open
for breakfast, lunch and dinner. Pupus are
served from 7:00 p.m. to midnight. Happy
hour is 3:00 to 6:00 and again 10:00 p.m. to
midnight.

Lahaina Provision Company

Hyatt Regency Maui, Kā'anapali, 661-5679,
Continental, **$$$**

The Lahaina Provision Company is an open-
air dining room overlooking the magnificent
pools of the Hyatt Regency and the Pacific
Ocean. For lunch you can choose among
sandwiches, soups and a seafood salad bar.
At dinner, the menu has a selection of grilled
steaks, fresh seafood and chicken specialties.
A decadent Chocoholic Bar is served nightly
and may be indulged a la carte or with
dinner. Reservations are recommended.

Local Boy's Drive In

Lahaina Square Shopping Center,
Plate lunch, **$**

This is a good place to get plate lunches
served in generous portions. Their breakfast
menu includes spam omelette.

Longhi's

888 Front Street, Lahaina,
667-2288, Italian, **$$$**

Longhi's has been Maui's most successful
and popular restaurant since it opened in
1976. It's a two-story, open-air establishment
with black and white tile floors and casual
wooden tables. The restaurant receives a lot
of notoriety because the waiters and
waitresses pull up a chair and recite that
day's menu to the patrons. Longhi's sets a
high standard for choosing the freshest
available ingredients. They fly in ricotta and
mozzarella cheeses from New York and
import gorgonzola, provolone, parmesan, and
feta cheeses and Italian cold cuts. All the
pasta they serve is made in their own pasta
kitchen and they have their own pastry chef.
At night there's dancing on the second floor
and complimentary valet parking.
Reservations are recommended.

Makai Bar

Marriott Hotel, Kā'anapali, 667-1200, **$$**

Great sunset views, a live band, dancing and
huge pupu menu for nibbling late into the
night.

Maui Brews Lahaina Center

667-7794, Microbrewery, **$$**

Maui Brews is as popular for its
entertainment as it is for its 16 beers on tap.
Burgers fill out the lunch menu. Pizzas, pasta
and roast chicken complement the beer for
dinner. Live music and dancing are featured
nightly.

Moose McGillycuddy's

844 Front Street, Lahaina, 667-7758, **$$**

Open for breakfast, lunch and dinner, you can
choose between the air-conditioned dining
room or the lanai overlooking Front Street.
Mondays and Thursdays are all-you-can-eat
Alaskan King Crab nights and on Sundays
it's all the BBQ beef ribs you can eat.
Macadamia nuts are used liberally to flavor
fish and chicken dishes. They have happy
hour and early bird specials, a cigar bar, live
bands and dancing until 2:00 a.m.

Pacific'O

505 Front Street, Lahaina,
667-4341, Pacific Rim, **$$$**

This oceanside restaurant offers
contemporary Pacific cuisine for lunch,
dinner and late pupus. Pacific'O has won first
prize in the Taste of Lahaina's seafood
category repeatedly. A few selections from
their dinner menu include: banana "imu
style" fish, bamboo-steamed lobster and
roasted Maui onion and Puna goat-cheese
salad.

Pizza People
Lahaina Center, 667-7700,
Nāpili Plaza, 669-7788, **$**

Pizza People offers toppings not found at the average pizza joint such as clams and garlic. You can choose between tomato or pesto sauce and white or whole-wheat crust with optional sesame seeds. Add a salad and breadsticks, or try their volcano wings—active or dormant. They can deliver to any hotel room or condominium in West Maui.

Plantation House Restaurant
2000 Plantation Club Drive, Kapalua,
669-6299, Continental, **$$$**

Perched on the hills above Kapalua and surrounded by the Plantation Golf Course, this restaurant offers a blend of the best of the "warm climate" cuisines of Hawai'i, the Mediterranean, the Caribbean, and the Asia-Pacific Islands. Open for breakfast, lunch and dinner. Dinner reservations are recommended.

Roy's Kahana Bar & Grill
4405 Honoapi'ilani Highway, Kahana,
669-6999, Pacific Rim, **$$$**

This is the older of the two restaurants owned by one of Hawai'i's most celebrated chefs, Roy Yamaguchi. He is often featured on the PBS series *Hawai'i Cooks*. His network of restaurants spans the Pacific from Asia to California. Roy's Kahana puts a spicy Asia-Pacific spin on fish, meats and pasta. Reservations are recommended.

Roy's Nicolina Restaurant
4405 Honoapi'ilani Highway, Kahana,
669-5000, Southwestern, **$$$**

Roy's Nicolina (named after Roy Yamaguchi's daughter, Nicole) is right next door to Roy's Kahana Bar & Grill in the

Kahana Gateway Shopping Center. Both restaurants share an identical fixed menu, each featuring its own specials. The specials in Roy's Nicolina are Southwestern dishes like grilled chicken with Anaheim chili hash and grilled coriander pork loin with gingered potatoes and sweet spiced currant sauce. Reservations are recommended.

Sansei
115 Bay Drive, Kapalua,
669-6286, Japanese, **$$**

Although serving traditional Japanese fare like tempura, soba noodles and sauteed shitake mushrooms, Sansei is best known for its excellent sushi bar. Open 5:30 p.m. to 2:00 a.m. Located at the Kapalua Shops shopping center.

Sunrise Cafe
Front Street and Market, Lahaina,
661-8558, Hawaiian, **$**

This small cafe with an outdoor courtyard can be found hiding behind Lapperts Ice Cream on Front Street. They'll serve up tasty Hawaiian dishes like kalua pork and mango BBQ chicken in just five minutes. Open 6:00 a.m. to 6:00 p.m.

Swan Court
Hyatt Regency Maui, Kā'anapali, 661-1234,
Continental, **$$$$**

Lifestyles of the Rich and Famous named the Swan Court among the "Top Ten Most Romantic Restaurants in the World." Swans glide by a cascading waterfall as continental cuisine like steamed Maine lobster or Hunan marinated rack of lamb are served. Breakfast buffets and Sunday buffets are also served. Reservations are recommended. A jacket is required for dinner.

South Maui Restaurants

Alexander's Fish, Chicken and Ribs

1913 South Kīhei Road, Kīhei, 874-0788, American, $

This fast-food restaurant's name more or less describes its menu. You pick the type of fish you want and get it either broiled or fried. If it's chicken you want, you can also get it either broiled or fried. Open 11:00 a.m.–9:00 p.m. Located across from the whale at Kalama Park.

A Pacific Cafe Maui

1279 South Kīhei Road, Kīhei, 879-0069, $$$

Chef Jean-Marie Josselin brings the cooking styles of Hawai'i, India and the Mediterranean to his Maui restaurant. Patrons are treated to dishes like mahimahi with garlic-sesame crust and lime-ginger sauce, and smoked chicken with Thai rice, pineapple, and lemon-jalapeno marmalade. The spacious and elegant dining room is decorated in shades of sea green and copper, elegantly belying the restaurant's mundane location in Azeka II shopping center. Reservations are recommended.

Bistro Molokini

Grand Wailea Resort, Wailea, 875-1234, Italian, $$$$

Bistro Molokini offers open-air dining in the finest European tradition with distinctively tropical surroundings. Enjoy lunch or dinner within view of the Grand Wailea Pool and the ocean beyond. Whitewashed wood tables, big wicker chairs and colorful Italian tableware serve to set the mood. Meals are presented in simple, clean and classic arrangements. Several high-protein, low-calorie selections are included in the menu as spa specials. Dinner reservations are recommended.

Buzz's Wharf

Mā'alaea Harbor, 244-5426, Seafood, $$$

Buzz's has a great waterfront location where you can watch the fishing and tour boats entering and exiting Mā'alaea Harbor with Haleakalā beyond. They have an extensive fish menu including their specialty, called prawns Tahitian. Their Tahitian baked papaya (baked with Tahitian vanilla beans) won first prize at the Taste of Lahaina competition. Reservations are recommended.

Cafe Kiowai

Maui Prince Hotel, Mākena, 875-5888, Continental, $$

The Cafe Kiowai offers casual but elegant open-air dining overlooking the gardens and koi ponds at the Maui Prince Hotel. Open for breakfast with a buffet.

Hapa's Brew Haus & Restaurant

41 East Līpoa Street, Kīhei, 879-9001, Microbrewery, $$

This Kīhei hotspot serves an Italian menu of pizza, pasta and calzones along with steak and the fresh catch of the day. You can wash down your meal with just-brewed Black Lava, Paradise Pale or Maui Moon lagers.

Kea Lani Restaurant

Kea Lani Hotel, 4100 Wailea Alanui Drive, Wailea, 875-4100, Pacific Rim, $$$

This open-air restaurant with a sunset view treats its diners to an elegant atmosphere. The menu, which changes monthly, is full of exquisite dishes made with fresh ingredients grown in an organic garden on the premises. Reservations are recommended.

Kincha Japanese Restaurant

Grand Wailea Resort, 875-1234, Japanese, $$$$+

Located in the Grand Wailea Hotel, this tranquil Japanese restaurant was created from 800 tons of rock from Mount Fuji. Lush gardens and peaceful lagoons backdrop the exquisite cuisine and service. Kincha offers sushi and tempura bars, private tatami rooms and features authentic, full-course kaiseki dinners. This cuisine, from appetizers to desserts, uses fish and shellfish along with seasonal fruit and vegetables while improvising cutting techniques and color schemes. Suitable shapes, colors and materials are selected to match the tableware used for each delicacy and are skillfully and decoratively arranged to produce a seasonal appearance. Thus, the changing seasons as seen in Japan are portrayed in one dish.

Even the restaurant's decor lends to the true Japanese experience. In order to assure authenticity, both architectural design and crafting were completed in Japan and then reassembled in Wailea. Average meal price per person is $500!

Maui Tacos

Kama'ole Beach Center, Kīhei, 879-5005; Nāpili Plaza, Nāpili, 665-0222; Lahaina Square, Lahaina, 661-8883, Mexican, $

Healthy Maui-Mex food is the keynote feature at the three Maui Tacos locations. They use lean steak, skinless chicken, and vegetable oil in preparing their meals. The meats are marinaded in pineapple juice and Mexican spices and no MSG is used. Items for vegetarians and dairyless diets are available.

Pacific Grill

Four Seasons Resort, 3900 Wailea Alanui Drive, Wailea, 874-8000, Continental, $$$

The Pacific Grill has all-day, al fresco dining in a relaxed setting on patios with ocean views. The restaurant opens at 6:30 a.m. with a breakfast buffet that includes an array of fresh island fruits and juices. Lunch menus feature grills, sandwiches, pastas and salads. East meets West on the dinner menu with specialties prepared in full view in the Oriental exhibition kitchen. Reservations are recommended for dinner.

Sea Watch Restaurant

Wailea Gold Course Clubhouse, 100 Wailea Golf Club Drive, Wailea, 875-8080, Hawaiian Regional, $$$

The Sea Watch Restaurant features several distinctive dining areas each complimented by the soft pastel colors of the walls and furniture. The Grill Room is adorned with two Arthur Johnson murals that reflect the vivid natural colors of the Sea Watch location, 200 feet above sea level. For a spectacular and expansive view, dine on the lānai at sunset. The menu consists of Hawaiian Regional cuisine with Classical French influence including crab cakes, spinach salad, fresh Island fish, miso-chili glazed tiger prawns and vanilla bean cheesecake. Reservations are recommended.

Seaside

Four Seasons Resort Maui, 3900 Wailea Alanui Drive, Wailea, 874-8000, American, $$$$

Nearly one million dollars was spent to transform the former poolside restaurant Cabana Cafe into the swanky, oceanfront Seaside Restaurant. Seaside offers light American cooking with fresh fish including Tombo (albacore tuna), Nairagi (striped marlin), and Shutome (swordfish). Meat-lovers can enjoy whole-roasted chicken with rosemary-and-caper mashed potatoes, and roast leg of lamb flavored with thyme and garlic. One of the dessert specialties is apple tart with rhubarb ice cream. Seaside is open for lunch from 11:30 a.m. until 3:00 p.m. daily. An extensive pupu menu is available from 3:00 p.m. to 6:00 p.m., followed by dinner from 6:00 p.m. until 9:00 p.m. Hawaiian entertainment highlights sunset each evening. Reservations are recommended.

Seasons Restaurant

Four Seasons Resort, 3900 Wailea Alanui Drive. Wailea, 874-8000, American, $$$$

A dramatic open design brings ocean vistas and breezes to your table in the premiere restaurant of the Four Seasons. The menu features seasonal California cuisine and fresh island seafood. Open daily for dinner at 6:00 p.m. with dancing every evening until 10:30. Reservations are recommended.

Stella Blues Cafe

1215 South Kīhei Road, Kīhei, 874-3779, American, $

Stella Blues Cafe has a casual atmosphere, an extensive menu and reasonable prices, making it a favorite with locals and visitors alike. They use fresh ingredients from local Kula growers and feature a large selection of vegetarian dishes along with meats, seafood and desserts. They can be found in the Long's Shopping Center and are open 8:00 a.m. to 9:00 p.m. daily.

'Ukulele Grill Maui

575 South Kīhei Road, Kīhei, 875-1188, Hawaiian, $$$

Found in the Maui Lu Resort, the 'Ukulele Grill's menu combines traditional Hawaiian favorites with some regional twists, evidenced by the kalua pig quesadilla or the ahi poke Napoleon. Open 7:00 a.m. to 10:00 p.m. daily.

Central Maui Restaurants

Bentos and Banquets by Bernard

85 Church Street, Wailuku, 244-1124, Local, $

Local plate lunch eatery with teriyaki chicken or steak, roast pork and a variety of noodle dishes.

Fujiya Restaurant

133 Market Street, Wailuku, 244-0206. Japanese, $

A good place for inexpensive Japanese food, including sushi, located in the heart of Wailuku.

Mama Ding's Pasteles

255 East Alamaha Street, Kahului, 877-5796, Puerto Rican, $

If you looking for something different this might be the place for you. The specialty is pasteles, which are steamed green banana skins filled with pork, vegetables and spices.

Mama's Fish House

799 Poho Place, Pā'ia, 579-8488, Seafood, $$$

Mama's Fish House is located one-and-a-half miles east of Pā'ia. The restaurant is actually a converted beach house opening to a palm tree-studded lawn and the ocean. Hinged windows open to let in the sea breezes. A low wood-slatted ceiling, candle light, tables covered with tapa-print cloths, walls decorated with Maui memorabilia, original landscapes and old photographs gives Mama's a casual, authentic feel. Their menu is dominated by seafood items. The catch of the day can be prepared sauteed in garlic-butter with white wine and capers, grilled with a sauce of tomato, orange, basil and garlic, sauteed with macadamia nuts, sauteed with coconut milk and lime juice, seared with honey-lime sauce or grilled with mildly spicy wasabi sauce. Open daily from 11:00 a.m. to 9:30 p.m. Reservations are recommended.

Marco's Grill & Deli

444 Hāna Highway, Kahului, 877-4446, Italian, $

At the Dairy Road corner of the Hāna Highway, this is a handy place to grab a meal on your way to or from the airport in Kahului. Lots of omelettes for breakfast and big New York style deli sandwiches and Italian dishes like lasagne and pasta for lunch and dinner are available.

Nazo's Restaurant

1063 Lower Main Street, Wailuku, 244-0529, Local, $

Lots of local and Filipino dishes that include bento plates, oxtail soup and pork adobo.

Pā'ia Fish Market

101 Hāna Highway, Pā'ia, 579-8030, Seafood, $

A good, inexpensive, seafood restaurant for travelers on a budget, featuring chowder, fresh local fish and fish sandwiches.

Picnics

30 Baldwin Avenue, Pā'ia,
579-8021, Health Food, **$**

Picnics has customized its business to cater
to the people driving the Hāna Highway for
the day. Their "Excursion Meal" includes
slices of ham, roast beef and turkey, roasted
chicken, cheeses, rolls, fruit salad, potato
salad, boiled eggs, Maui Style potato chips,
macadamia nut cookies and beverages—all
presented in a basket with cooler, tablecloth
and a cassette tape of "Road to Hāna" tour.
Open from 7:00 a.m. to 7:00 p.m.

Simply Healthy Cafe

J. Walter Cameron Center, Mahalani Rd.,
Wailuku, Local, **$**

A non-profit group that focuses on the health
of native Hawaiians operates this lunch cafe
featuring low-fat, low-salt meals. The Simply
Healthy Cafe uses island produce such as poi,
taro leaves, fish and sweet potato in meals
prepared without frying or seasoning with
sugar, butter or salt. They don't use coconut
and avocados, which have a high fat content,
and mangoes, which are high in sugar and
carbohydrates. Missing from the menu is
kalua pig, which contains 13 grams of fat per

three ounces or worse yet, Spam, which
contains 26 grams of fat in a 3-ounce slab.
The chef has achieved her goal of making
healthy food tasty, to which the large,
lunchtime crowds will attest. Simply Healthy
is open to the public from 11:30 a.m. to 2:00
p.m. Most menu items are $5 or less.

Sharktooth Brewery
Maui Steakhouse

Ka'ahumanu Mall, Kahului,
871-6689, Microbrewery, **$**

A good place for lunch or an inexpensive
dinner. They brew four of their own beers.

Sub Paradise

395-E Dairy Road, Kahului,
877-8779, Sandwiches, **$**

A large selection of submarine sandwiches.
This is a good place to pick up sandwiches to
take with you on a trip to Hāna.

The Vegan

115 Baldwin Avenue, Pā'ia,
579-9144, Vegetarian, **$$**

This is the most popular restaurant on Maui
for those who shun meat.

Upcountry Maui Restaurants

Casanova Italian Restaurant and Deli

1188 Makawao Avenue, Makawao, 572-0220, Italian, **$$**

Traditional Italian dishes including lasagna, homemade pasta, seafood, and pizza made in a wood-burning oven. Late night live entertainment and dancing are thrown in too.

Courtyard Cafe

Baldwin Avenue, Makawao, **$**

The self-serve Courtyard Cafe is open for breakfast and lunch. Diners can choose to eat out in the courtyard or inside on antique chairs and tables. Omelettes are the mainstay of the breakfast menu along with waffles and Maka muffins, which is ham and cheese on an English muffin. Lunch fare includes ham, tuna or turkey sandwiches, soup and fruit smoothies. Parking is available at the rear.

Hali'imaile General Store

Highway 371, Hali'imaile, 572-2666, Hawaiian Regional, **$$$**

This enormously successful restaurant was a camp store in the 1920s. The building has a white and green tin exterior and seems to be standing out in the middle of nowhere in a pineapple field. Owners Beverly and Joe Gannon have created a menu of contemporary cuisine as well as seasonal island fare. Standouts are such appetizers as brie and grape quesadilla with sweet pea guacamole, and sashimi Napoleon—a tower of crispy wontons layered with sashimi, smoked salmon and ahi tartare. Specialties include Szechuan barbecued salmon and rack of lamb Hunan style. Reservations are recommended.

Polli's Mexican Restaurant

1202 Makawao Avenue, Makawao, 572-7808, Mexican, **$**

This small restaurant gives good value for its meals and quick service. That's probably why its 14 tables are filled by 6:00 every day. They serve a varied selection of Mexican dishes as well as burgers, salads, BBQ ribs, chicken and vegetarian dishes. Open every day for breakfast, lunch and dinner.

Sportswatch Sportsbar and Grill

1127 Makawao Avenue, Makawao, 572-1380, Italian/American, **$$**

The only sports bar in Upcountry, the Stopwatch has several large-screen TVs to watch while eating burgers, mahimahi sandwiches, roast beef, soups or salads.

Upcountry Cafe

Aewa Place, Pukalani, 572-2395, American, **$**

The Upcountry Cafe serves lunch and dinner, featuring fresh fish, salads and pastas, but their claim to fame is their hamburger.

SHOPPING

State excise tax for most purchases is four percent. Because businesses have to remit four percent of their total sales including tax collected, they usually charge customers 4.167 percent.

Ka'ahumanu Center

275 Ka'ahumanu Avenue, Kahului, 877-3369

The Ka'ahumanu Center is Maui's largest shopping mall with more than 100 stores and restaurants. Anchoring the mall are Liberty House, Sears and JCPenney department stores and the Japanese retailer Shirokiya. Beside the many chain stores that you'll find in every other mall in the U.S., there are several specialty shops selling locally made products. The mall has movie theatres and a food fair.

Maui Marketplace

Dairy Road and Hāna Highway

On Dairy Road in Kahului is the recently completed Maui Marketplace. Featured retailers are Eagle Hardware, Old Navy, Office Max, Sports Authority, Samsonite, Nine West and Borders Books and Music. Borders has a good selection of Hawaiian music and books as well as a Starbucks. Across the road from Maui Market place are KMart and Costco.

Lahaina Cannery Mall

1221 Honoapi'ilani Highway, Lahaina 661-5304

Looking similar to an old pineapple cannery with its metal walls, the Lahaina Cannery Mall is distinct in Maui because it is fully enclosed and air conditioned. There are about 50 stores in the mall—mostly specializing in clothing, children's wear and artwork. Besides Longs Drug Store, some of their specialty stores include: Lahaina Printsellers, Crazy Shirts, Royal Hawaiian Heritage Jewelry and Kite Fantasy. Every Tuesday and Thursday at 7:00 p.m. there is an exhibition of Polynesian dancing at the mall's center court.

Lahaina Center

900 Front Street, Lahaina, 667-9216

Behind the Hard Rock Cafe on Front Street you'll find a collection of buildings housing mostly clothing shops such as Banana Republic, Waterwear, Arabesque Maui, Hilo Hattie's and a four-screen cinema. An unusual tenant for this shopping center is an indoor gun range. Businesses at Lahaina Center will validate your parking if you make a purchase.

Front Street Lahaina

The strings of shops jammed together on Lahaina's Front Street sell everything from tacky to exquisite to the thousands of strolling tourists. On Front Street you can find every kind of T-shirt to prove to the folks back home that you were in Maui, or you can buy shimmering, black pearl jewelry, or you can get a tattoo. Several art galleries are concentrated here. Each week, they promote "Friday Night is Art Night" from 7:00 to 10:00 p.m. Many of the artists featured in the galleries are on hand to talk to customers and show off their work.

Whalers Village

2435 Kā'anapali Parkway, Kā'anapali 661-4567

A recent renovation has doubled the size of chic and trendy Whalers Village. Upscale shoppers can browse in Louis Vuitton, Hunting World, Tiffany & Co., Gianni Versace and the Chanel Boutique. The Whalers Village Museum of Whaling is housed here (see West Maui Sights). Free Hawaiian entertainment is presented at the center court at 7:00 p.m. every Monday, Wednesday, Friday and Saturday.

Shops at Wailea
Wailea Resort

The 20-year-old Wailea Shopping Village was torn down to make way for the new and posh Shops at Wailea. The 15-acre, two-story shopping center will have upscale outlets such as Louis Vuitton— befitting its tony neighborhood.

Ohana Farmers and Crafters Market
An open-air market where you can buy fresh Maui-grown fruit, vegetables (including organic), exotic tropical fresh-cut flowers, local crafts and gourmet foods. Every Wednesday from 7:30 a.m. to 1:00 p.m. at Kahului Shopping Center and Fridays from 9:30 a.m. to 5:00 p.m. at Ka'ahumanu Shopping Center.

Gift and Craft Fair
Kalama Park, Kīhei

Every Sunday from 9:00 a.m. to 4:00 p.m. local artists, craftspeople and importers set up tables and tents to display and sell their wares.

Maui Galleries

Coast Galleries
Hotel Hāna Maui, 248-8636; Hyatt Regency, Kā'anapali, 661-2777; Outrigger Wailea, 879-2301

The Coast Galleries have three showcases for original Island art. Local artists and artisans include canoe builders, sculptors, woodworkers, stoneworkers, bowl turners and painters.

Curtis Wilson Cost Gallery
Kula Lodge, 878-6085

Curtis Wilson Cost is a well-known and accomplished Maui landscape artist. The Cost Gallery is located in the Kula Lodge on the road to Haleakalā, 15 minutes from the artist's studio in Kula. The paintings hang in a room that has the feel of a European wine cellar.

Dolphin Galleries
Lahaina Cannery Mall, 661-5000; Whalers Village, Kā'anapali; Grand Wailea Resort

Traditional Maui marine subjects are represented by the bronze sculptures of Barclay Hill, the whale paintings of Don McMichael and the colorful tropical fish and sea turtles painted by Sherri Reeve.

Élan Vital's Art World
1134 Makawao Avenue, Makawao 573-8181

With more than 8,000 square feet, Élan Vital owns the largest art studio-gallery in the Pacific. Vital specializes in commissions of monumental scale in painting and sculpture. He sculpted the life-size humpback whale in Kīhei's Kalama Park. Vital is a nonrepresentational artist whose creations are truly one of a kind. The artist turned to engineering and technology to invent new ways of handling color. His paintings are produced with an oil-based polymer that suspends pure pigments in a transparent medium. This allows the artist to mix colors that remain pure, untainted by other pigments in close proximity. Vital pours the pigment/polymer mixture, which has the consistency of honey, across a new canvas. Then he allows gravity to create the design by elevating and lowering the canvas. As the mixture hardens, areas in the painting are manipulated to further enhance the appearance, then the surface is polished to reveal its luster and beauty.

Gallerie Lassen
844 Front St., Lahaina, 667-7707; 700 Front St., Lahaina, 661-6606

Featured are originals and graphics by famous Maui artist Christian Riese Lassen.

Lahaina Art Society Under the Banyan Tree

Lahaina

Every Saturday and Sunday from 10 a.m. to 5 p.m., society members exhibit their creations.

Lahaina Galleries

728 Front St., Lahaina, 667-2152; 123 Bay Drive, Kapalua, 669-0202; www.lahainagalleries.com

Offered is work by nationally and internationally prominent artists including contemporary paintings and graphics by Adolf Sehring and Aldo Luongo, marine art by Robert Lyn Nelson and Raymond Page, Island scenes in oil by Ronaldo Macedo, impressionism by the Makk Family, surrealism by Andrea Smith and Robert Watson, classic surrealism by Loren Adams, abstract expressionism by Lau Chun, whimsy by Guy Buffet and wildlife by Gary Swanson.

Larry Dotson Gallery

Pioneer Inn, 658 Wharf St., Lahaina, 661-7197

Featured are oils by Larry Dotson and Oscar Flores, watercolors by Henry Howell, Tracy Taylor and E'Drie, sculpture in wood and brass by Dennis Williams and woodblock prints by Haruyo and Yuriko.

Madeline Michaels Gallery

816 Front St., Lahaina, 661-3984

This gallery specializes in three-dimensional pop art from a variety of local artists. Collections include ceramic and papier-mache sculpture and jewelry.

Royal Art Gallery

752 Front St., Lahaina, 667-1982

The Royal Art Gallery features visions of Japan and China by Caroline Young, impressionistic Island scenes and florals by Linda Andelin, underwater scenes and seascapes in oils by Dy'an, marine sculpture by Richard Steirs and Jerry Joslin, and marine life, scenic paintings and prints by Anthony Casay, Dave Archer and George Sumner.

Village Galleries

Ritz-Carlton, Kapalua, 669-1800; 120 Dickenson St., Lahaina; Lahaina Cannery Mall, 661-4402

Exhibits in oil feature Island people and florals by Macario Pascuale and Susan McGivney Hansen, scenes by Hiroshi Tagami, Michelle Taylor, Hajime Okuda, Joyce Clark and Betty Hay Freeland and harbor scenes by George Allan. Watercolors include scenes by Peter Jacka, Fred Kenknight, Diane and Wayne LaCom, Pamela Hays and Bob Dahlquist.

Wyland Galleries

697 and 711 Front St., Lahaina; 136 Dickenson St., Lahaina; Whalers Village, Kāʻanapali, 667-2285

Originals and limited edition prints include marine life by Wyland, scenes by Tabora, mixed-media marine paintings and surrealistic fantasies by Pitre, nostalgic Hawaiiana by James Coleman and marine life in bronze and acrylic by Wyland and Douglas Wylie.

ARTISTS FIND THEIR MUSE ON MAUI

MAUI HAS LONG held a special attraction for artists. More than 1,000 serious artists, many of whom have earned notoriety for their treatment of the island's landscapes and life, work and live on Maui. Maui's artists portray and celebrate the colors and light of the island with oils, watercolors, wood carving, pottery, scrimshaw and sculpture.

The shoreline sunsets of Christian Riese Lassen's paintings bring beaches alive. Impressionists Joan Clark, Betty Hay Freeland and George Allan use Maui's colors and unique light to render their landscapes. Humpback whales are featured in the paintings of Robert Lyn Nelson and Wyland, who combine a vision of life above and below the ocean surface in a single work. Anthony Casay takes Nelson's motif to outer space. Transplanted Frenchman Guy Buffet produces whimsical works with a childlike perception of the world.

ACCOMMODATIONS

Rates quoted are for lowest-priced room for two people in low season without ocean view. Top-end prices for most hotels can double these rates. State excise tax and the transient accommodation tax will add 11.25 percent to the cost for both hotels and condominiums. The diamond ratings are from the American Automobile Association, five diamonds being their top rating.

Luxury Resorts— West Maui

Ritz Carlton
One Ritz Carlton Drive, Kapalua
AAA ◆◆◆◆◆
Phone: (808) 669-6200
Website: www.ritzcarlton.com
Rooms: 548
Rates: $260+
Beach: D.T. Fleming

Kapalua Bay Hotel
One Kapalua Bay Drive, Kapalua
Phone: (808) 669-5656, (800) 367-8000
Website: www.kapaluabay.com
Rooms: 191
Rates: $295+
Beach: Kapalua

Royal Lahaina Resort
2780 Keka'a Drive, Kā'anapali
Phone: (808) 661-3611, (800) 222-5642
Website: www.2maui.com
Rooms: 541
Rates: $215+
Beach: Airport

Sheraton Maui
2605 Kā'anapali Parkway, Kā'anapali
Phone: (808) 661-0031
Website: www.sheraton.com
Rooms: 510
Rates: $290+
Beach: Kā'anapali

Westin Maui
2365 Kā'anapali Parkway, Kā'anapali
AAA ◆◆◆◆
Phone: (808) 667-2525
Website: www.westinmaui.com
Rooms: 761
Rates: $265+
Beach: Kā'anapali

Maui Marriott
100 Nohea Kai Drive, Kā'anapali
AAA ◆◆◆◆
Phone: (808) 667-1200, (800) 228-9290
Website: www.marriotthotels.com
Rooms: 720
Rates: $280+
Beach: Kā'anapali

Hyatt Regency Maui
200 Nohea Kai Dr., Kā'anapali
AAA ◆◆◆◆
Phone: (808) 661-1234, (800) 233-1234
Website: www.hyatt.com
Rooms: 808
Rates: $275+
Beach: Kā'anapali

Luxury Resorts— South Maui

Renaissance Wailea Beach Resort
3550 Wailea Alanui Drive, Wailea
Phone: (808) 879-4900, (800) 468-3571
Website: www.renaissancehotels.com
Rooms: 347
Rates: $320+
Beaches: Mōkupu, Ulua

Outrigger Wailea
3700 Wailea Alanui Drive, Wailea
AAA ◆◆◆
Phone: (808) 879-1922
Website: www.outrigger.com
Rooms: 516
Rates: $229+
Beach: Wailea

Grand Wailea Resort
3850 Wailea Alanui Drive, Wailea
AAA ◆◆◆◆◆
Phone: (808) 875-1234, (800) 888-6100
Website: www.grandwailea.com

Rooms: 761
Rates: $380+
Beach: Wailea

Four Seasons Resort
3900 Wailea Alanui Drive, Wailea
AAA ◆◆◆◆◆
Phone: (808) 874-8000, (800) 334-6284
Website: www.fourseasons.com
Rooms: 380
Rates: $295+
Beach: Wailea

Kea Lani Hotel
4100 Wailea Alanui Drive, Wailea
Phone: (808) 875-4100, (800) 659-4100
Website: www.kealani.com
Rooms: 413
Rates: $295+
Beach: Polo

Maui Prince Hotel
5400 Mākena Alanui Road, Mākena
AAA ◆◆◆◆
Phone: (808) 874-1111
Website: www.westin.com
Rooms: 310
Rates: $260+
Beach: Malu'aka

Grand Wailea Resort

Traveler's Palm decorate the Kea Lani

Luxury Resorts— East Maui

Hotel Hāna Maui
Hāna Highway, Hāna
Phone: (808) 248-8211, (800) 321-4262
Rooms: 96
Rates: $395+
Beach: Hāmoa

Hotels— West Maui

Nāpili Kai Beach Club
5900 Honoapi'ilani Road, Nāpili
Phone: (808) 669-6271, (800) 367-5030
Website: www.Nāpilikai.com
Rooms: 162
Rates: $170+
Beach: Nāpili Bay

Embassy Suites Resort
100 Kā'anapali Shores Place, Kā'anapali
Phone: (808) 661-2000, (800) 669-3155
Website: www.embassy-maui.com
Rooms: 413
Rates: $260+
Beach: Kā'anapali

Kā'anapali Beach Hotel
2525 Kā'anapali Parkway, Kā'anapali
AAA ◆◆◆
Phone: (808) 661-0011
Website: www.kaanapalibeachhotel.com
Rooms: 430
Rates: $160+
Beach: Kā'anapali

Maui Islander Hotel
660 Waine'e Street, Lahaina
AAA ◆◆
Phone: (808) 667-9766
Rooms: 372
Rates: $82+

Pioneer Inn
658 Wharf Street, Lahaina
Phone: (808) 661-3636
(800) 457-5457
Rooms: 34
Rates: $119+

Hotels— South Maui

Maui Coast Hotel
(808) 2259 South Kīhei Road, Kīhei
AAA ◆◆◆
Phone: (808) 874-6284, (800) 426-0670
Website: www.westcoasthotels.com/mauicoast
Rooms: 260
Rates: $129+
Beach: Kama'ole I

Maui Oceanfront
2980 South Kīhei Road, Kīhei
Phone: (808) 879-7744, (800) 367-5004
Website: www.castle-group.com/
maui_oceanfront
Rooms: 85
Rates: $85+
Beach: Keawakapu

Aston Wailea Resort
3700 Wailea Alanui Drive, Wailea
Phone: (808) 879-1922
Rooms: 516
Rates: $219+
Beach: Wailea

Diamond Resort Hawaii
555 Kaukahi Street, Wailea
Phone: (808) 874-0500
Rooms: 72
Rates: $170+

Hotels— Central Maui

Maui Beach Hotel
170 Ka'ahumanu Avenue, Kahului
Phone: (808) 877-0051
Rooms: 147
Rates: $93+

Maui Palms
150 Ka'ahumanu Avenue, Kahului
Phone: (808) 877-0071
Rooms: 98
Rates: $60+

Maui Seaside
100 Ka'ahumanu Avenue, Kahului
Phone: (808) 877-3311
AAA ◆◆
Rooms: 250
Rates: $80+

Hotels— East Maui

Hāna Kai-Maui Resort
1533 Uakea Road, Hāna
Phone: (808) 248-8426
AAA ◆◆
Website: www.hanakaimaui.com
Rooms: 18
Rates: $125+
Beach: Hāna Bay

Condominiums

Maui has more than 7,000 condo units available for rent by vacationing visitors. Being more economical to rent than hotel rooms and offering more space, condos are the preferred choice for many traveling families.

Although they don't provide the services of a hotel, vacation condos generally are located near beaches, golf courses and other recreation spots. Full-service condo resorts often have their own rental offices, restaurants and recreation facilities. Their rates can reach the levels of luxury hotel resorts. Condos rented directly from owners who list with vacation rental services on the Internet can be had for as little as $60 per night. Vacation rental condos come with fully equipped kitchens which allow guests to save even more money by preparing their own meals. Another good source of condo rentals is the classified ad section of *Hawai'i* magazine.

Internet Vacation Rental Listing Services

Vacation Spot:
www.vacationspot.com

Vacation Rentals by Owner:
www.vrbo.com/vrbo/maui.htm

Great Rentals:
www.greatrentals.com/HI/HI.html

A1 Vacations:
www.a1vacations.com

Royal Vacations:
www.royalvacations.com/maui.htm

1st Choice Vacation Properties:
www.choice1.com

10,000 Vacation Rentals:
www.10kvacationrentals.com

Full-Service Condos— West Maui

Kapalua Villas
500 Office Road, Kapalua
Phone: (808) 669-8088, (800) 545-0018
Rates: $185–$400
Units: 150
Website: www.kapaluavillas.com

Nāpili Shores Resort
5315 Honoapi'ilani Road, Nāpili
Phone: (808) 669-8061
Rates: $135–$200
Units: 100

Nāpili Point Resort
5295 Honoapi'ilani Road, Nāpili
Phone: (808) 669-9222
Rates: $154–$279
Units: 108

Nāpili Sunset
46 Hui Drive, Nāpili
AAA ◆◆
Phone: (808) 669-8083
Rates: $75–$265
Units: 41

Kahana Village
4531 Lower Honoapi'ilani Road, Kahana
Phone: (808) 669-5111
Rates: $160–$320
Units: 42

Kahana Reef
4471 Lower Honoapi'ilani Road, Kahana
Phone: (808) 669-6491, (800) 253-3773
Rates: $105–$130
Units: 88

Sands of Kahana
4299 Honoapi'ilani Road, Kahana
AAA ◆◆◆
Phone: (808) 669-0423, (800) 332-1137
Rates: $110–$310
Units: 128
Website: www.sands-of-kahana.com

Kahana Beach Condominium

4221 Lower Honoapi'ilani Road, Kahana
Phone: (808) 669-8611, (800) 222-5642
Rates: $125–$225
Units: 81
Website: www.go2maui.com

Noelani Condominium Resort

4095 Lower Honoap'ilani Road, Kahana
AAA ◆◆◆
Phone: (808) 669-8374, (800) 367-6030
Rates: $97–$197
Units: 43
Website: www.noelani-condo-resort.com

Maui Park

3626 Lower Honoapi'ilani Road, Honokōwai
Phone: (808) 669-6622, (800) 367-5004
Rates: $104–$198
Units: 186
Website: www.castle-group.com/maui_park

Papakea Beach Resort

3543 Honoapi'ilani Highway, Kā'anapali
AAA ◆◆
Phone: (808) 669-4848
Rates: $119–$239
Units: 50

Maui Eldorado

2661 Keka'a Drive, Kā'anapali
AAA ◆◆
Phone: (808) 661-0021
Rates: $150–$325
Units: 98

Kā'anapali Ali'i

50 Nohea Kai Drive, Kā'anapali
Phone: (808) 667-1666, (800) 642-6284
Rates: $265–$700
Units: 207
Website: www.classicresorts.com/unit_kalii/index.html

Kā'anapali Royal

2560 Keka'a Drive, Kā'anapali
Phone: (808) 879-2205
Rates: $175–$250
Units: 13

Maui Kā'anapali Villas

45 Kai Ala Drive, Kā'anapali
AAA ◆◆◆
Phone: (808) 667-7791
Rates: $135–$280

Maui Kai

106 Kā'anapali Shores Place, Kā'anapali
Phone: (808) 667-3500, (800) 367-5635
Rates: $120–$265
Units: 58
Website: www.mauikai.com

The Whaler

2481 Kā'anapali Parkway, Kā'anapali
AAA ◆◆◆
Phone: (808) 661-4861
Rates: $168–$455
Units: 159
Website: www.thewhaler.com

Lahaina Shores Beach Resort

475 Front Street, Lahaina
Phone: (808) 661-4835, (800) 642-6284
Rates: $120–$245
Units: 154

Full-Service Condos— South Maui

Sugar Beach Resort

145 North Kīhei Road, Kīhei
AAA ◆◆
Phone: (808) 879-2778
Rates: $95–$240
Units: 119

Kīhei Bay Vista

679 South Kīhei Road, Kīhei
Phone:(808) 879-8866
Rates: $129–$149
Units: 60
Website: www.marcresorts.com

Kauhale Makai, Village By The Sea

938 South Kīhei Road, Kīhei
Phone: (808) 879-5445, (800) 822-4409
Rates: $70–$150
Units: 90
Website: www.vacationweb.com/hawaii/
maui-condos/Kihei/kauhale_makai.html

Luana Kai Resort

940 South Kīhei Road, Kīhei
Phone: (808) 879-1268, (800) 669-1127
Rates: $79–$159
Units: 80

Maui Sunset

1032 South Kīhei Road, Kīhei
Phone: (808) 879-0674
Rates: $85–$205
Units: 100

Kīhei Akahi

2531 South Kīhei Road, Kīhei
Phone: (808) 879-1881
Rates: $70–$145
Units: 70

Maui Vista

2191 South Kīhei Road, Kīhei
Phone: (808) 879-7966
Rates: $119–$199
Units: 53
Website: www.marcresorts.com

Aston At The Maui Banyan

2575 South Kīhei Road, Kīhei
Phone: (808) 875-0004
Rates: $115–$305
Units: 30

Kama'ole Sands

2695 South Kīhei Road, Kīhei
AAA ◆◆◆
Phone: (808) 874-8700, (800) 367-5004
Rates: $115–$340
Units: 315
Website: www.castle-group.com

Mana Kai Maui Resort

2960 South Kīhei Road, Kīhei
Phone: (808) 879-1561
Rates: $80–$190
Units: 67

The Palms At Wailea

3200 Wailea Alanui Drive, Wailea
Phone: (808) 879-5800
Rates: $170–$245
Units: 77

Wailea Ekahi Village

3300 Wailea Alanui Drive, Wailea
Phone: (808) 879-2770, (800) 367-5246
Rates: $140–$370
Units: 55
Website: www.maui.net/~drh/ekahi.htm

Wailea Ekolu Village

10 Wailea Ekolu Place, Wailea
Phone: (808) 879-2222, (800) 367-5246
Rates: $150–$245
Website: www.maui.net/~drh/ekolu.htm

Polo Beach Club

20 Mākena Road, Mākena
Phone: (808) 879-8847, (800) 367-5246
Rates: $295–$450
Website: www.maui.net/~drh/polo.htm

Mākena Surf

96 Mākena Road, Mākena
Phone:(808) 879-1595, (800) 367-5246
Rates: $360–$700
Website: www.maui.net/~drh/Makena.htm

MAUI ON THE WORLD WIDE WEB

News

The electronic editions of Maui's newspapers are good places to check on upcoming events for the dates you will be on the island.

The Maui News
www.mauinews.com
Maui's daily newspaper.

The Lahaina News
www.westmaui.com
Weekly newspaper with news pertaining to West Maui.

Haleakalā/Kīhei Times
www.mauisfreepress.com
Bi-weekly alternative newspaper.

The Hawai'i News List
www.aloha.net/~prophet/NewsList
Subscription service that will e-mail news of Hawai'i to you.

Information

Maui Weather Today
hawaiiweathertoday.com/mwt/
mwt_weather.htm#weather
Maui weatherman Glenn James brings his weather forecasts and comments on life on Maui to the Internet three times a week. The site has several links to satellite shots of the islands.

Virtually Hawai'i
hawaii.ivv.nasa.gov
Has computerized virtual tours of all the Hawaiian Islands and the latest views from space.

Live Cameras

Molokini
www.WebCam.InMaui.com

Lahaina Seawall
www.mauigateway.com/~video

Spreckelsville
www.windcam.com/index.html

INDEX

*The author welcomes any comments, contributions, or updates
to information contained in this book. He may be contacted at: exploreparadise@msn.com*